Reader's Digest

Complete Book
of
Home
Decorating

Reader's Digest
Complete Book
of
Home
Decorating

Inspiring Ideas and
Practical Techniques for Making
Your House Your Home

THE READER'S DIGEST ASSOCIATION, INC.
PLEASANTVILLE, NEW YORK / MONTREAL

A READER'S DIGEST BOOK

Designed and edited by Eaglemoss Publications Ltd

Copyright © Eaglemoss Publications Ltd 2001
Based on *Creating Your Home* and *Home Magic*.

READER'S DIGEST PROJECT STAFF
Project Editor: Don Earnest
Project Designer: Jennifer R. Tokarski
Editorial Manager: Christine R. Guido

READER'S DIGEST ILLUSTRATED REFERENCE BOOKS
Editor-in-Chief: Christopher Cavanaugh
Art Director: Joan Mazzeo
Director, Trade Publishing: Christopher T. Reggio
Senior Design Director, Trade: Elizabeth L. Tunnicliffe
Editorial Director, Trade: Susan Randol

Picture credits
Front cover: (top left) Marie Claire Idées/Fleurent/Chastres, (top center) Elizabeth Whiting and Associates,
(top right) IPC Syndication/Homes & Gardens, (center left) Crown Paints, (center right) Harlequin Fabrics,
(bottom left) IPC Syndication/Homes & Gardens, (bottom center) Abode Interiors Photography Library,
(bottom right) Eaglemoss/Paul Bricknell. Back cover: (left) Eaglemoss/Steve Tanner, (center) Swish,
(right) Creative Publishing International.
Page 3: Eaglemoss/Martin Chaffer.
The credits and acknowledgments that appear on page 304
are hereby made a part of this copyright page.

Library of Congress Cataloging in Publication Data

Reader's Digest complete book of home decorating : inspiring ideas and practical
techniques for making your house your home.
    p. cm.
  ISBN 0-7621-0330-2
    1. Interior decoration—Handbooks, manuals, etc. I. Title: Complete book of home
decorating. II. Reader's Digest Association.

NK2115 .R35 2001
747—dc21

2001019611

Printed in Singapore

1 3 5 7 9 10 8 6 4 2

CONTENTS

INTRODUCTION

The key to successful home decorating is a combination of inspiration and practical know-how. With *Reader's Digest Complete Book of Home Decorating* at your side, you'll have all the ideas, advice and expertise you need to turn your decorating dreams into reality.

First, you need to take a long, hard look at your home in order to plan an approach that not only looks good, but is functional too. Perhaps you have an open-plan living space that can be divided up into sitting, dining and working areas simply by arranging your furniture in self-contained units. Discover how to maximize the space you have by turning a spare room into a combined home office and guest bedroom, and using that awkward area under the stairs for storage.

Next you must decide on the style and overall look and feel you want to create for each room – bold and dramatic or understated and elegant, folksy country charm or sophisticated urban chic. Sections on style details break each approach down into manageable chunks and highlight the individual elements – including furniture, color schemes and accessories – that are combined to produce each look.

Colors and patterns are probably the two things that excite interior design experts the most, but they are also the things that instill most fear into new home decorators – choosing the right scheme can seem daunting, and mistakes can be costly and depressing to live with. *Reader's Digest Complete Book of Home Decorating* helps you to use colors and patterns with confidence. Photographs of real interiors show how different combinations work in different situations – how warm and cool colors can energize or relax, and make a room seem larger or smaller; how patterns add interest to the plain, or can be co-ordinated with differently scaled prints and stripes for unusual effects.

On a more basic level, you will need to draw up a wish list of furnishings, from curtains and carpets to storage units and sofa beds. These items are likely to be the most expensive of any home-decorating make-over, so you must be sure to consider all the options and choose carefully. Visual identification guides and charts that compare and contrast the pros and cons of each item help you to choose the best option for you from the wide range available.

Then it's the moment to put it all together. If you have the time and the inclination, the most rewarding and cost-effective option is to do it yourself. Illustrated instructions explain every job step by step – how to put up wall coverings, paint a window, refinish a wooden floor and more.

Finally, you can sit back and enjoy the fruits of your labor, and admire your smart new stylish home!

1
PLANNING

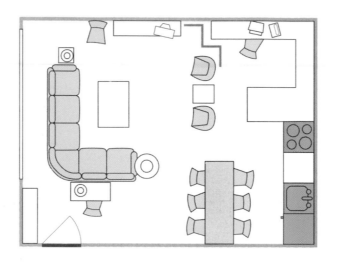

MAKING A PLAN

*Whether you're buying new furniture, planning a fresh look for
your home, or moving into a new house, drawing plans of your rooms
is a good way to save effort and avoid expensive mistakes.*

A scale plan – a simple drawing setting out the important dimensions of a room – has several uses. If you are moving into a new home, plans of the new rooms can help you work out the best furniture layout and tell you whether doorways or low ceilings will prove awkward during the move. If you want to replace or add to existing furniture, a plan quickly shows you what will work in the available space. For buying paint or wallpaper, the same plans can be used to estimate correct quantities of materials.

Plans can also provide useful information to pass onto workers. Movers will know where to put furniture. Contractors, electricians, and plumbers can familiarize themselves with a room before working in it and can also be informed of your exact requirements.

The main types of plan that are useful for these purposes are floor and wall plans. Floor plans give a bird's-eye view of the room and

show its length and width. They are useful for working out how much floor covering to buy and where to situate furniture.

A wall plan shows the height of a room and details features such as doors, windows, and alcoves. These plans are drawn wall by wall. They can be used to estimate quantities of paint and wallpaper and to work out where to locate built-ins.

A perspective drawing gives a three-dimensional view of how a room looks and is useful when precise planning is needed – for example, for a kitchen with built-ins. However, these plans are complicated and are best left for a professional to provide on a computer. Draw up your final plans accurately and keep them for future occasions – you'll be surprised how often they'll be useful.

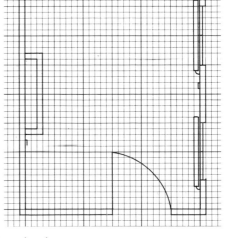

▲ *When there's a lot of furniture to
be arranged in a limited space, it helps
to detail the dimensions and shape of
the room on a scale plan first.*

DRAWING A FLOOR PLAN

YOU WILL NEED

- PAD OF ¹/₁₀, ¹/₂, AND 1IN GRAPH PAPER
- RETRACTABLE STEEL TAPE MEASURE
- PENCIL AND RULER
- STEPLADDER
- CALCULATOR

Start by making a rough outline sketch of the room on which to record its measurements as you take them – the plan doesn't have to be accurate at this stage.

Mark in the position of doors, windows, radiators, electrical outlets, light switches, chimney breasts, alcoves, fireplaces, and other permanent features. It is also important to show the arc of the doors – which way they open – and note down whether the windows hinge, slide, or pivot, since this affects the positioning of the furniture.

MEASURING UP

You may find it easier to work with a partner, so that one person can hold the tape measure while the other extends it along the length of the wall. This also allows you to read off the measurements more easily.

Start at one corner of the room and run the tape along the floor, keeping it straight and parallel to the wall you are measuring. Mark each measurement onto the plan.

If there is a fireplace or other feature jutting out from the wall, take four separate measurements:
- The overall length of the wall, measuring in front of the feature
- The width of the feature itself
- The distance from one side wall (or corner) to the feature

- The distance from the feature to the other side wall (or corner)

Add up the last three measurements to ensure that they equal the overall one. Then measure from the wall to the front of the feature on each side and note down how far it projects into the room.

Also measure the width of the doors, door frames, windows, and their frames. Work out the door arc by measuring how far the door protrudes into the room when it is fully open. Put these measurements on the floor plan and draw an arc to connect the side of the door frame to the far edge of the open door.

THE FINAL PLANS

Once you're happy that your measurements are accurate, transfer the rough sketches of the plans onto graph or squared paper. Select a graph paper that makes your calculations easy; ¹/₁₀, ¹/₂, and 1in paper is good to work with because the squares are large enough to be seen comfortably. Choose a scale that enables you to fit everything onto one sheet and always note down your chosen scale on any plans that you draw.

◀ *A rough sketch plan of a bedroom is a help in visualizing the best place to put the bed, while leaving enough space for other furniture and to open drawers and doors.*

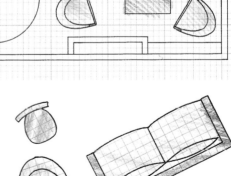

◀ *In theory, there are many ways of arranging the same sofa, chairs, tables, and cupboard in a room, some more practical than others. Juggling paper cutouts of furniture about on scaled plans allows you to explore various options until you hit on the most workable answer.*

FURNITURE TEMPLATES

By making simple templates you can test changes of furniture layout in a room more easily than by shifting heavy pieces about. Measure the width and length of each item and, using the same scale as the floor plan, draw outlines of overhead views of this furniture. Draw a dotted line in front of the solid outline of cupboards or chests of drawers to show the drawer or door opening space, or the activity space needed around bathroom fixtures. Color in or label the pieces before you cut them out to help you to identify them.

Move the templates around on your floor plan to work out the various layout options for your room and its furniture. It is easiest to position the bigger pieces first and then arrange everything else around them. Try out several arrangements to see which one suits you best.

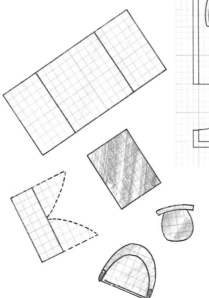

DON'T FORGET THE UTILITIES

When possible, note the position of electrical fixtures, radiators, gas connections, plumbing, and any important drainage on your plan. If any of these form an obstruction to a proposed layout, they will need moving. Electrical outlets are easier to move than drainage pipes but you may still have to do some replastering or redecorating.

▲ *Furniture templates can be as detailed as shown above, but in practice they need to be quite simple in outline. For instance, if a sofa or cabinet is rectangular, a plain rectangle, drawn to scale, is all you need for your planning.*

DRAWING A WALL PLAN

▼ A wall plan is very helpful when plotting the neatest way to arrange shelving against a wall and put stereo equipment near power outlets.

A wall plan is useful, particularly when dealing with built-in furniture or working out quantities of wallpaper. To draw one, make a sketch of the wall, noting down the wall's measurements, including the heights and widths of doors, windows, picture rails, wainscoting, and baseboards. When you have collected all your measurements, draw up a final scale plan of the wall – called an elevation.

Bear in mind that rooms rarely have walls that are equal in length or in height, or have corners at right angles. If the walls are slightly different and your plans aren't for built-in furniture, you can usually ignore the differences. If you are drawing plans for built-ins, it's important to take accurate measurements.

When measuring the lengths of walls or alcoves, take measurements in at least three places and measure wall heights at several places along the wall. Professional cabinet makers always take their own measurements to double check yours, but if you are doing your own carpentry, taking multiple measurements ensures that you are prepared to make allowances if any of the walls are out of true.

To find the area of a wall for wallpapering and so on, multiply its length by its height. If you need to know the wall area of a whole room, work out the area for each wall and add the totals together.

Use the floor plans in a similar way to work out ceiling and floor areas. Simply multiply the length of the room by the width. For an L-shaped room, divide the space into two rectangles and work out the area for each rectangle, adding the two figures together. You can use the same method to measure the area of an alcove or a bay.

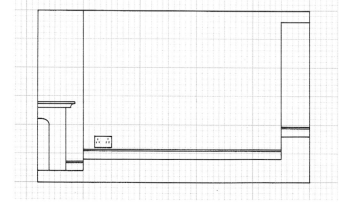

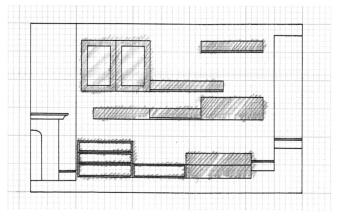

MIXED LIVING AND DINING

*The most comfortable dual-purpose living and dining
rooms are both welcoming and well planned, offering an agreeable
atmosphere for relaxing, eating, and entertaining.*

A separate room devoted solely to dining represents something of a luxury in many households, but dinner parties and family gatherings are more likely to be relaxed, informal gatherings these days than in the past. For many people, incorporating an eating area within the main living room is a sensible arrangement and provides congenial surroundings for meal times.

With any dual-purpose room, good planning helps you make the best use of the space at your disposal. To avoid a clash of interests and to maximize comfort and convenience, it's important to pay particular attention to the layout. The shape of the room may suggest an obvious way of separating living space from a dining area but you can also mark the distinction decoratively or in the way the furniture is arranged.

A dining area set up in a living room can provide an additional place to study, use a sewing machine, or tackle paperwork. Sympathetic lighting and flexible furnishings enable you to allow for different pursuits and create a harmonious, integrated look.

Before you begin planning a dual-purpose arrangement, sketch a plan of the room and mark on all existing features, such as fireplaces, windows, doors, and power outlets. Cut out paper shapes of your major furniture items and move them about on your plan to experiment with different arrangements.

▲ *Well-placed furniture is the key to making a dual living and dining space functional. Often an item of furniture can make an effective room divider – here the dining area becomes an intimate corner when it is defined by the bold red sofa.*

PLANNING THE LAYOUT

The basic room shape may suggest where to site a dining area. The alcove formed by a bay or bow window is a good location. L-shaped rooms divide naturally in two; any change in level in a room can be used to signal the boundary between different activities. If the room is a generous size, it may be worth adding some form of partition, such as a freestanding double-fronted cabinet or an open shelving system, to create a visual break between the two areas.

If the architectural features of the room don't offer a solution, you will have to rely on the way you arrange the furniture to make the distinction clear. A sofa, a line of low storage cupboards, a folding screen, or even a large potted plant strategically arranged can all partially enclose a dining area and give a hint of separation.

It's important to remember that there should be enough clear space around the dining table for chairs to be drawn back comfortably and food to be served. A clear route to the kitchen is vital, or serving a meal becomes an obstacle course. If the kitchen is immediately adjacent, consider making an internal window in the dividing wall as a version of the traditional serving hatch for passing dishes back and forth.

A pleasant view adds to the enjoyment of food, so try to place the table near French doors or a window where it also benefits from natural light.

◀ *The room itself may have a feature that provides a natural division. The change in level in this spacious room is utilized to the full extent. The lower level makes a cozy seating area, while the lighter aspect of the upper level is pleasant for dining.*

▶ *Sometimes a few well-chosen accessories are all it takes to give each area a sense of purpose. The small, but vivid blue rug clearly claims the seating area, while the pendant light sets the mood over the table. As a unifying touch, the same range of lighting is repeated throughout.*

▼ *The plan below explains the relative positions of the kitchen, dining, and living areas shown in the picture above left.*

THE DECOR

There are two basic approaches to decorating dual-purpose areas. The first is to keep everything simple and employ a single range of colors, fabrics, and finishes throughout the entire area, which helps increase the sense of space in a small room.

The second approach, which works better in larger spaces, is to emphasize the distinction between the living and dining areas through subtle contrasts of texture. Avoid decorating the two parts of the room in wildly different styles, or the result is visual confusion.

It makes good sense to opt for a tougher floor covering in the dining area because eating brings the inevitable risk of food spills. A washable, cotton rug under a dining table offers some protection in a fully carpeted room, or if you extend wood flooring throughout the room, a large, soft rug in the living area provides extra warmth and comfort. Alternatively, partner carpeting in the living space with easy-to-clean tiles or woodstrip flooring in the dining area, keeping the colors as tonally close as possible for a sophisticated look.

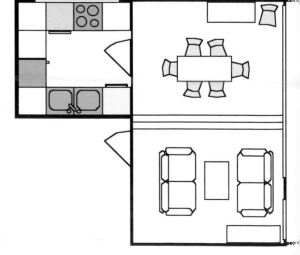

▶ Comfortably arranged around a luxurious rug and chest-style table, these sofas form a convivial conversation group. The position of one of the sofas, at right angles across the room, acts as a physical barrier, and creates a natural route to the kitchen.

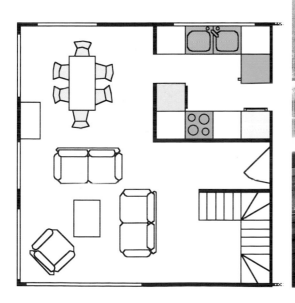

LIGHTING

Flexibility is the key factor here. For general background illumination, wall-mounted sconces or torchères are discreet and subtle. For directional lighting, choose spotlights fixed to the wall or ceiling, angled to highlight the table or displays. Tiny halogen spotlights enhance the colors and textures of food and table displays, while a single pendant light over the table defines the eating area.

Strategically placed around the room, table and floor lamps emit a warming glow which is flattering and easy to live with. Include additional local light for reading and any other pursuit that calls for good light. It's also worth fitting all the lights with dimmer switches so you can vary the mood.

FURNITURE

In a dual-purpose space, a large dining table is usually impractical and too imposing. The best solution is to choose a table that you can extend as required to accommodate more people, and chairs that you can fold or stack to save space. Alternatively, canvas directors' chairs, wicker chairs, bentwood, or ladderbacks work well as additional living-room seating.

The aim is to keep the accessories of dining – tableware, glassware, cutlery, and linen – near the table so that they are easily accessible. Corner cupboards, sideboards, storage units, display shelves, or low chests can accommodate a range of items. Combine hidden storage with open display areas for china and glassware. Storage furniture can double as a means of dividing space or a serving area.

▲ *A number of devices set the dining area apart: a large dresser and painting on adjacent walls form a corner for the table. The pendant light gives the corner a sense of permanence.*

◀ *In a very small area, maximum use of space is made with an ingenious table that extends from the shelving. The choice of cane chairs for dining is practical, as they double as extra seating in the living area.*

OPEN-PLAN AREAS

Taking full advantage of the space available in an open-plan living area calls for a thoughtful approach to arranging the furniture and the interior decorations in order to accommodate a variety of activities.

In some homes, an open-plan living area is built into the layout of the ground floor area by design; in others, walls have to be knocked through to combine two or more small rooms into one large open area. In a restricted space, the absence of clearly defined rooms produces an illusion of spaciousness and makes a greater floor area available. In larger homes, an unpartitioned layout engenders a feeling of unlimited space with limitless design potential.

When decorating an open-plan area, you are aiming not only to create an attractive-looking room but also to make the large living space workable. You may have the luxury of a fabulous amount of space to play with but, unless you have a very large house, you also have to fit a lot of activities into it – certainly living and dining facilities and sometimes the hall, stairs, and/or kitchen, too. So in your planning you need to allow for socializing, watching television, relaxing, working, and dining – in some cases maybe even cooking and sleeping as well.

It helps to get the layout of the activity areas and the furniture placement sorted out before you finalize the color scheme and soft furnishings. You can demarcate functional areas within the broader scheme using furniture, flooring, lighting, or screens. Then you can use colors and patterns either to unify the various zones or to reinforce their moods and functions. Time spent at an early stage, working out how the open-plan area will look and function, makes the world of difference to the ease with which you can use it.

▲ *The ideas in this open-plan area can easily be adapted for a more modest size of room – the space is divided into separate zones while still keeping an overall cohesion, and castors on armchairs and coffee table add extra flexibility.*

DIVISION OF SPACE

The key to a successful open-plan layout lies in keeping it simple. Sometimes your freedom to maneuver is limited. The location of a fireplace, for example, largely determines the best place to site the easy seating. Windows, doors, and other rooms also impose themselves on the layout of the space. For instance, it makes sense to site the dining section at the end of the area nearer the kitchen. If possible, it is pleasant to position the dining table near a window where it will catch the sunshine at breakfast time. On the other hand, you want to place the television where the screen doesn't catch the glare of the sun through a window.

ARRANGING FURNITURE

A few well-chosen pieces of furniture – a sofa, a dining table and chairs, maybe a desk, side tables, and storage units – are preferable to crowding the space. Strategically positioned, they help to create a structure for the area and accommodate all the people using it. A sofa bed offers the sleeping option. Ample storage makes it easier to preserve an uncluttered look.

Practical positioning Arrange the furniture so that people will use it rather than reorganizing it every time the room is occupied.

Traffic flow It is important to work out a convenient traffic flow through the whole room. When the open-plan living area is the only route from the front door to the kitchen, you want to avoid having to make a detour around a table or cutting across a group of armchairs to get there.

Creating zones A table, chest, sofa, or sideboard placed across the open-plan space sets up a spatial and visual break to differentiate activity zones without destroying the sensation of roominess.

Organizing the dining area If you prefer to use most of the open-plan area as one large living room, a folding dining table that you can push against a wall until you need it is a good idea. When you want a distinct dining section, instead of leaving the dining table surrounded by chairs, disperse some to other parts of the room for a more informal look and extra seating.

CREATING DIVIDERS

If you find you need more privacy in a particular area of the living space, erect a formal room divider. Before rushing into building a permanent divider or buying a freestanding screen, experiment with an improvized divider to make certain that the new arrangement fits the bill. Floor-to-ceiling curtains, for example, drawn across between two sections of the room, muffle sound and create a sense of division and coziness. You must position the partition carefully so that it does not cut across a window, make a room disagreeably dark, slice into an elegant plastered ceiling, or obstruct movement around the room.

▼ In this multi-functional family room a striped rug placed diagonally creates a pathway to the balcony door, visually separating the living and dining areas, while the storage unit for the study area doubles as a stylish room divider.

DECORATING THE AREA

Color and pattern are crucial to the success of the whole layout. Overall cohesion is best maintained by the use of the same or coordinated wall coverings, fabrics, and flooring throughout the area. The flow of colors between sections of the room visually holds the space together.

On the other hand, you can positively emphasize a change of shape or function in the room with color or pattern. By following an obvious structural division, such as the line of a former dividing wall or an alcove, you can modify the color scheme and atmosphere in each activity area. Avoid too many changes, or the area can look cluttered and lose the sense of space.

Flooring Floor coverings usually play a significant part in reinforcing the overall or subdivided nature of an open-plan space. In general, it is best to keep to the same tone throughout the area, even if you vary the material. You can combine a pale carpet in the living space, for example, with woodstrip flooring over the dining section, or vinyl tiles in the kitchen area.

It's worth remembering that footsteps tend to reverberate in a large area. All-over carpet or natural-fiber flooring, laid on good-quality padding, muffles the sound and forms an excellent background for decorative rugs. If you prefer the bare-floorboard look, scattering a few rugs over the floor helps to deaden the sound.

Well-placed rugs are also useful for demarcating definite territories in the room – perhaps in front of a fireplace to anchor a seating arrangement or under a dining table to mark out the eating area.

Dressing the windows Many open-plan conversions result in a room with a window at each end, often of a different shape and size. The same window treatment may not be appropriate for both. However, using the same or complementary fabrics to make a blind or perhaps a valance for a small window at the back of the house and more lavish curtains for the front windows establishes continuity between the two ends of the room.

Accent features Dashes of the same eye-

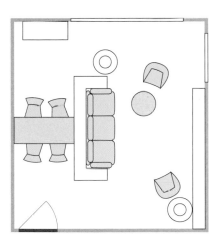

▲ *Here the furniture arrangement divides the room neatly into separate zones for dining and relaxing. Waist-high units built around the back and sides of the sofa help to screen the table and provide storage as well as cozily encompass the seating.*

catching color, appearing on cushions, ornaments, pictures, plants, and rugs dispersed around the area, are all excellent devices for drawing attention to specific zones while unifying the whole scheme.

LIGHTING SCHEMES

A flexible lighting system is vital to making the whole open-plan area work effectively. The immense diversity of activities that go on in an open-plan area calls for general, task, and accent lighting.

Efficient background lighting, supplied by sconces or other wall-mounted lights and spotlights on the ceiling, is supplemented by localized task and accent light sources in separate activity areas. Table lamps, desk lights, floor lamps, and freestanding torchères are portable light sources and flexible design tools that create warm pools of light around the room wherever you want them. At the dining area, concentrate most of the light on the dining table. A rise-and-fall pendant which lifts out of the way when not in use is an ideal light source, as long as you remember it is fixed and governs the table position.

An outlet sunk into the floor under a sofa or armchair means that you can have table or floor lamps close to the seating area without the need for a light cord trailing dangerously across the floor from the wall. For a variable atmospheric effect, fit dimmer switches. These let you adjust the level of lighting in different areas of the room to suit the occasion and to balance natural and artificial light.

▼ *This room seems full of color, yet the walls are a restrained cream and the color is simply introduced with a few well-chosen pieces of furniture. The furniture and furnishings demarcate the different functional areas. The push-together soft seating creates a generously large, right-angled sitting area around the coffee table, while a useful occasional table backs on to the seating.*

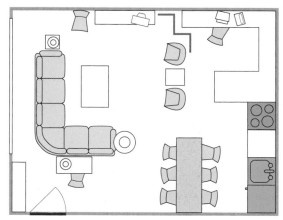

▲ *A large, freestanding item of furniture such as a big sofa can also do duty as a room divider. Here, the sofa separates the open-plan kitchen area from the living space. An attractive half wall with "windows" screens the dining area.*

ROOM DIVIDERS

From half walls to a well-placed sofa, use room dividers to make the most of the space in your home, creating manageable activity areas that still let you enjoy the benefits of open-plan living.

Most rooms in the house have to serve more than one function – whether you have open-plan areas or not – all of which are equally important. The living room may embrace a host of different activities, from quiet reading to music practice, from watching television to formal dining. The kitchen is often the place where family meals are eaten as well as prepared. Bedrooms double as dressing areas, playrooms, or studies; children's rooms are often shared.

Multi-purpose areas require some form of internal organization to avoid chaos and confusion. Room dividers don't increase the space at your disposal, but they make better sense of it.

A room divider can be as permanent as a half-height wall or as temporary as a freestanding screen.

Furniture that you already possess, such as a shelf unit or sofa, can be pressed into service to distinguish one part of a room from another. Dividers that provide practical advantages of their own multiply the benefits. For example, a counter that hides kitchen clutter can also serve as a breakfast bar; open display shelves offer additional storage space for ornamental pieces and books while partially enclosing a section of the living room.

Make sure the dividers don't undermine the basic qualities of the room – you need to plan carefully to avoid blocking light or creating traffic bottlenecks. Equally, it's important to work with the inherent proportions and decorative character of the room so the final effect appears well considered rather than makeshift.

▲ The work area in this living room is separated by an almost ceiling-height shelf unit that can be used from both sides. On entering the room, you see the comfortable seating area. The home office becomes visible only when you move beyond the unit.

PLANNING THE ARRANGEMENT

Before you begin, make a rough sketch of the room to assess how best you can divide it. Pay special attention to entrances, windows, and traffic routes through the space. Ideally, place dividers so that each portion of the room receives natural light. This means the position of the windows is a crucial factor in your layout. Also take care not to obstruct main entrances or make it difficult to move around the room.

Think about how much space to allocate to each activity. Study areas can be quite compact, for example, whereas a dining area requires more space so that chairs can be moved comfortably back from the table. Dividing a shared bedroom usually means splitting the room in half to provide each person with an equal amount of space.

Dividers don't have to follow straight lines. A curving counter is an attractive way of separating a kitchen area in an open-plan space. In a similar way, a pair of narrow dividers projecting out from opposite walls to frame an area can provide more visual interest than a single divider extending some way across the room.

▼ *A blind hanging from the ceiling to the kitchen counter separates the kitchen from the living area; raising the blind unites the two areas. This is the perfect arrangement for entertaining – with the blind raised you can join in the conversation while you cook. Simply lower the blind while you eat to screen dirty pots and pans from view.*

PERMANENT DIVIDERS

Permanent dividers make sense if you can commit yourself to a fixed room arrangement for the foreseeable future. Low walls are relatively simple to construct and you can finish and decorate them to match the rest of the room. Alternatively, you can fit one side of the divider with built-in shelving or cupboard space to provide additional storage. Counters to screen the cooking and preparation areas of a kitchen may need to be slightly higher to provide effective concealment.

Half-width, as opposed to half-height, partitioning is also a possibility. In a bedroom, a narrow partition at right angles to the wall can separate a

bed from a study alcove. On the study side, you can add shelves for books and files.

Display shelves make effective dividers when you want to make a visual distinction between areas but don't necessarily want to block views. Sturdy storage units, open on both sides, are good for separating living from dining areas and provide extra storage space for books and knickknacks. Bear in mind that units must be sturdy enough to withstand being toppled over if you accidentally knock into them. Alternatively, you can construct an open wall of shelving that is fixed securely to both the floor and ceiling.

◄ *You can separate areas within a room effectively by just hinting at a division. This shelf running at picture-rail height across the width of the room supports a collection of grape ivies. Left to grow, their trailing creepers will create a curtain of foliage.*

▼ *This angled counter attractively separates the open-plan kitchen from the rest of the living room. A plate rack suspended from the ceiling further divides the space and makes up for any lack of wall space in the kitchen area.*

IMPROVISED DIVIDERS

One of the simplest ways of dividing space is to position a dominant piece of freestanding furniture, such as a sofa, cabinet, sideboard, or chest, strategically across a room. If you place a table or console behind a sofa that has its back to a portion of the room, the effect will look more considered.

Plants make good improvised dividers, too. You can mass together groups of large plants, such as croton, coffee plant, schefflera, or podocarpus, or use a freestanding weeping fig tree or palm to divide the area. Plants trained on wooden trellises, stakes, or canes, such as philodendron, creeping fig, or grape ivy, grow over time to create a wall of green between two areas.

For a subtler effect, construct a trellis by running lengths of string or wire from the plant pots or floor to the ceiling and train the plants to grow up the framework.

Hanging baskets can also be used to divide the space. Suspend two or three from strong ceiling hooks. House plants such as hoyas, Swedish and grape ivies, and spider plants make good hanging displays and are easy to look after.

◄ *The shelving built to fit against the sloping ceiling of this room creates a tidy corner that can be used for dressmaking. As well as visually dividing the room, the shelving provides a practical surface for the sewing machine to rest on.*

FLEXIBLE DIVIDERS

In some circumstances, permanent dividers are too restrictive. If you want to retain the option of changing the focus of the room at a moment's notice, movable dividers make better sense. Display units on castors provide one solution; standing screens are equally versatile.

Folding screens can offer just enough privacy for a reading corner or dressing area, without committing you to a fixed arrangement. The advantage of screens, aside from their flexibility, is that you can buy them or decorate them yourself to suit the character of the room.

Choose Japanese-style screens paneled in opaque paper and framed in black wood molding for a contemporary setting; fabric-covered screens – either upholstered or with tied or ruched-on fabric panels – for a countrified look; or cover a plain screen with a collage of découpage images to create a Victorian-style accessory.

Sliding panels or folding screens that retract into a door or window jamb or special housing or open accordian-style flat against the wall allow you to partition a room in an instant. This solution makes good sense for children's shared rooms, for example, where you may wish to provide a degree of privacy for each child at night, without sacrificing the use of the entire space during the day.

▶ *A boldly draped curtain hung across an alcove and swept up into a wrought iron tieback gives this telephone corner a sense of privacy.*

◀ *A portable screen is a good way to section off part of a room dedicated to other activities. Here, the fabric screen encloses a sewing area. Pockets sewn onto one side provide useful storage for sewing accessories.*

LOCATING A TV AND STEREO

Choosing where to place your television and stereo system is as important as selecting the equipment itself – follow a few simple guidelines to make sure you get the best out of these home-entertainment purchases.

Almost every household has a television and sound system, from the smallest CD player with miniature speakers to large-scale televisions with stereophonic sound. Getting the best from your home-entertainment equipment depends as much on how you position the units as on the systems themselves.

Once you've decided where to site your stereo and television, you need to decide how to store and display them. Many living-room storage systems offer a module for the television, separate video recorder, and stereo; some stand-alone units are specifically designed to house them.

If your home is high-tech and modern you can make a virtue out of your viewing and listening equipment and choose it to suit the style and decoration of the room. However, for more traditionally furnished homes, the overwhelming modern style of audio-visual systems can spoil the atmosphere, so you may decide to hide the equipment away completely.

Before you buy storage for a stereo system, think about how you use it, whether there is adequate access to it – stereo systems often require access from the front and top – and where in the room you want to place it. The key to enjoying your system at its best is to position the speakers where they give the highest quality sound. This depends to a large extent on the shape of the room and the type and size of speaker – some are designed to sit on the floor, some on a shelf or mounted on a wall, and others are designed to be used with a rigid stand.

The most important aspect of television storage is to make sure it is located where you can see the screen easily. When you buy a storage unit, check that it is the right size and height to house the television and the video recorder if that is separate.

▲ *Home-entertainment equipment should be sited to get the best sound and picture without letting it dominate the decorating scheme. Here a television is housed in a pine cupboard, once a wardrobe. Simply shutting the doors changes the room's focal point to the seating area and coffee table.*

POSITIONING THE STEREO

The operating height of the stereo is an important consideration. You should position the system either low enough so that you can kneel in front of it or high enough for you to stand comfortably while loading tapes or CDs.

Some storage units include room for speakers, but while these look neat, they probably don't give you the best sound quality. The most effective position for the speakers is on the floor or high up on a wall in a corner of the room. Here, the sound output is reflected by the corner walls and the floor or ceiling. If this is not possible, the next effective option is to position them on the floor or near the ceiling against one wall. The further the speaker is from the corner, the more the sound is reduced.

In a small room, the speakers are often so close to the seating area that it is impossible to have any background music without it interfering with the conversation. In such a case, placing the speakers off the floor – either wall-mounted or on a shelf – can help. Wherever you decide to place your speakers, it's a good idea to take time to experiment with a few arrangements to find out by trial and error which one suits you best.

Some of the more expensive speakers are supplied with detailed instructions about where they should be placed. These are the result of exhaustive listening tests by designers, so it's as well to follow them to the letter.

Carpets, curtains, even items of furniture can all affect the quality of sound from the speakers. Bare walls and floors reflect the sound, making it much clearer and bigger, while thick carpets and curtains have a muffling effect.

▼ *The sound system and television play the most important role in this room, so they are very much features of the decor. The speaker cabinets – which match the rest of the storage – and the television are all on castors, so you can move them to get the best sound and an uninterrupted view from any seat in the room.*

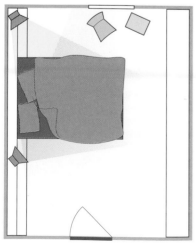

▲ *This is the perfect bedroom for music lovers. A clever shelf arrangement by the head of the bed doubles as bedside tables and stands for the two speakers. The wall-mounted shelves over the bed make space for the stereo, so you can put on music without getting up. A stylish television on a wheeled stand at the foot of the bed is the height of luxury.*

◄ *Speakers on the floor are angled upward to direct the sound into the middle of the room. An attractive, freestanding shelving unit provides room for both the stereo and a collection of records and CDs.*

▼ *Shelves cover the whole of one wall in this living room, making room for both the stereo and speakers positioned along their length. Putting the speakers at opposite ends ensures that the sound reaches all parts of the room.*

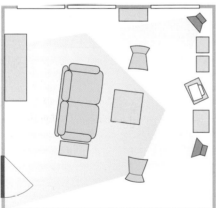

SITING THE SPEAKERS

Each speaker has a cone of sound – the area near the speaker where the sound quality is best. By drawing a plan of your room complete with the main items of furniture, and marking on the speakers and their respective cones of sound, you can work out where you should ideally place them.

▶ *In general,* *if you draw a line through the center of the cone of sound coming from each speaker, the point where the two lines cross is the optimum position to sit and listen to music played on the system. For really serious listening, the distance between the two speakers must equal the distance between each speaker and the listener, forming a triangle of equal sides.*

▶ *In a long room,* *it is more difficult to position speakers successfully, but it does present more options. If you want a quiet area in the room, for dining perhaps, place one or both speakers part-way down the wall, facing into the listening area; the space behind the speakers is quieter.*

▶ *In a square room,* *speakers facing diagonally in from the corners of one wall give the whole room sound.*

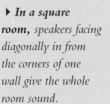

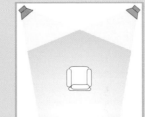

POSITIONING THE TELEVISION

Your television should be easy to view from the most comfortable seats in the living room, but it shouldn't dominate the room. You can meet both of these conditions by placing it on a cart or keeping it in a cabinet or cupboard with closing doors. However you house it, do make sure that it is on a stand of some sort or placed on a surface to keep it off the floor. The recommended minimum height from the base of the set to the floor is 48in (120cm). This allows you to maintain a good seating posture while viewing. Unfortunately, some commercial stands are much lower than this, forcing you to crane your neck forward or slump in your seat in order to see the screen.

Make sure the television is positioned so that there is minimum reflection off the screen from both the window and any lighting. At the same time, though, it is a good idea to have some lighting near the television when viewing, as looking away from the screen from time to time helps to reduce the eye fatigue caused by focusing on it for a long time. This relief is most effective if you look at something of a similar brightness to save your eyes from having to readjust to different levels of light.

▲ *Unobtrusively placed on a shelf, this television is in a perfect position and at the ideal height to be viewed from the sofa, but surrounded as it is with a collection of pots and books and with a large print on the wall above, it doesn't dominate the area.*

▲ *The space between these built-in cupboards and the shelving above is just the right size for the television and stereo with its speakers. All the equipment stands in one spot, so it doesn't interfere with the rest of the room's decorating scheme. Simply turn the television toward you when you want to watch it.*

▶ *This television is cleverly hidden in a built-in storage system. When you want to watch it, you simply open the door and angle the pull-out stand so it is in the best position for viewing.*

DUAL-PURPOSE BEDROOMS

*With a little planning, you can turn a spare room into a
welcoming and comfortable guest bedroom that doubles as an extra room
for the family to use when it is unoccupied.*

A genuinely spare room is a rare feature. Space is a luxury and few people can afford to underuse any room. There are, however, certain times – perhaps before you have children, and after they've left home – when a room won't have a permanent occupant.

If you have frequent visitors, it is a good idea to create a comfortable bedroom. A well-appointed guest room lets you cater for a variety of social occasions without disrupting the entire household. With careful planning and adaptable furnishings, the room can fulfill other functions between visits.

Your spare room may be occupied by guests for a few weeks of the year, so for the rest of the time why not use the room as a study or hobby area? A room that works well for guests also provides the right surroundings for activities such as reading and sewing that require peace and quiet – or for music practice, in which case it maybe everyone else who wants peace and quiet.

If you require a more permanent base for a home office, using the guest room is not a good idea. However infrequently it is occupied, you need guaranteed access to the space every day.

▲ *Everything in this
charming spare room has
a double purpose. Kept
bright, light, and simple,
it serves as a study, a
bedroom, or just a place
to curl up with a book.*

GUEST-ROOM DECOR

The guest room is unlikely to be top of your decorating priorities, but it is worth devoting some time and money to creating a pleasant, hospitable atmosphere. Sympathetic decoration also helps to dispel some of the limitations these rooms may have.

The natural choice in most homes is to allocate the largest and sunniest bedrooms to the permanent residents of the household – which means that a guest room is likely to be small, dark, and chilly or awkwardly shaped, or a combination of these.

If the room is small, but there is plenty of light, opt for a fresh, natural look using white, cream, or pastel backgrounds to increase the sense of space. Keep it simple with natural fabrics in soft, textured weaves on the bed and at the window and a neutral-toned carpet or plain, polished wood underfoot.

On the other hand, if the room is fairly dark, a pale color scheme won't remedy the situation and may make the room look even bleaker. In this case, a dash of color is needed to revive the spirits and supply warmth and coziness. Paint walls in stronger shades of terra cotta, Wedgwood blue, sea green, or sunflower yellow and choose fabrics that reinforce the brighter palette.

Pattern is often just as appropriate for a small room as a large one. Patterned wallpaper helps disguise awkward angles and unifies a room. Alternatively, you can make a feature of one pattern – introduce a bright scatter rug, a dramatic bed cover, or lively window treatment – and keep everything else fairly subdued.

Carpet is the most sensible choice for the floor, supplying warmth, comfort, and sound insulation. Alternatives include stained or polished boards and natural-fiber coverings in sisal or coir. Rugs such as dhurries and kelims add decorative interest.

A houseful of guests means lines outside the bathroom door. A connected bathroom is a real luxury, but installing a small handbasin in a guest room is relatively inexpensive and straightforward and can help to ease pressure on the main bathroom.

For guest rooms that are also work areas, avoid overly fussy looks which are primarily bedroom-oriented. Choose striped, checked, or textured fabric for curtains and blinds and keep covers and upholstery crisp and tailored.

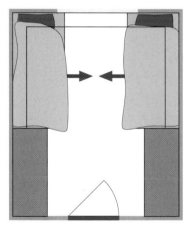

◄ *Every inch of this small room is used to provide a comfortable room for two, and simultaneously provide storage for the household's needs. The single beds are on rollers and can be pushed together to make a double bed. As a bedside table would hinder this transformation, a chair-molding-height shelf runs around the room as a useful substitute.*

CHOOSING A BED

In a guest room, the most important item of furniture is the bed. You don't need to lay out huge sums for the highest quality on the market since the bed is unlikely to be slept in every night. Plain daybeds of average quality are sufficient. A pair of singles may be more flexible than a double. You can dress daybeds up with a headboard or wall hanging – or play them down with a tailored bedcover and scatter cushions to serve as additional daytime seating.

Sofa beds are a popular choice for accommodating overnight guests. If the room is used more often as a work or study area than as a guest room, a sofa bed is unobtrusive and practical. Most sofa beds do not have very high-quality mattresses, which makes them fine for infrequent use.

A Japanese futon looks good in contemporary settings and offers an alternative to a sofa bed. However, choose with care as some people find futons unyielding and uncomfortable, and don't enjoy sleeping so close to the floor. Foldaway cribs that can be stored out of the way between visits can also be useful as extra beds for children.

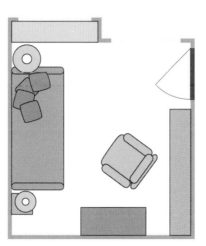

◄ *By virtue of its clever lighting and the attractive window-seat, this room is more than just a place to put up the occasional guest. Matching the fabric on the bed and the window-seat pulls the decorating scheme together, while covering the cushions, mattress, and base of the bed in the same fabric gives it a more sofalike appearance.*

FURNISHINGS

Don't use the guest room as a repository for pieces that don't fit anywhere else in the house. Keep furnishings simple and customize second-hand finds with paint for a coordinated look. Apart from the bed, it is a good idea to include:
• A limited amount of hanging space in a small wardrobe or closet
• A small chest of drawers for folded clothes
• A comfortable chair
• A flat surface, such as a table top or low chest, for unpacking suitcases
• Bedside lamps

In a dual-purpose room, you may also need a work table or desk, a bright task light near the work surface, and plenty of storage. A wall of shelving provides efficient organization for items that look good on display; you can incorporate a worktop into this built-in scheme for a tidy, integrated look. Hide clutter behind closet doors or pull-down blinds. Disguise a sewing table beneath a floor-length cloth when not in use. Store sewing equipment under the table and hide it from view behind the cloth.

◄ *Rule number one in successfully using a room for more than one purpose is to keep it simple. The blue and white decor, natural floor covering, and unfussy furnishings like the built-in, blue-washed cabin bed and painted tray table do this to perfection, resulting in a versatile room.*

FINISHING TOUCHES

Any room that remains empty for prolonged periods inevitably lacks atmosphere. Decorative objects, framed prints, and cushions help to provide some character and vitality. Often a few small touches will go a long way to making your guest's stay a happy one, such as chilled mineral water and glasses in the room, a box of tissues, and other small luxuries. Make sure there is a mirror and lay out several fresh towels. A bowl of fruit and a vase of fresh flowers will bring the room to life and make your guests feel welcome, and a little light reading – books and magazines – piled up on a night table is always appreciated.

▶ *The window area in this attractive cream and pale gray room has been put to excellent use as a luxurious window-seat complete with built-in bookshelves. The drawers below hold the linen and blankets needed to turn the seating area above into a cozy and attractive bed.*

▼ *A wicker sofa bed with its coordinating chair adds charm to this light, striped room. When the sofa bed is folded up, the room can be used for study or sewing.*

CHILD'S ROOM (3–12 YEARS)

A child's room caters for all sorts of activities, from sleep to play, homework to creative fun. To plan a room that does this and keeps pace with a child's growing needs requires a fair degree of ingenuity.

Children grow at a surprising rate. Luckily, you don't need to redecorate and re-equip your child's bedroom nearly as often as you update their wardrobe or replace a pair of shoes. But furnishing and fitting a child's bedroom does mean keeping an eye on the future and building in enough flexibility to cope with the stages to come. Investing in full-size good-quality furniture that lasts for years is the only really cost-effective solution.

Storage is a key consideration. The smaller the room, the more important places for organizing toys and games, clothes, and books become.

Children need the freedom to make a mess, but you can also teach them the advantages of keeping their belongings tidy if you give them the means to do so. For children who share a room, good organization also helps to give each of them their own territory.

All children identify strongly with their surroundings. Bright, cheerful decoration makes a positive environment for play. Display areas for posters, drawings, and favorite toys allow children to express their interests and personalities, while practical, tough surfaces and finishes make life easier for you.

▲ *Try to combine practicality with a sense of fun in your child's room. Here, a comfortable mattress fits into a loft bed. A child can use the space underneath as a den, climb up the ladder into bed, but use the slide to get down. The walls' painted stripes are similarly innovative.*

FURNISHINGS

Arranging the room The floor is the key play area in a child's room. Arrange furniture to leave as much clear space as possible for setting up train sets, romping with friends, making a fort or hideaway, or having a doll's tea party. Most children enjoy the security of having their bed pushed against a wall, so maximizing floor space is not difficult. Where two children share a room, beds on opposite sides of the room help to create separate personal territories.

If the room is big enough, you can tailor storage and layout so there are distinct play areas: a home corner with dolls and accessories, a work area for study and creative play, and a quiet corner with a bean bag, or big, overstuffed floor cushions for looking at books or listening to tapes.

Beds Young children need more sleep than adults. They spend up to half their lives in bed. A good-quality bed and firm mattress that supports the spine are essential for a child's health. Small beds are a false economy. An under-five may look a bit lost in a big bed, but not for long.

Bed frames do not need to be elaborate, but they should be sturdy and well constructed to proper safety standards. Daybed bases, metal frames, or plain wooden bedsteads are widely available and reasonably priced. Invest in a good mattress and, if your child is not reliably dry at night, provide extra protection with a padded, washable mattress cover.

The move from a crib to a proper bed is a momentous point in a child's life. You can ease the transition by letting your child choose his or her own bedspread or duvet cover – bed linen depicting favorite cartoon characters and cuddly animals is widely available. Filling up extra space at the bottom of the bed with soft toys and teddies also helps transform the bed into a more friendly place.

Loft beds, incorporating a desk or play area underneath, are good space savers and provide endless scope for imaginative play. Ensure the basic framework is sound and well-anchored, and the ladder and guard rails are strong and steady. Most manufacturers recommend that loft or bunk beds not be used for very young children. Where older children share a room, bunk beds are always popular.

◀ *A sunny yellow color scheme is suitable for children of all ages. Simply changing a few accessories here allows the room to mature with the child. Plenty of clear floor space means room to play.*

▶ *The curtain strung across the width of this room is drawn at night to make a cozy niche for a child to sleep in. You can keep it closed during the day to screen off the bed and turn the room into a full-fledged playroom.*

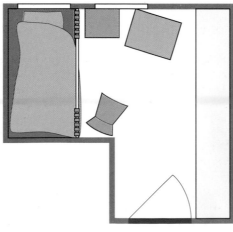

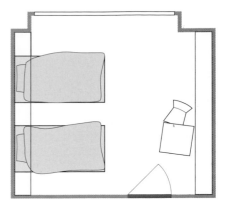

◂ *It is the curtains, border, and bedcovers that make this room such a delight. They are easy to change for a more grown-up look as the children get older. Storage areas on either side of the beds give each child closet space, while the section next to the ceiling holds less frequently used items.*

◂ *Loft beds are perfect for a smaller room and are a good choice for children, who often like such closed-off spaces. Here, the area underneath is used for studying.*

Storage Children and clutter are inseparable. A single toy box or cupboard may be fine for a toddler's possessions, but a few birthdays and Christmases soon change all that.

Successful storage must be adaptable. A child's interests change, so a flexible storage system which serves a variety of uses more than earns its keep. Full-size furniture is better than nursery pieces, which, although undoubtedly appealing, have a short practical life. You can reorganize cupboards or closets fitted with adjustable rails or shelves as the child grows taller and clothes take more space. Shelves on movable metal brackets are indispensable for keeping games and books in order.

Other solutions include:
- A chest of drawers for folded clothes and linen
- A blanket box or trunk for toys and sports equipment
- A big basket for dress-up clothes, soft toys, or dolls
- Individual stacking crates or plastic boxes for blocks, Lego, or Tinker Toys, or creative equipment such as paints, clay, paper, and crayons
- Peg rails or coat hooks for hanging up outdoor clothes, nightwear, or painting smocks
- An open display area for treasured possessions, curios, and collections

If possible, arrange storage so that the child can reach everything. You can stow baskets and boxes under beds, put up peg rails within arm's reach, and keep clothes in lower drawers for easy access. Toys stashed away on upper shelves either won't get played with, or may encourage dangerous mountaineering.

DECORATION

A child's room should have a distinctive flavor of its own. Not many children feel at home in a bland, neutral space. They are naturally attracted to bright color and like to personalize their rooms with representations of favorite objects. For girls, pictures of animals are always appealing, while boys are often smitten by rockets, planes, boats, cars, and trains. Relentlessly themed rooms can be oppressive, but your child is bound to be delighted if you include some reminder of his or her favorite interests in the decor.

Walls Use paintbox shades for a cheerful environment. Alternatively, you can set off pale walls with more intensely colored woodwork. Simple stylized murals or stencil designs are perfect for young children and are easy to paint over when the child develops more mature tastes.

Choose semigloss latex paint or washable vinyl paper for easy maintenance. Set aside some wall space as a display area for artwork, photos, notices, and mementoes. Felt-covered pin boards or corkboards are useful for this. Consider a wall-mounted blackboard or even a lower wall painted with blackboard paint to provide room for creative scribbling. Covering the lower part of the wall with white melamine board supplies another good surface for children to draw on with washable felt-tipped pens.

Theme wallpapers are big business and most children go through a stage when they are completely entranced by a cartoon character or storybook hero. Bear in mind, however, that such enthusiasms are often fairly short-lived. A paper border, duvet cover, or poster featuring the flavor of the month isn't so dominating and is economical to replace at a later date.

Floors Carpet is a good all-rounder, kind on the knees, warm underfoot, and a useful means of sound insulation. Rugged cord or dense twisted low pile make the best choices – avoid thick-cut pile which stains easily. Washable cotton rugs protect flooring from the inevitable spills.

Windows Roller blinds or simple gathered sill-length curtains are the best options. Interline curtains with blackout material for extra light control. There are many charming fabrics specially designed for children. Using them to make curtains or blinds is an excellent way of introducing a favorite pattern into the room.

▸ *A made-to-measure work and hobby area like this could make even homework a pleasure. It combines plenty of surfaces with enough shelving to store both books and toys, and introduces a sense of fun at the same time with shelves made up to look like a house. It would be easy to customize store-bought furniture in a similar way.*

◂ *The modular furniture in this room is ideal for a young child. You can swap around some of the pieces as the child gets older to give the room a more grown-up feel.*

▸ *Bunk beds are a real favorite with children. Even for an only child, it's nice to have somewhere for friends to stay. Here, the lower bunk is a sofa area with part of the frame converted into a desk and shelf.*

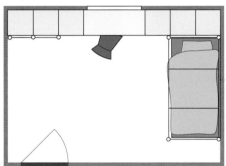

▲ *Good storage is all important. Kit shelving in pine covers the walls of this room. Animal motif fabric hides any untidiness from view and drapes over the bed to create an attractive canopy.*

SAFETY

- Ensure bunk beds have adequate guard rails and a firmly attached ladder. Keep small children on the lower bunk and don't allow children under five to play unsupervised on high-level beds.
- Fit windows with safety catches and install safety glass on large windows or ones that extend below waist height.
- Secure freestanding shelving or storage units firmly to the wall.
- Low Surface Temperature (LST) radiators are ideal for use in children's rooms. Fit safety guards over conventional radiators to prevent burns.
- Provide plenty of electrical outlets to avoid trailing light cords and fit all outlets with safety covers.
- Place non-slip mats under all loose rugs.

▲ Storage never needs to be boring — simple paint techniques jazz up these shelves. Stenciling the boxes in bright colors gives a child somewhere private to store treasured possessions.

▲ This is a great way to add storage to a room. Boxes of toys slide out of the way underneath a low-level platform that gives the child a play area with a difference. You could turn the platform into a comfortable reading corner with the addition of a few scatter cushions.

▶ Brightly colored crates are perfect for storing a child's many toys. Here they are kept under a low-level shelf that doubles as child-sized seating. The castors underneath each crate mean that even a child can pull the containers out from under the shelf.

REVAMPING A BATHROOM

*Brightening up your bathroom needn't be a time consuming
or expensive business – with a little imagination and effort you can spruce
up the most lackluster of rooms.*

To create a new look for your bathroom you don't have to rip everything out and start again. Often all you need to do is replace one or two key items – perhaps lay new flooring or install different lighting – and make a few cosmetic changes, such as introducing a fresh color scheme and new accessories.

If you are keeping some or most of the existing features, it's not always easy to pinpoint exactly what you need to do to a room that lacks inspiration. You may find it helps to leave a notebook and pencil in the bathroom for a week or two, and make a list of things that are inefficient, irritating, or just plain dreary.

In the meantime see what's available. Make notes of color schemes and accessories that appeal, but avoid impulse buys – there are so many accessories and other bits and pieces in a bathroom that it's all too easy to spoil a coordinated effect if you don't exercise restraint.

If the room leaves a lot to be desired, work according to short- and long-term aims. You will then have the immediate satisfaction of seeing some quick improvements – towels in fresh colors, for instance, or a new bath screen or shower curtain – while you wait for other longer term jobs to be finished, such as a new tiled border or built-in bathroom cabinet.

▲ *You can transform an ordinary bathroom into something quite spectacular with a few deft touches. The pine shelf provides an anchor for the unusual brass globe lights and a useful storage area for towels and decorative boxes. An attractive pine-topped vanity unit accommodates the washbasin while the bath brushes and oval mirror continue the pine theme. Choosing a coordinating color for the tile border and Roman blind is another inspired touch.*

QUICK CHANGE

The practicalities Deal with anything that's even remotely dangerous first: put a non-slip finish on the bathtub base, and provide a mat for ceramic floor tiles that get slippery when wet; install a childproof medicine cabinet if necessary; and if there's room, install a grab rail by the bath.

Once the safety work is completed you can set to work on the irritating inefficiencies: replace the waterproof seal around the bath or basin; stop drips and dribbles by replacing washers or faucets and installing a new shower hose, and consider installing an exhaust fan if condensation is a serious problem. In a small room, rehanging a door with hinges on the other side may make better use of space.

With the room in working order, you can set about improving the style and adding color.
Walls Tiles are the most practical of finishes for bathroom walls, but what if they're in an uninspiring design or color you no longer like? With tiles that are in poor condition, either remove them completely, or cover them with some form of paneling – wooden tongue-and-groove panels for example.

There are two ways to tackle tiles that are sound but unattractive: remove them and put up new tiles, or – much quicker and often just as satisfactory – simply tile over them. A third option, not normally recommended for an area subject to damp but worth considering as a short-term cover-up, is to cover the offending tiled surface with a tile paint. This solves the problem if you are planning a complete overhaul but have other priorities to see to first.

If the tiles are merely dull rather than an eyesore, make them more interesting by adding a tiled border to the existing tiles or, for a low cost facelift, experiment with tile transfers.

If you prefer wallpaper, choose a waterproof vinyl, which copes well with condensation and damp zones. Alternatively, paint is a quick way of freshening up walls – look for a type that's specifically made for bathrooms.
Floors Carpet tiles are easy to lay and comfortable underfoot – choose a type suitable for the damp conditions in a bathroom. Also worth considering are well-sealed, floor-quality cork tiles and vinyl sheet flooring or tiles.

▶ *Color coordination plays a huge part in improving the look of this bathroom. The existing aqua walls and bland cream tiles have been linked by a decorative wallpaper border in the two colors. The shower curtain and bathmat in a deeper, richer turquoise add much-needed color. For increased efficiency, the shower attachment has been wall-mounted. Installing a pine cupboard under and next to the washbasin has tidied up the overall look. Open shelving, perfect for displaying attractive lotions and bottles, has replaced the stark chrome bathroom cabinet.*

◀ *Dashes of aquamarine add pizzazz to an all-white bathroom. The free-standing washbasin is contained in a narrow aqua-colored cupboard that provides valuable storage space.*

▼ *A few alterations have changed this bathroom from an uninspired space to a streamlined haven. The larger mirror and sophisticated lamps add light and spaciousness, while the glass shelves fixed over the mirror provide a space to display decorations, bottles, and guest towels. The basin towel rail has been repositioned at a more convenient level.*

Bathroom suite It's possible to buy individual bathroom appliances without replacing the whole suite – you can usually get a good color match for the most popular colors, even from different manufacturers. If the suite is still in fairly good condition, look at ways of updating it. Consider boxing in the bath, for example, and installing a new toilet seat in matching wood. Replace the faucets – there's a wide range of modern and traditional designs available.

Windows One of the easiest ways of adding color and character is with window treatments. Blinds work well in many bathrooms – choose from Venetian or Roman blinds, or softer, more ornate ruched styles. If you are making new curtains, use the same fabric as an over-curtain to hang on the dry side of your shower curtain.

Lighting Good lighting is essential, but it must conform to safety regulations – check with your supplier. Consider something different – special down lights on the ceiling or Hollywood-style bulbs around a mirror. For a look that's both efficient and stylish, install fluorescent tubes concealed behind a translucent ceiling panel.

FACELIFTS

- Introduce color with bright towels, bath mats, and rugs.
- Add character with a themed collection – shells, old bottles, colored glass, or framed prints all make an effective display.
- Collect up all your clutter and stow it in a wicker basket, blanket chest, or similar container.
- In a small room, keep details simple and coordinated.

- Give the room an overall style with matching accessories in china or wood, such as soap dishes, towel rings, and toilet-roll holders.
- Large mirrors are attractive and useful; they reflect light in a dark bathroom and make a small room appear more spacious.
- Improve plain hardboard panels around a bath with inset panel effects using strip molding.

▲ Purely cosmetic improvements – striped wallpaper, a lace swag at the window, a lacy shower curtain, lace-trimmed towels, and a wall-to-wall carpet in blue – combine to give a sophisticated, luxurious look.

▲ It's easy to get a jazzy look by dressing a window in bright and breezy fabrics. The wooden pole, stained a bold orange, adds to the sense of fun, while the windowsill is put to good use to display color-linked accessories.

▶ A coat of blue paint creates a stunning bathroom. A stylish feature has been made of an alcove by painting the recess in deep blue and inserting glossy white shelves. Simply framed photographs, glassware, and some unusual plaster casts help create an interesting focal point.

SINGLE-LINE KITCHENS

*Compact and easy to run but often tight on space,
single-line kitchens need to be planned with ingenuity if they
are to offer a workable layout.*

In a narrow or small kitchen, a single-line layout, with units along just one wall, is often the only possible design option. Although this may seem restrictive, it is possible to make the most of available space with careful planning. This sort of arrangement works equally well in a multi-purpose kitchen/dining/living room, as units and appliances can be neatly contained in one area, leaving the majority of the floor space free.

The key to success in a single line arrangement lies in keeping as much counter space free as possible, and in having a flexible approach to storage, using wall and base units, and the mid-way space between the two. Space saving ideas worth considering include bi-fold, sliding, or roll-up doors. With ingenuity, you may be able to make use of the facing wall in a single-line kitchen, with narrow shelves, a fold-down table, or a grid system for wall storage.

◄ An uninterrupted stretch of work surface above well-organized storage space is the key to a successful single-line kitchen. A refrigerator at the end of a row of units should be hinged so that the door opens away from the counter space for easy access.

PLANNING THE LAYOUT

You need at least 4ft 6in (140cm) of free floor space in front of a single-line of standard-size kitchen units, to leave enough room to move around comfortably and open doors.

Start your plan with the sink. This is best positioned in the middle of the row, leaving space on either side for the range and the refrigerator. It is a sensible idea to situate the sink as close to the original drains and supply pipes as possible to avoid extensive re-plumbing.

Ideally, there should be space for a counter between the sink and the range. If this proves impossible, make sure the drain side of the sink is next to the cooking area so that there is somewhere nearby to put down hot dishes.

RANGE AND FRIDGE

To keep as much counter space free as possible, choose either a slip-in range – a freestanding unit that slides in between the cabinets – or a built-in undercounter oven that has a cooktop above. If you have a very narrow kitchen, make sure you allow enough room for an oven's flap-down door to open.

Even in a tight space, under-counter refrigerators are too small to suit most cooks. A standard refrigerator, with separate fridge and freezer compartments in a single tall unit is much easier to use. Position it at the end of a row of units. This will probably be next to either a door or a window. In both cases, the appliance door should open fully to give you enough space to transfer items to and from the fridge to the work surface with ease.

WASHING APPLIANCES

Finding space for a washing machine is difficult when there is just one wall along which to arrange all the units. You may have to think of an alternate place to install it, perhaps in the garage, if this is attached to your house, or under the stairs.

A dishwasher is useful in any kitchen, but is again hard to accommodate when space is tight. An undersink model, which washes fewer place settings than a regular unit, is ideal in this situation because it uses the space under the sink so efficiently.

With a dishwasher, you may be able to do without a draining board and fit a single sink – or a pair of sinks, if space permits – with a wall-mounted draining rack.

▲ *Try to provide heatproof counter space on at least one side of the range, on which to rest hot dishes as they come off the cooktop or out of the oven. If space is restricted, place the drain side of the sink unit next to the range.*

◄ *This type of layout makes sense in the larger space of a multi-purpose room, such as a combined dining room/kitchen, for example, in a studio or efficiency apartment.*

▶ *Ideal for narrow single-line kitchens, tambour doors are made from wooden slats and roll up from the bottom, allowing full access to the storage space without intruding on the space in front of the unit.*

▲ *Although a central sink is ideal, installing it as close as possible to the original drains and water pipes saves money. Use corners for broom closets or refrigerators.*

SPACE-SAVING DOORS

Ordinary side-hinged doors are not the only or most compact options. Here are some space-saving ideas to think about if you are planning a single-line kitchen:

• Piano hinge or bi-fold doors are hinged in the middle to fold back on themselves, offering access to the whole cupboard. Some bi-fold systems link four or more doors, others just two.

• Sliding doors take up even less space but allow access to only half the cupboard at a time.

• Tambour doors are made from joined pieces of slatted wood and roll up from the bottom, allowing access to all the cupboard. This is a stylish option available on more expensive kitchen cabinets.

STORAGE SPACE

With the essentials in position, you can devote the remaining space to storage.

Wall units Take wall units right up to the ceiling to make the best possible use of the space available. Use the top shelves for infrequently used items. Where a window breaks the row of wall units, incorporate it in the overall design by hanging cupboards at either side level with the top of the frame, then join them with an overhead storage shelf.

Base units Pull-out racks help to make the contents of base units more accessible but do take up space. Installing narrow wire racks to the inside of the doors is useful for small jars and bags, without affecting the storage capacity of shelves.

Midway space Don't forget the wall space between the wall units and countertop. Many kitchen manufacturers make small midway units or narrow shelves for this area. Alternatively, you could install storage grids for hanging utensils, or buy a specially made storage rail with fittings such as a cookbook stand, kitchen towel holder, and wire shelves for spice jars. Utensils can be hung from the rail using S-shaped hooks.

A microwave is an asset in most households, but takes up counter space. Make use of the midway space by mounting the microwave on a shelf, or by installing it to a pivoting bracket. If you want a microwave but can't afford either wall or counter space for it, consider an electric multi-function oven which also includes a microwave. This is an expensive option but offers two appliances in one.

◀ A double stack of swivel-out, wedge-shaped metal baskets takes up no extra space under the counter at the end of a single line of units and appliances. Perforated for ventilation, they keep fruit and vegetables fresh and easily accessible.

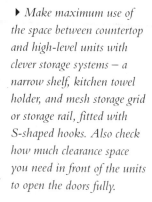

▶ Make maximum use of the space between countertop and high-level units with clever storage systems — a narrow shelf, kitchen towel holder, and mesh storage grid or storage rail, fitted with S-shaped hooks. Also check how much clearance space you need in front of the units to open the doors fully.

◀ *Intense sky blue, midway between low- and high-level storage units, provides an airy backdrop for a hanging dish rack, glass rack, knife rack, kitchen towel holder, and spice shelf. High-level, open shelves are ideal for attractive but little-used items.*

◀ *This stylish butcher's table on lockable wheels supplies flexible and mobile work and storage space. Side panels can be extended for additional counter surface, and collapsed for compact storage when not in use.*

VISUAL TRICKS

• You can fit integrated doors to the front of appliances to match the base units, giving a neat, uncluttered line. The drawback is that integrated appliances cost much more than their free-standing equivalents, even though the essential features are exactly the same. You can save money by using a wider than normal countertop, which projects about 3in (7.5cm) beyond the front of appliances and base units, so that you can install matching fronts to hide the dishwasher, washing machine, and refrigerator. Doing this leaves a handy service space behind units which can be used for gas and water pipes and wiring.

• An efficient range exhaust hood is a must in a small kitchen where a build up of cooking smells can soon become unpleasant. This also keeps surfaces free of airborne grease. Make the range hood into a focal point by choosing an eyecatching stainless steel chimney model, or by housing it in a chimney hood to match units. You can fit slimline pull-out range hoods beneath a wall closet. It is also possible to buy a range hood with a microwave built in above it.

• Mix glass-paned and solid-front wall units with open shelving to avoid a boxy look. Mixing colors is another possibility. Cream and natural wood, red and black, black and white, and green and yellow are all stylish combinations.

THE FACING WALL

Don't ignore the facing wall in a single-line kitchen. With ingenuity, you can make excellent use of the space.

• Narrow shelves fitted from floor to ceiling add invaluable extra storage space. Put cuphooks beneath upper shelves and use them for hanging cups and mugs.

• Fix a hinged shelf to the wall with a fold-down supporting leg beneath. You can use it as extra working space or as a breakfast bar and fold it up when not in use.

• Install storage grids on the wall. Timber storage grids are strong enough to hold pans. Make sure the grid is attached securely to take the weight.

• Base units measure 2ft (600mm) from back to front. Wall units measure 1ft (300mm). If there is enough space for doors to open easily, you can fit cupboards along the facing wall by turning wall units upside down and fitting them with a countertop. You could also stack units to provide a double layer of useful storage space. Mix glass-paned and solid wood doors for an interesting effect.

▲ *Sliding doors fronting a tall shelf unit are very economical on space. When closed, they protect a handsome collection of china from dust and kitchen grease.*

▲ *Use recesses in the facing wall for fitted shelves and/or closets. Mounting the telephone and kitchen accessories on the walls keeps counters free of clutter.*

▶ *A duck-board hanging rack fixed to the facing wall and fitted with S-hooks adds strong visual interest as well as endless possibilities for storing utensils and herbs. The duck-board can also camouflage a less-than-perfect wall surface.*

ISLAND KITCHENS

If you have enough space, a well-planned central island can become the functional heart of a kitchen, providing extra storage, work surfaces, or a venue for quick meals.

An island kitchen is essentially one that is large enough to allow a central working unit. This can be as complex as a custom-built unit, possibly on more than one level, with or without built-in appliances, or as simple as a wheeled work trolley or a table. The island need not be square or rectangular. Depending on the space available, it can be circular, oval, geometric, angled, or an L shape with a cooktop on one arm of the L and a sink or breakfast bar on the other.

Installing an island in a large kitchen can help to avoid the problem of an over-extended work triangle as services can be positioned close to each other by installing the cooktop, sink, or cooling equipment in the island. Piping and wiring will need to be run under the floor which will increase installation costs. Because of this disruption, it often isn't practicable to add an island fitted with appliances or a sink to an existing kitchen.

An island without appliances can be just as useful as one with. The base can be a mix of cupboards and open storage, such as pull-out wicker baskets for vegetables, a space for baking trays, a wine rack, and open shelving. The counter can be extended beyond the base at one side to make a breakfast bar, and extra storage can be created by hanging a utensil rack from the ceiling. The possibilities are endless, even if your budget is limited.

▲ *Although usually flat-topped, island units can also be multi-level. This unit features a built-in wooden chopping block and cool marble surfaces, ideal for rolling out pastry, above ample storage space.*

FINDING SPACE

Island kitchens are not suitable for very small rooms as space is needed all around the island to allow cupboard doors both on the island and on the facing runs of base units to open easily.

The size of the island depends on the space available, but generally it shouldn't be any smaller than 23½ x 35½in (600 x 900mm). Too big an island can involve unnecessary walking, so don't be tempted to install a large unit just because there's enough space for one.

The island doesn't have to be square or rectangular. In a smaller room, a curved island with no corners to knock against may be more convenient than a square or rectangular shape. In a very large room, you could opt for an island based around a rectangle with angled wings at each end, or a multi-purpose, multi-level island with a granite or solid wood work surface at one side and a table at the other for eating.

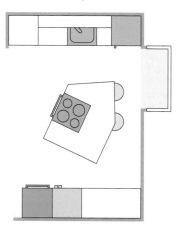

▼ *An asymmetrical shape of island unit may make the most of the space in a kitchen. Installing a range hood above an island cooktop is perfect for removing steam and cooking smells, but is expensive in an existing kitchen.*

▲ *In the planning stages, remember that sufficient surrounding space is necessary for access to the island's and adjacent units' drawers and closed cupboards, and overhead lighting is useful.*

▶ *A kitchen sink fitted into an island unit, such as this small round sink useful for washing fresh fruits and vegetables, should always be in addition to the main sink.*

USING THE ISLAND

A simple island can provide valuable extra working space, or you can opt for something more elaborate fitted with a sink or a cooktop. The top of the island can be made from laminate, solid granite, artificial stone, solid wood, or tiles. If you plan to use the surface for food preparation, choose real or artificial stone with a solid wood butcher block inset. It's easy to damage a laminate top by forgetting to use a chopping board and although tiles are attractive they can be impractical as a work surface. Using real or artificial stone is sensible if you want to include a cooktop.

Where electricity is being run to an island, it's a good idea to make the most of it by installing a couple of outlets, either mounted in the top or on the side, so that you can use small appliances. Top-mounted sockets must be protected from spills and liquid by a flap cover.

USING THE TOP

The top can include a sink or a cooktop but existing floor coverings may have to be lifted so that gas and water pipes and electric wiring can be brought to the island.

It's sensible to site the island opposite the existing sink position to minimize piping. Connections can be run across a concrete floor before the final topping is laid, or run beneath floorboards.

Secondary sink The island sink is normally secondary to the main sink and can be used for washing vegetables or for preparing drinks. It isn't really a good idea to make the island the site for the main sink – there's unlikely to be enough room for anything more than a single bowl.

Cooking center You could use the island as a cooking center by installing a cooktop into the surface. An island is the perfect site for an additional cooking unit such as a deep fat fryer or an indoor barbecue. These small units take up less space than a normal 23½in (600mm) wide cooktop, which does not allow enough work space on each side.

These small specialized cooktops can be used alone or in combination. A typical unit includes an indoor barbecue, griddle, deep fat fryer, two zone gas, electric or halogen burners, and a two zone gas cooktop with a wok burner.

If you want to install a cooktop, you need a ceiling-mounted range hood above the island. A dramatic stainless steel chimney range hood, or an integrated range hood hidden in a handsome wooden canopy, helps to turn the island into an interesting focal point. A ducted range hood that carries cooking smells, steam, and smoke is more efficient than a recirculating model – in an island installation, the ducting can be hidden in the ceiling cavity.

Even expensive range hoods can be noisy so if you intend to use the room for living and eating in addition to cooking, consider a remote motor model.

WORKING HEIGHT

Make sure the island is at the right working height for you. Standard working height is 36in (900mm), but some feel that the ideal height for cooking, kneading bread, and other culinary tasks is 31½–33½in (800–850mm). Achieve this by either reducing the whole island height or part of it. If you want it to double as a breakfast bar, lower the cooking and working areas only so that the top is on two levels.

ON TOP

If you are installing an additional cook-top into the countertop, the range hood will help to make the island into a focal point. There are several other ways to give dramatic overhead impact to a simple working island.

• A hanging canopy makes the perfect home for trailing green plants such as English or grape ivy. Both flourish in a warm, steamy kitchen atmosphere. If the canopy is slatted, you can hang utensils from the underside.

• Make a utensil hanger from an old-fashioned clothes drier. Make sure that it is securely fixed to the ceiling with butterfly bolts or it might collapse under the weight of pots and pans.

• Hang a simple wooden or metal rail from chains and use it for tying up bunches of dried flowers and herbs, and strings of garlic and onions.

• Fit a billiard table-style light or a pull-down light fixture above the island to illuminate the surface.

▶ *Overhead racks make good use of space and, if well designed and suspending handsome utensils, enhance the appearance of the island unit.*

THE BASE

Make the base of the island unit really work for you with these simple ideas:

• Attach wooden rollers to the side of the island for kitchen towel, dish towels, foil, and food wraps.

• Install a kick space heater in the plinth for instant warmth.

• Leave a space between units or appliances for trays or wooden chopping boards. Fit the space with telescoping rails if you need somewhere to hang dish towels and oven gloves.

• If space is limited, use sliding or bi-fold doors on island base cupboards.

• Deep drawers are useful for storing casseroles, saucepans, baking tins, and electrical appliances.

• If you collect cookbooks, fit bookshelves to the base – small, shallow ones for standard paperbacks; larger, deeper shelves for bigger books.

◀ *A sturdy freestanding kitchen unit with low-level shelf space can make a movable island unit, to be positioned wherever it is most useful.*

HOME OFFICES

*Working from home offers many benefits, not least
that you can create a comfortable and stylish environment to
suit your own personal needs.*

More and more people are working from home, sometimes for convenience, but often purely out of preference. There are many benefits – you save both time and money by not traveling to an office and you can plan your working environment to suit your particular needs. Even if you're not running a business from home, space-consuming, or messy hobbies benefit from having their own area.

Conflicting interests between domestic and business tasks can make working at home difficult, and this applies as much to planning a home office as to allocating your own time. It's hard to ignore dirty dishes or an unmade bed if your desk is in an open-plan kitchen-dining area or bedroom. So it is important to try to shut yourself away from such routine distractions. On the other hand, it is unfair to spread your clutter around a room which is used by the rest of the family.

The solution lies in a disciplined approach to allotting and planning a room for your home office. How much space do you need? Is peace and quiet essential? Do you use noisy equipment that might disturb the rest of the family? The answers may lead you to consider ways of getting away from it all in a converted loft, basement, or garage, for example, or even by building an extension. But if these are not feasible options, you can always transform a spare bedroom or an under-used dining room into a home office.

▲ *A home office can operate
efficiently without looking
utilitarian. Here, the pine
furniture includes attractive
shelving fitted around the
window. The desk is placed
under the window for
optimum light, while the
radiator underneath keeps
the area warm. A Venetian
blind controls the amount of
light entering the room.*

CREATING A WORKING ENVIRONMENT

Decor Real offices are usually painted in neutral, unobtrusive colors, but working from home offers an opportunity to apply some color psychology, letting you choose the tones that make you feel like working – calming pastels if you like lots of light or deeper tones for a more traditional atmosphere. Use flowers, plants, and photographs to make the room look inviting.

Lighting Good artificial lighting helps to avoid eye strain and headaches. Your office should be well lit so that you can work at any time of the day or night – remember, you're no longer confined to traditional office hours. You need desk lamps for close work and for when it grows dark. Angled desk lamps and wall-mounted or clamp-on spotlights all give excellent local light. Versatile overhead lighting is provided by down lights. These are either recessed or surface-mounted on the ceiling. They produce a pool of glare-free light on the surface immediately below and so minimize the risk of reflection. You can angle eyeball down lights to shed light exactly where you want.

Placing your desk so that it faces a window provides you with lots of natural light – the best to work in. Avoid sitting with your back to the window, as the sunlight may be reflected from a computer screen. Venetian blinds are useful for light control, especially if your computer is affected by glare, as you can adjust the amount of light entering the room. Not only that, but they're useful for hiding distractions such as the lawn that needs mowing, sociable neighbors or toddlers who would much rather you were playing outside with them than working.

Sound The purpose of a home office is to provide the user with privacy and solitude, but peace and quiet for the rest of the family is just as important. Computer keyboards, printers, and knitting or sewing machines are less disturbing with a degree of soundproofing, which can be as simple as lining the wall closest to them with cork or an insulating wall covering. Placing the machines on rubber pads also helps to cut down on sound and vibration.

Warmth It is expensive to heat the whole house throughout the day for the benefit of a single person. If your central heating is switched off during the day in winter, consider adding some form of back-up heating just for your office – an electric convection fan or radiator heater may prove to be an economical solution.

▲ *This light, bright alcove extension built onto a living room is separate from the main living area. Patio doors on one side and floor-to-ceiling opaque glass windows on the other give the area an open, spacious feel.*

◀ *Ideal for teaching or academic work, this office has a complete wall of open shelving, so books and files are easy to locate. A worktop fixed right across the room under the window allows space to spread out. There is more than enough room for two people to sit and work together.*

◄ *This is the perfect home office if you need to entertain clients or conduct business meetings. There is enough room around the island desk for people to gather, while the sofa provides seating for more informal moments.*

▲ *Full use is made of the stunning windows in this room, setting two desks side by side in front of them. The desks are built-in with useful storage cubicles running along the tops and sides.*

SAFETY

Ensure that your home office is a safe place to work. Watch out for:
- Trailing light cords
- Overloaded power outlets
- Inadequate lighting
- Poor ventilation
- Inadequate heating
- Chairs that are the wrong height for the desk

FURNITURE ESSENTIALS

Regardless of whether you opt for the fitted or the freestanding look, all home offices need a desk, a chair, and somewhere to store work, stationery, and equipment.

The desk The size of the desk you need is dictated by how much space you have to play with and whether or not you use a computer. Computers take up a lot of desktop space, so you may prefer to add a separate computer table with a swing out section for the keyboard and a shelf for the printer and paper as well as a desk.

Almost any kind of table – including a shelf fixed securely into an alcove – can serve as a worktop, even if it has no drawers underneath. Traditional roll-top or knee-hole desks are attractive and provide generous drawer storage.

The chair A good, comfortable chair is one of the best investments you can make for your home office. An unsuitable chair can give you backache, while one that is too low makes using the desk awkward.

Ensure your desk and chair are the right size for each other – your best bet is an adjustable chair. If it has arms, make sure these don't prevent you from getting close enough to the desk to work comfortably. You may also need an extra chair or two for visitors.

Storage This needs to be well organized and easily accessible to avoid wasting time and effort unpacking and clearing away equipment before and after each working session.

Built-ins offer good storage, but you may prefer to buy attractive freestanding pieces that you can take with you if you move. Solid doors for lower units keep messy clutter out of sight, while open shelves above are attractive if they include, for example, the odd plant between files and books. Self-assembly or simple do-it-yourself shelving are good, inexpensive options.

Filing cabinets are a good idea if you have a lot of papers to keep. A lockable drawer allows you to keep important or private files safe.

▶ *Traditionally furnished, this small room has a luxurious feel, making working more pleasurable. The antique knee-hole desk faces the window which, with its elaborate curtain treatment, is the focal point of the room. A mixture of open and closed custom-made built-in storage runs along two walls of the room.*

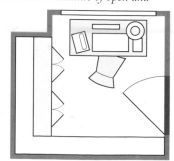

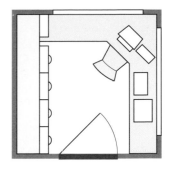

◀ *Building the work surface around two walls of the room makes the most of the space. The knee-hole area in the corner provides adequate leg room, allowing the rest of the room to be saved for storage.*

▼ *A large amount of this room is given over to the pine table and filing cabinet, allowing you space to spread out. But, with its upholstered leather stool and the framed map on the wall, the room escapes a spartan feel.*

▲ *Specially designed office furniture makes for a workman-like office without sacrificing style. You can pick and mix the units to suit your needs.*

BUILT-IN FURNITURE

If you want the look and feel of a real office, opt for made-to-measure built-ins designed specifically for the home office. You can arrange a selection of the many storage options on offer to make the best use of the space available; they fit into awkward corners and around out-of-true walls.

If you decide on built-in office furniture, get professionals to help you choose and arrange it. The cabinetmakers will visit your home, measure the room, ask about your requirements and make suggestions about the type of furniture you need, where to site the desk and whether any additional lighting and power outlets are necessary.

There is usually a choice of different styles of furniture, ranging from oak or beech to mahogany veneer or high-gloss colored laminates.

IMPROVISING AN OFFICE

You don't need to invest in an expensive built-in system to create a good working atmosphere for your home office. Improvised solutions can be very effective. You can use a trestle table as a desk and place a small chest of drawers under it to one side to provide all the storage space you need. Alternatively, use a large sheet of plywood or a length of kitchen worktop as a desk surface and balance it between the tops of two hip-height filing cabinets.

If you need more storage space, you can add it very simply by fixing shelves to the wall with brackets. Paint and decorate the area using any techniques that strike your fancy, then add a chair plus any equipment and stationery you need, and you have an effective home office.

▲ *A highly polished table like this one is perfect as a work surface. It has more than enough depth to allow you room for a computer and keyboard, if necessary, and looks just right in the traditional setting.*

▶ *This improvised desk made from filing cabinets, mini bookcases, and a double worktop provides a huge amount of storage and fits perfectly into the area under a sloping roof. Positioned under a skylight, the setup makes the most of the daylight.*

◀ *Wall-mounted shelves on each side of the window take care of storage needs, while the desk has space for a computer, printer, and room to work, but it is the vibrant color of the walls that really makes this home office something special.*

UNDER THE STAIRS

Create a compact home office, telephone alcove, or airy, orderly storeroom under the stairs and relieve pressure on other areas of your home at the same time.

The area under the stairs is often neglected. Once you recognize its potential, however, you can transform it in a variety of ways. With a little thought you could turn it into an efficient storage area, designed around your particular needs; or you could open it up into a room or hallway, thus increasing available space and giving your home a more open-plan feel.

Depending on the pitch of the stairs, there may be enough room at one end to stand, in which case the space can be put to many uses. If the water supply and

drain lines are close, you could install a shower or toilet, or even turn the area into a mini-utility room, fitted with a washing machine and dryer.

However you decide to use the space, aim to unify it with the surrounding decor by painting it in the same colors or papering it in similar wallpaper. Continue the existing floor covering, if possible, or keep closely to its tone and style, even if you are using the space for storage. That way the newly converted area looks a planned part of your home, rather than an afterthought.

▲ *Opening up the area under the stairs in this narrow hallway increases the sense of space and forms a secluded alcove for additional seating. Scatter cushions add to the decorative look of the seating area.*

OPENING UP THE SPACE

The ease with which you can open up the area under the stairs depends on the type of staircase and its position in the house. In many instances the space under the staircase is already enclosed by paneling and opening it up simply involves removing the wood panels. Before you start though, it is important to assess the construction of your staircase.

CAN IT BE DONE?

The simplest type of staircase – a straight staircase supported at the top against a wall – is the easiest to open up because the timbers under the stair serve only to support the paneling. A straight staircase between two side walls (with access to the space from an adjoining room) is the most difficult to open up as both walls are likely to be load bearing. In this situation you need professional advice and

help, and perhaps a building permit, before you can remove the walls.

With quarter-turn, half-turn, and some straight staircases that extend onto a landing, the top of the stairs and intermediate landings are supported by a large timber post called a *newel*. You can easily identify it because it is much bigger than the timbers that support the understair area, and usually lines up with the corner post of the stairs above.

You should never remove a newel post without consulting an architect or builder first, as it is a complicated structural conversion that may require a building permit. If you do go ahead and remove it without professional advice, the stairs above could fall down on you. However, you can remove the paneling which screens off the area under the stairs without any fear of collapse, and then plan how you use the space around the newel post.

▼ *Careful furnishing of reclaimed space under the stairs makes it a focal point of the room and a useful display area for family treasures.*

▶ *Continuity in the wall color, flooring, and paintwork ensures this under-staircase library is an integral part of the room.*

USING THE SPACE

Opening up the area under hall stairs adds a feeling of spaciousness to the entrance area and gives you more room to put the hall to practical use. The same goes for opening stairs up into a room – you create a visually interesting niche, framed by the staircase, which you can use in any of the following ways:

A library If you have a fairly large space and lots of books and magazines, how about setting up a mini-library? Line the walls under the stairs with shelves – adjustable ones are a good idea, allowing you to vary and alter the spacing to store all sizes of books and magazines. Painting the shelves to match the baseboard and other moldings gives the space an integrated feel. Use recessed spotlights or angled floor lamps to illuminate the books as well as to provide reading light. For a really high-tech touch, fix up strip lighting on the shelves themselves to highlight the books.

If space permits, add a comfortable chair, looking out into the room or hall. The stairs themselves often protect the space underneath from drafts, making it a cozy place to sit and browse through the books.

A work space You don't need much room for a compact home office. Install a desk or fitted work surface with roll-out filing cabinets or a stack of baskets underneath. Fix shelves to the walls above the desk and add a swivel chair on castors. Provide a telephone jack and power outlets for electronic equipment. Multi-purpose office machines, such as a combination phone, fax, and answering machine, fit into some remarkably small spaces.

Good lighting is essential, especially if you sit with your back to the natural light source. Wall-mounted bracket lighting may be more practical than a desk lamp, which takes up some of the valuable, but limited, space on your work surface.

A telephone corner Set up a private telephone area under the stairs. All you need is a phone and phone jack, a comfortable chair, and a telephone table – use one with a shelf or drawer underneath for message pads, pens, and telephone books. A wall-mounted adjustable spotlight or torchère with a dimmer switch gives you enough light to read phone numbers, but allows you to dim the lights to a pleasant glow for a chat to family or friends.

A display area Shallow under-stair spaces fitted with shelves are ideal for displaying collections of attractive objects, such as glass or china. Put up open shelving or place precious collections behind glass. It is also a good place to display collections of watercolors, delicate needlework or fabrics because they are usually protected from damaging exposure to direct sunlight.

▼ *Soft lighting, fitted carpet, and wood paneling make this under-stair space perfect for a study area. The white-painted, sloping wall stops the space from feeling claustrophobic and reflects the light from the table lamp.*

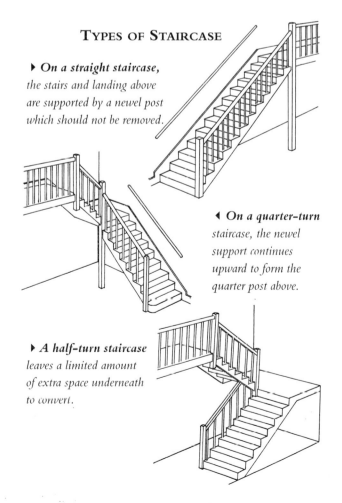

TYPES OF STAIRCASE

▶ *On a straight staircase, the stairs and landing above are supported by a newel post which should not be removed.*

◀ *On a quarter-turn staircase, the newel support continues upward to form the quarter post above.*

▶ *A half-turn staircase leaves a limited amount of extra space underneath to convert.*

CLOSED-IN SPACE

You may decide to close in the space under the stairs instead. Using wooden panels, tongue-and-groove boards, or sheets of plywood effectively creates a useful storage closet. If you equip the area with plenty of hooks and shelves, you can store a large quantity of household paraphernalia away under there. For easy access, fit a full-size, outward-opening door a little away from the end wall, so that you can put shelves behind the door as well. Make sure that the space is adequately lit, locating the light switch by the door.

Utility space You may even be able to keep large kitchen appliances, like a freezer, tumble dryer, or washing machine under the stairs. Check out the practicalities of installing power outlets and plumbing first, of course. Also ensure that you can comply with the regulations for adequate ventilation in windowless spaces by installing a ventilating kit for the dryer and an exhaust fan to the outside.

Cloakroom space In many homes, there is enough room to add a toilet or mini-shower room under the stairs, as long as it is practicable to supply power outlets, plumbing, and ventilation. Consult a plumber for professional advice and be sure to get a quote for the work before embarking on the conversion.

▶ *An unusual V-shaped door provides generous access to a narrow, under-stairs space. Plenty of hooks and shelves ensure it is a great place to keep regularly used household items.*

◀ *The door under these stairs leads into a small cloakroom. Finishing the staircase, the door and the surrounding paneling in exactly the same dark-wood effect gives the hallway a pleasing continuity.*

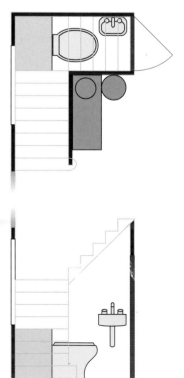

2
ROOM STYLE

CLASSIC LIVING ROOMS

Elegant and comfortable, classic style is a popular choice for a living room, creating a restful ambience for relaxing, or an impressive setting for entertaining.

A classic living room has an air of effortless style and comfort, as though all the contents have been cherished and handed down over the centuries. Soft, gentle color schemes give an impression of space and light, while period architectural details, such as a marble fireplace or decorative cornicing, add to the look of a well-established home.

Deeply upholstered sofas and armchairs are surrounded by antique-style furnishings – a sparkling glass chandelier, an old brass-handled chest used as a coffee table, and richly draped curtains all reflect an earlier era of gracious living. Small details are important too, such as dainty tassels that finish a tablecloth corner or dangle from a window shade. Complete the effect with formal groupings of pictures, lavish flower arrangements, and precious-looking china, glass, and silver.

➤ *Soft blues and yellows create a calm and sunny scheme, carried through on walls, furnishings, and floor. Elaborately swagged curtains frame the window, and an elegant stripe mixes with pretty florals on the sofa. Touches of black in the picture frames and the lacquer chest coffee table add a sophisticated touch.*

CREATING THE LOOK

Choose easy, gentle shades for walls, keeping to pale shades if the room isn't large. Creamy yellows, shades of rose, off-white, or beige make good backgrounds for stronger accent colors, and contrast well with rich, polished woods. Plain latex or interesting paint effects are suitable, with detail added in the form of plaster moldings, paneling, or wainscoting. Pick out any details in a delicately contrasting color, or rub them lightly with gilt wax for a faded sheen.

A period fireplace makes an important focal point; an Regency-style plaster surround has a graceful effect, while marble looks imposing – you can imitate this successfully with paint. Carved and polished wood has the right look too. A number of firms specialize in original fireplaces – check out architectural salvage companies before buying an expensive imitation.

Wallpaper designs are traditional – smart stripes, scrolled designs, or stylized flower and leaf prints all flatter the look, but patterns should be fairly subtle. Keep woodwork pale – white gloss looks fresh and crisp – or strip back to the wood, then stain and polish to an aged mahogany or oak effect. Make sure details such as door handles and finger-plates are all in period style – opt for gleaming brass or crystal rather than chrome.

STYLE POINTERS

 WALLS Pale/matte: plain pale latex; decorative paint effects – ragging, marbling, or dragging; symmetrically paneled areas with plaster beading, or wainscoting; white, pale gloss, or stained and polished woodwork.
Wallpapers: formal stripes, subtle florals, or small traditional motifs such as wreaths or classical urns; ornamental borders or trompe l'oeil effects of classical moldings.

 WINDOWS Elaborate: full-length lined curtains on imposing wood or brass rod; elegant swags and tails; formal pleated valances or shaped cornices; fringes, tassels and braids.
Shutters/blinds: folding shutters; simple roller shades in plain cream with tassels.

 FLOORING Traditional: polished wood or parquet; fitted carpet in subtle neutrals or small all-over scrolling designs.
Rugs: traditional Persian and Turkish-style in rich, toning colors; tapestry rugs in gentle browns, pinks, and blues.

 FABRICS Rich/traditional: gleaming damasks, silks, glazed chintz, woven stripes; small woven motifs or velvets for chairs; tapestry or needlepoint cushions.

 FURNITURE Period style: comfortable sofa and armchairs; upholstered ottoman, stool, chairs; polished wood or Chinese lacquer occasional tables; small antique-style desk; fitted glass-fronted cupboards or shelving.

LIGHTING Grand: central chandelier in gilt and cut glass; period-style wall sconces; brass or wooden floor lamp with large pleated silk shade; table lamps; candles in silver candlesticks.

 ACCESSORIES Antiques, objets d'art: delicate porcelain and china; silver; gilt-framed pictures and mirrors; leather-bound books.
Flowers: large formal displays of seasonal blooms with trailing greenery; small flowers in tiny jugs; bowls of dried flowers or potpourri.

▼ **Yellow striped wallpaper** *gives an impression of height and airiness, and sets a sunny tone for the color scheme.*
Period-style architectural detailing – *the paneling, wainscoting, and decorative molding on the bookcase are typical of the classic style.*
An imposing marbled fireplace *with an overmantel mirror provides a formal focal point in the room.*
Elaborate swags and tails, *extravagantly trimmed with a tasseled fringe, create a grandly formal effect.*

▶ *A subtle color scheme gives this classic style room an air of distinction, creating a harmonious background for carefully chosen furniture and accessories. The gothic arches on the shelving, marbled paintwork below, pillared fireplace, and framed mirror help create the period look.*

FURNISHINGS

Elegance and comfort are essential elements of the classic style living room. Choose a boxy-shaped sofa with comfortable, soft cushions covered in a longwearing woven stripe or damask. Team it with a selection of different seating styles, covered in toning but different fabrics. This looks more natural than a matching suite, and you can pick up bargains to revamp. A chesterfield or chaise longue adds an authentic touch.

Glass-fronted cupboards are perfect for displaying favorite china or old books. Chests and trunks with upholstered tops – or draped with a shawl or throw – provide a useful surface, and hidden storage space, too. Modern items such as the TV and stereo are best tucked away in built-in storage systems.

Look for small decorative tables to hold lamps and collections of silver-framed photos; or buy inexpensive particleboard tables and disguise them with matching floor-length circular cloths trimmed with deep fringing.

Create a soft, atmospheric glow with careful lighting. If you have a central chandelier, fit a dimmer switch so you can create a candle-like glimmer. Wall lights, table lamps, and floor lamps, or candles set around the room, create pools of warm light. Large Chinese-style vases in blue and white or green provide good lampbases; wood stained to a mahogany or ebony finish on brass bases are also ideal. Fit them with a simple parchment or pleated silk shade.

Large, gilt-framed landscapes or portraits look suitably imposing, together with a large framed mirror over the fireplace. Architectural engravings or botanical prints in narrow black frames add a sophisticated touch. Hang them in groups, perhaps linked with a picture bow or stick-on, printed classical swags and borders.

Choose ornaments carefully, avoiding a cluttered look; a single big plaster bust – some museums sell copies of original antiquities – placed on a side table or in the hearth, has real impact. Symmetry is an important element – matching stylized china dogs or cats either side of the hearth is a typical classic look; or place matching china figurines on the mantelpiece.

▼ *A tasteful collection of bric-a-brac makes an artless set piece on a gleaming wood fireplace. The textures and images create a classic period feel – polished wood, brass, a paisley scarf, and images of country sports.*

▲ *A warm and welcoming glow suffuses this room, from the mottled peachy walls and shadow-striped curtains to the richly colored Turkish rug. One antique piece in good condition, such as the gothic-flavor glass-fronted cupboard, gives the whole room an authentic classic look.*

▲ *Pale neutrals have an air of luxury, and make a flattering background for precious objets d'art. Vary textures and patterns to keep the interest around the room. Here, a wreath-strewn beige wallpaper is teamed with plain cream curtains, swagged and rosetted, and the cream sofas have an obvious satin stripe.*

▶ *With the precision of a stage set, pairs of swags, tails, rosettes, lion plinths, armchairs, and needlepoint cushions march forward in ranks from a bay window. Each pair contributes something distinctive to the picture – a flash of yellow, a classical reference, or an intricate detail.*

DETAILS

Small touches can create the impression of graceful living that typifies classic style. Flowers are always important; create a big, splashy formal display of greenery and twigs, and supplement it with fresh flowers in season. Place bowls of scented dried flower heads or potpourri on tables for a drift of perfumed air.

Handworked items, such as tapestry cushions, old silver, and leather-bound books, create a sense of the past. Group objects together carefully to complement each other.

▲ *Distinctively monochromatic, a black-on-beige shadowy stripe wallpaper has a Jacobean-style floral motif. The faux green marble effect on the fireplace adds classic style detail and makes a dramatic background for gilt and brass.*

▲ *A plump needlepoint cushion in a fruity design is aglow with rich color. Needlepoint and tapestry create a classic feel, reinforced by the classically inspired basket of fruit design on the cushion.*

▼ *Two pictures complement this cool turquoise scheme. One has a dainty gilt bow – easily made in fabric dipped in stiffener, then gilded – and a carefully matched turquoise mount. The other has a molded gilt frame around a simple engraving. Both draw the eye to a sculptured and pleated curtain tieback.*

▶ *Classic blue and white china always has a fresh appeal. Place a Ming-style lampbase with a pleated shade on a tiny table to illuminate a dark corner.*

GLAMOUR LIVING ROOMS

*To give your living room a sumptuous image, indulge in
a spot of glamour styling. The results are as relaxing as they are impressive
and luxurious but, despite appearances, don't have to cost a fortune.*

Classy and chic, but never vulgar, glamour styling creates a sophisticated, comfortable living environment. To the envy of anyone with young children or boisterous pets, pale neutral and pastel shades are used exclusively on walls, floors, and upholstery, with reckless disregard for practicalities. There is a larger-than-life, film-set side to the look that favors accents of gilt and sparkling glass on furniture, soft furnishings and themed accessories, to accentuate a sense of grandeur and luxury.

The impression of spaciousness on a broad scale is another defining feature. Within reason, you can create space by leaving out more than you put in, and by maintaining symmetry and a strict orderliness.

In glamour styling, there is a healthy cross-fertilization between styles and periods. The look borrows an overall feeling of elegance from the town house idiom, and sets it in delicate, light color schemes and clean-cut furniture arrangements gleaned from the Scandinavian style.

Once the scene is set, it is the detailing that truly enriches the look. A seemingly incongruous mix of highly ornate and ultraminimalist furniture and accessories distinguishes the image. You can expect to see eighteenth century French-style giltwood chairs combined with Art Deco-style tables, all illuminated by modern light fittings. Far from becoming a mishmash, a carefully rationed selection and purposeful placement ensures glamorous exclusivity.

▲ *The very epitome of glamour styling, this majestic living room exudes class and luxury in every respect – from the enormous white-upholstered sofas to the magnificent mirror and the monumental onyx and glass coffee table.*

CREATING THE LOOK

Color and pattern scheming The first commandment of glamour styling stipulates that all surfaces and soft furnishings are pale or shiny. Discreet self-colored jacquard and damask fabrics and brocade shot through with gold thread are favored over conspicuous, colorful patterns.

The notable exception to the pale-only rule is the use of a little black or dark navy for dramatic contrast on woodwork, furniture, or upholstered furnishings.

A prolific use of gilt and gilding adds a rich gleam to instill a vital feeling of luxury and extravagance into the look. To replicate the effect, you can use inexpensive gold wax polishes or paint to accent the detail on moldings, furniture, and picture frames.

Walls Creamy neutral or pale pastel shades dominate the look – peachy pink is a favorite color. Wallpaper is subtly colored, maybe with a faint self-colored stripe or a damask-style or moiré pattern. To capture some of the architectural extravagance of stately homes, you can use trompe l'oeil wallpaper borders that mimic cornicing or balustrades between the wall and ceiling or around the wainscoting.

Floors Thick pile, wall-to-wall carpeting, again in pale colors, is a quintessential part of the luxurious impression the room is designed to create. It doesn't stop there because there's often a liberal scattering of large, subtly colored rugs.

Fireplaces An imposing fireplace, preferably in real or mock marble, provides a significant focal point for the room. Embellishing your existing fireplace with corbels and moldings, then painting the whole assemblage white gives it an appropriate sense of grandeur. Alternatively, a simple arrangement of two large corbels supporting a glass mantelshelf looks very effective.

Lighting In true theatrical fashion, atmospheric lighting dispensed from stylish light fittings enhances the glamorous setting in the evening. Overhead chandeliers or Art Deco-style torchères are ideal for general lighting. Magnificent table lamps and lampshades contribute localized illumination at strategic points around the room.

ELEMENTS OF THE STYLE

The handsome living rooms shown here and on the following pages represent an attractive and attainable view of glamour styling that you can easily introduce into your own living room.

FLOORS

It's unnecessary to forgo all practicality for comfort. Wall-to-wall berber carpet, echoing the biscuit coloring of the room and looking suitably luxurious, is very longwearing.

WALLS

A fine striped wallpaper adorns these walls, topped with a wide paper border depicting a lavish three-dimensional effect of festooned fabric. A pale neutral or pastel paint can achieve a similar light effect. Woodwork is typically painted white or cream.

WINDOWS

This room is blessed with a huge picture window which is quite modestly but stylishly dressed with neatly pleated swags and tails and a navy blue roller blind. More flamboyantly draped, full-length curtain treatments help smaller windows live up to their illustrious surroundings.

FIREPLACE

Decorated with moldings and painted to match the woodwork, a large fireplace makes an imposing focal feature for the room.

FURNITURE

The room is fairly simply furnished with a pair of sturdy sofas covered in a pale damask, a large fabric-covered coffee table, and a lacquered chest. Bookshelves are tucked into the fireside alcove.

ACCESSORIES

A glint of golden color is significantly conspicuous on a lamp base, picture frames, brass-trimmed boxes, ceramics, a clock, and candlestick. Flowers and pot plants are compatibly large and exotic.

FURNISHINGS

Arrangement Plenty of space, light, and airiness, or at least the impression of spaciousness, is extremely important to the image, so avoid crowding the room with furniture and accessories. Given the significance of the fireplace as a focal point, the seating and allied occasional tables tend to be ranged around the hearth.

Furniture Quality and size count more than quantity in glamour living. Remember, this is a look that is out to bowl you over with its audacious use of deep sofas and elaborately carved and gilded console tables, commodes, or sideboards. Including the occasional delicate Louis XVI-style giltwood chair or side table underscores the magnificence of the proportions.

Pale or muted damask, moiré, and jacquard fabrics figure largely in the upholstery. You can establish the basis of the look quite economically with two roomy sofas covered in crinkled cream or white washable cotton fabric.

Generally, any wood trim or wooden furniture is quite light, either limed, painted in subtle colors with touches of gilding, or veneered in golden walnut. For an absolute contrast, black lacquered wood trim on chairs and tables can look dramatic, especially when the details are accented with gilt paint or polish, although dark mahogany is too somber for the effect.

Lustrous metals, sparkling glass, and polished stones, such as marble and onyx, are three definitive elements in establishing the richness and splendor of the style. Metallic effects can range from a gentle golden gleam to the eye-catching twinkle of polished chrome. Glass appears frequently as mirrors and as table tops.

Windows For classic, ostentatious glamour, copious amounts of fabric are poured into ceiling-to-floor length curtains and trimmed with cord and tassels. Although fully fringed swags and tails work well for the look, they're not obligatory; brass tiebacks, goblet headings and Italian stringing are just as acceptable. However, in a fuss-free setting, you can use plain, neatly folded Roman blinds very effectively.

In keeping with the walls, floors, and furniture, curtain fabrics are generally light in color but heavy by weight and rich in texture. Interlining the curtains adds extra substance and stresses the luxurious quality of the style. A darker contrast in linings and valances is permissible as it draws more attention to prominent window treatments.

◀ *Dedicating a whole wall to sheets of mirrored glass has a wonderfully glamorizing effect. Not only does it afford a larger than proscribed measure of shiny, reflective surface but it also makes the room appear twice its real size. The extra-long settee, silk cushions and elegant Italian strung curtains reinforce the feeling of grandeur.*

◀ *In the hands of a glamour stylist, plain walls, a few massive pieces of furniture, a disparate assortment of accessories, and classical ornaments are miraculously unified into a cultured, welcoming living area.*

▼ *Whether as cushions, throws, rugs, or upholstery, mock animal prints bring an element of the exotic to the look.*

▼ *Atmospheric lighting and stylish light fittings – preferably in polished metal or glazed ceramics with a hint of gilding to reflect the gleam – are intrinsic aspects of glamour styling.*

DETAILS

Stardom beckons when it comes to adding the ornaments and accessories that conjure up the characteristic glitz and gloss of a glamorous look. A few key pieces of fine ceramics, the odd flash of polished metal, glass, and stone, with touches of plush fabric, hit just the right note.

▶ *The contrast between a muted color scheme and glowing lighting plus plenty of shiny accessories sets up glamorous vibes in a comfortable living room.*

▲ *Adorned with fine china, a picture frame and the ever-present table lamp, an occasional table, and a mix of textured fabrics on the sofa typify the aims and ideals of glamour accessorizing.*

◀ *Burnished brass, gilt wax or paint, and gold threads add a rich flavor of luxury to the plainest of walls, fabrics, and ornaments.*

GLOBAL DINING ROOMS

*Dining room decor should lift the spirits to complement
the food you are serving. Global styling is ideal for creating an exciting sense
of theater that livens up the experience of eating at home.*

Hospitable and comfortable, the global style combines informality with strong handling of the decorating basics – confident color, characterful texture, and lively pattern. The look is simple and natural yet exuberant, with the emphasis on straightforward materials and unfussy detail. Rugged, natural surfaces and finishes marry with cheerful handmade accessories to create dining rooms which are practical as well as enjoyable. The informal approach goes well with today's casual lifestyles and the latest trends in decorating.

Global styling is also economical and easy to assemble. You needn't travel far to find most of the ingredients for the look – homespun furnishings, handprinted textiles, handcrafted baskets, bowls, and tableware are as accessible as they are affordable. It's always worth keeping your eyes open for ethnic craft items with bold profiles or striking designs, such as pottery jugs or metal candelabra, that look good on the dining table.

Unless you want to achieve a particular regional look – a minimalist oriental scene or a sumptuous Indian setting, for example – you can mix and match artifacts from different countries of the world and combine colors, patterns, and textures with abandon. In this relaxed styling, there's no need to agonize over what goes with what, since most elements blend well together whatever their country of origin. If you like to travel, global style provides the perfect excuse to display your treasured souvenirs.

▲ *In a dining room
decorated in global
fashion there is a strong
bias in favor of earth
colors and natural
wooden furniture and
fittings, enriched with
handcrafted accessories.*

CREATING THE LOOK

Walls The look is fundamentally bold, rather than pristine, warm rather than cool. Rich earthy tones, from ocher to brick red, epitomize the look. If you prefer a more reticent background, chalky white makes a good foil for dark wood and lively patterns.

For once, less than perfect wall surfaces actually suit the look. Paint loosely washed over rough plasterwork provides a wonderful textural dimension while layers of glazes or washes add luminous depth to the finish. You can accent the main divisions of the wall, at the top, bottom, or wainscoting level, with a handpainted trim.

Floors Dining room flooring should be easy to maintain. With its bias toward natural materials, the global style is best expressed in plain sanded or stained floorboards, natural stone or brick flooring, plain terra-cotta quarry tiles or natural fiber coverings such as seagrass, coir, or sisal.

As an extra layer of comfort, you can partner basic no-nonsense flooring with bright scatter rugs or runners.

Indian dhurries, kelims, and Mexican serapes come in a wide range of colors, patterns, and price ranges. Natural fiber floor coverings can be made up in room-sized mats or runners, loosely laid over a non-slip backing.

Windows Window treatments are best kept simple and uncluttered. Slatted wooden louver shutters, natural split-cane blinds, or wooden Venetian blinds filter the light interestingly. If you prefer fabric at the window, choose a homespun or handprinted textile, such as batik or tie-dyed designs. You can catch up a length of ethnic fabric, including saris, in front of the window with clips or drape it over a wooden, bamboo, or metal rail for an instant, no-sew window treatment.

Lighting For atmospheric dining, combine a chandelier over the table with soft wall lights, table lamps, or discreet torchères. Plain modern fittings are best, while lamp bases in polished metal or glazed ceramics fit in well. Metal candleholders with tiered branches look right on the table.

ELEMENTS OF THE STYLE

In this natural version of the global style dining room, the emphasis is firmly on a neutral color scheme, rugged furniture, and coarse fabrics, set into a worldwide framework with authentic ethnic artifacts. For further inspiration on recreating the look, and more exuberant, colorful renditions, explore the pictures on the following pages.

WALLS

Plain neutral or earthy shades suit the look well, possibly with a broken color paint effect to suggest roughened plaster. White painted or stripped woodwork complements the rugged, rustic feel best.

ACCESSORIES

Whether it's a metal sculpture of dancing figures, an intricate wire fruit bowl or lamp base, or a length of kelim patterned fabric thrown over the back of a chair, ethnic artifacts establish the global connection.

FURNITURE

A solid wooden dining table presides over the room, accompanied by a set of dark wood dining chairs. Each chair is treated to its own cover, in a variety of coarse fabrics to match the color scheme.

FLOOR

Bare wooden floorboards, stained and varnished, help to define the style. A natural fiber runner under the table is a good compromise instead of carpet in a dining room; it fits in well with the soft furnishings and is too narrow to catch many accidental food spills, yet helps prevent the floor getting scuffed by diners' feet.

WINDOWS

Unfussy window treatments are the order of the day. Tabbed sheers and a length of coarse, hand-decorated fabric draped over a bamboo rod are ideal. Stiff bristle finial-like ends to the rod are an apt ethnic detail.

FURNISHINGS

Furniture Global style is essentially an international country look with pieces gathered from around the world. Rustic rather than refined, global dining furniture displays a forthright use of natural materials, such as wood and metal. Many retailers produce ranges of simple, sturdy furniture which work well with the style, or you could look out for similar designs in secondhand shops and flea markets. Plain or painted planked wooden tables, wrought metal chairs, benches, and farmhouse chairs with rush seats make good global basics. Tie-on cushions or loose covers give extra comfort.

For dining-room storage, choose a large wooden cupboard, armoire, or series of wooden wall cupboards to house linen, cutlery, glassware, and crockery. Strip old pieces of previous finishes and lightly stain or wash them with paint for a distressed look.

Table settings Mix ethnic ceramics, metal platters, carved wooden bowls, and woven baskets for serving dishes and containers. Tableware should be chunky and colorful; spotted, striped, or plain earthenware in vibrant colors looks cheerful and unpretentious. You can cover the table with a patterned cloth or use individual place mats in rich or bright weaves. Many home stores stock a range of characterful dining accessories, from handmade wood ladles to handblown colored glass, that display the global theme.

Accessories The definition of the global style relies on a few well-chosen accessories, rather than a mass of small curios and trinkets. Be bold and choose a few large decorative pieces, such as stoneware urns, embroidered wall hangings, and carvings to create points of interest. Too much clutter is claustrophobic and will detract from the center of attention, the table.

On the walls, display a collection of ethnic style prints, an oriental hanging, or rich appliquéd embroidery. A mirror adds drama to the dining room, especially with a metal or mosaic frame.

▲ A carnival of bright colors fills this dining area with a sense of exotic gaiety. True to the global tradition of impromptu, handworked patterns, a border design is painted around the room at wainscoting level. Wrought-iron chairs and a floorstanding candelabra perpetuate the Central American theme.

◀ The global equivalent of classic dining-room red, this terra-cotta colored wall offers a rich, warm backdrop against which to dine off ocher-glazed crockery set on a color-coordinated tablecloth.

◀ *A cozy cottage interior is the ideal venue for global styling and vice versa. Chunky wooden furniture and vibrantly patterned fabrics from around the world are excellent at conveying rustic charm.*

▶ *Authentic ethnic designs are a great source of inspiration when it comes to incorporating colors into a global dining room. Here, the rich colors of the Madras check cloth are well distributed around the room. The color-matched metal and wicker chairs add a novel twist to the global scene.*

DETAILS

Collect a worldwide range of ethnic artifacts to establish a multi-cultural context for the style. Look out for handcrafted tableware from the area of the dish you are serving to generate an authentic atmosphere for the meal.

▲ *Serve wine or soft drinks from a galvanized pitcher or a glazed terra-cotta jug swathed in a bright neckerchief to continue the theme of the party.*

▼ *A divided basket made of woven cane is a convenient and appropriate way to present cutlery in the global style.*

▲ *Be on the look out for pottery in traditional ethnic shapes and patterns to give your dining an international flavor.*

◀ *Hand-carved wooden salad servers are a practical token of global dining.*

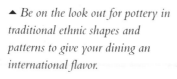

DRAMATIC DINING ROOMS

Making an impression is central to dramatic style, so the intimate setting of a dining room is the perfect place to express your creative flair – and to revel in the riches of color, pattern, and texture.

Dramatic style provides you with a bold canvas, whether your tastes are sleek and contemporary or steeped in the glamour and history of a period look. Ambience is important in any dining room, and creating a setting where your guests have a sense of well-being underlines its success. However, the mood in a dramatic dining room or dining area goes further, bestowing a sense of occasion and making any meal served in the room a memorable, almost theatrical experience.

The success of the style relies on an imaginative

approach rather than a large budget – creating a great visual effect is what matters. Capitalize on the attributes of the room , such as its natural light, height, or size. Even a particularly small dining room can be an advantage because you can emphasize its

▲ Good balance and proportion and a skillful use of color equal maximum visual impact in this richly patterned scheme. In such a powerful dramatic setting, strong keynote accessories, such as these golden wine goblets, earn their place.

cozy, intimate atmosphere. Highlight any key elements: extravagant drapes in luxurious velvets, silks, or brocades; crystal glass and sleek, gleaming tableware; large, ornate mirrors and candlesticks; and the most important element of all, strong, bold color combinations.

CREATING THE LOOK

Use color on the walls to establish a particular mood. If the mood is to be airy and romantic, pale shades, with gilding or shiny metal accents, will help to create the right ambience. For a classical twist, you could opt for graphic black and white.

If the mood is more exotic, or has a sumptuous, period feel, saturate the room with intense, warming color; reds, glowing earthy colors, faux stone, and rich, dark shades, all have the effect of "pulling in" the walls.

Deep purples, midnight blues, and vibrant malachite greens have this enclosing, haven-like effect, too, but these rich colors also convey a subtly different mood with an air of mystery and a hint of magic.

For floor covering, take the lead from your special theme. Stone slabs or faux effects and black and white tiles suggest many looks, from ancient or heraldic to classical and ethnic, and can also look very modern. Pile carpet, polished parquet, or custom-ized floor designs have a sophisticated, luxurious element to them.

Lighting, like color, captures the mood. Dramatic style relishes special effects, so choose lighting designs that work for your theme. Torchères, sconces, picture lights, table lights, as well as an imposing light positioned centrally over the table, allow you to create subtle changes. A dimmer switch gives you control. Candles are a vital prop, and are a must for an intimate atmosphere.

STYLE POINTERS

 WALLS Rich/sumptuous: vibrant contrasting color paint effects; colorwashes and glazes, stippling, faux effects; stone, marble, verdigris; murals, trompe l'oeil, bold plain color, gilding/metallics; ornate moldings.
Wall coverings: bold, flamboyant/exotic pattern; classical motifs.

 WINDOWS Flamboyant/curtains: lined, full-length, variations of dramatic classic styles; pelmets, swags, and tails; elaborately draped metal/wooden poles; extravagant tiebacks, sumptuous cord ties.
Blinds: sleek and architectural with slatted Venetians; or theatrical/exotic festoon styles.

 FABRICS Gorgeous/exotic: richly colored and textured silks; satins; moirés; saris; luxury devoré velvet/velvets; brocades; shimmery metallics; fur fabrics; bold graphic prints; floaty voiles; shiny plastic/PVC; leather; dramatic pattern prints, stripes, checks.

 FLOORING Luxurious/bold: wall-to-wall velvet pile carpet; animal prints; exotic/theme pattern; customized patterns/faux stone/ marble/linoleum effects; parquet; graphic black and white tiles.
Rugs: stylized contemporary/exotic patterns; natural/cream plains.

 FURNITURE Impressive/modern/period: theatrical flourish; glass and metal/black lacquer for contemporary looks; rich fruit woods, mahogany, oak, painted/distressed wood, painted motif for period look armoire, shelving, serving table/sideboard; metal grille-front radiator covers/bookcases.
Table and chairs: contemporary pale wood/glass and metal or heavy period styles for refectory, extending leaf, trestle styles; circular pedestal table; wrought metal/sleek wood chairs; flamboyant slipcovers; rich texture/color upholstered period chairs.

 LIGHTING Bold/atmospheric: sets the mood; extravagant looks for traditional or modern chandeliers; contemporary pendant shades/halogen spots; wrought iron candle fittings, character table lamps; dimmer switches; candles/nightlights.

 ACCESSORIES Impressive/eclectic: luxurious, streamlined contemporary or heavy traditional cutlery; metallic/bold color underplates; streamlined modern, ornate/metallic rim traditional dinner service; goblets; metallic/luxurious tablecloth/mats/napkins; elaborate floral/fruit display; striking mirror/picture frames; decorative screens.

▼ *A sumptuous color scheme* of fruity reds, pinks, and gold creates a warm and luxurious ambience with an unashamedly romantic, period flavor.

Lavishly draped silk curtains with their wide padded borders and corded tassel trims add a flamboyant style statement.

An ornate gilt mirror is a dramatic feature in its own right, and the reflection of the dining table adds visual interest and atmosphere.

Strikingly bold stripes for upholstery and accent furnishings prove that elegance need not be understated.

A crystal chandelier provides a glittering focal point, and echoes the intricate lines of the mirror frame.

▶ *Dramatically different, zebra stripes look surprisingly modern on these Art Deco dining chairs. The blue walls and the light cast by the torchère create an airy background, so attention is drawn to the warm tones of the maple wood.*

FURNISHINGS

All the colors, patterns, textures, and lighting in the dining room should provide a flattering setting for the dining table. Think of this as the star, center stage, and everything else, including existing features such as a fireplace or window, as important but supporting role players. Position the table for maximum impact, for example under a central, eye-catching light fixture, or framed by a window treatment or a handsome fireplace. Alternatively, create your own foil – position a sideboard or serving table to balance the dining table, and use the top for a dramatic display as on a mantelpiece, with lights or candles to each side. Other foils could be an elaborate screen, theatrically ornate mirror, bold picture display, specimen topiaries, potted palms, or other large, leafy plants.

As befits the most important feature in the dining room, the table should take pride of place; not only with tableware, linen, and accessories to enhance your theme, but because of its own impact. If your dining table and chairs are unexceptional or not compatible with your chosen style, transform them using spectacular patterned and colored fabric. A fabulous floor-length cloth, tailored to flatter the table shape, and chair slipcovers, will alter the whole look of the room. If all your chairs require is a simple change of color, lavishly upholstered seat pads will instantly focus attention where you want it.

▼ *Looking contemporary with an exotic touch, vibrant green and a rich blend of blues, yellows, and gold are balanced by refreshing white and the graphic lines of the wrought-iron furniture. The glass table top is an inspired choice as it promotes a feeling of space, as does the mirror, centered dramatically over the console table.*

◀ *Both traditional and contemporary elements are at the heart of this scheme's success. The dramatic floral centerpiece is classically formal, but its support looks very modern – a twist that is echoed with the eye-catching classical mural on the folding screen. The screen itself is used as a backdrop to streamlined furniture and bold, colored fabrics.*

▶ *Glorious, warm Tuscan colors seem to drench the walls with a sun-baked ambience, and create an escapist atmosphere where classical features combine with a comfortable earthiness. Elegant period details such as the Venetian glass chandelier and heavily textured fabrics are key features that enhance the drama of the setting.*

WINDOW TREATMENTS

Window treatments reflect and enhance the look, so be generous here with shape, color, and texture. Use rich velvets and glowing silks – saris are relatively inexpensive – swagged and draped in lavish folds, and trimmed with rich braids, fringing, and tassels. Alternatively, choose a more restrained elegance. Minimalist blinds, tailored pelmets and lambrequins, and graphic prints such as those with classical motifs or calligraphy, all have a dramatic undertone, and a bold, almost stark approach can be just as relevant in the right setting as lavish furnishings in sumptuous, period-inspired schemes.

◀ *Candlelight intensifies the intimate atmosphere of this warm, inviting setting, where muted colors and exotic spice-route patterns meet traditional western comforts. Cleverly coordinated formal swags and tails and elegant chair covers flatter the lavishly presented table with its color-matched napkins.*

DETAILS

Because dramatic style is larger than life and an element of fantasy is the norm, you can really indulge a passion for extravagance when it comes to choosing accessories and style details. Make sure each element earns its place visually in the scheme of things; fussiness means a loss of impact. Let your theme dictate a signature color choice for tableware, fabric covers, table mats or color accent underplates, and match crockery and cutlery to stemware where possible, whether it is elegant crystal or extravagantly tinted, gilded, or beaded in style.

Be indulgent with table centerpieces – use fruit, vegetables, flowers, or natural forms. These offer lots of dramatic potential. Incorporate candles into the scheme – arrange them at different heights for effect. The containers you use should echo your theme. Architectural pedestal urns, oversized, sleek, and modern glass vases, carved ethnic bowls, and antique-style metal or rustic clay and wicker, all speak volumes about mood and ambience.

▲ *A rich, Victorian-inspired color scheme with dark polished wood and deep jewel colors creates an imposing atmosphere – one where the dining table definitely takes pride of place. The contemporary fabric print, which is an imaginatively designed collage of classical details and botanical studies, is the key element in this dramatic scheme. Strong, plain colors provide flattering accents.*

▲ *Contrast checkered tiles have a dramatic visual quality, and seem to define a floor space as no other patterned covering can. Here, they are set off by the glass-topped table and the graphic lines of the wrought-metal furniture. The white accent chair seats and blue-rimmed plates are clever touches, as these contrast with the colors of food.*

◄ *An imposing gilt-framed mirror is almost a necessity in a dramatic, period-style dining room. Place it centrally over a mantelpiece, or on a wall where it can reflect the dining table and enhance the table setting. A large mirror helps to create a balance with other elements.*

COUNTRY BEDROOMS

*With its emphasis on hand-crafted natural materials,
informality, and simplicity, the country bedroom is
stylishly restful and refreshing.*

The hallmarks of the country bedroom – natural materials, unfussy and practical furnishings, airiness, restrained but rich color schemes, and a commitment to comfort – create an environment that is perfectly conducive to rest and relaxation at any time of day.

Whether stripped, stained, varnished, or painted, wood features heavily in country schemes as floor and wall surfaces, furniture, and smaller decorative objects. Other natural raw materials such as cane, wicker, and cotton play supporting roles. Colors such as teal blue, creamy yellow, conifer green, and rich Indian red are traditional, used on their own to cover broad expanses

of wall, or in small doses to give character to large expanses of white or pale neutrals. Furniture has a timeless practicality, based on a mixture of Shaker simplicity, American Colonial elegance, and a hint of toned down Victorian. Generously stuffed cushions, pillows, and quilts ensure that comfort is high on the list of priorities.

Ornamentation, from stencils to children's toys, is – in appearance if not in actuality – hand crafted. Likewise, fabrics have a slightly rough, homespun appeal, and patchworks and samplers continue the hand-crafted theme. The look is mildly eclectic rather than highly coordinated, but never chaotic – everything has its rightful place.

▲ *Wood in all its rich variety – stripped, stained, varnished, and painted – is one of the keys to creating a country bedroom. White walls with a hint of terra cotta and a touch of stenciling add to the look.*

CREATING THE LOOK

Walls Whether they are plastered, papered, or tongue-and-groove paneled, keep walls plain. Combining low-level, tongue-and-groove paneling with a plain painted surface above is traditional. Consider narrow, vertical tongue-and-groove paneling up to wainscoting level if funds allow, with wide, horizontal tongue-and-groove paneling above, or vice versa. The paneling can be left natural, stained, or painted in solid, matte tones.

Patterned wallpapers are unsuitable, as are chalky ice-cream pastel colors such as light pinks, blues, and mauves. Earth colors, natural dye colors, off-white, and white are ideal for the look – the latter two especially for small bedrooms. For an authentic touch, paint the woodwork – doors, architraves, baseboards, wainscoting, and picture rails – a rich color to counteract the impersonality of white or off white. Varying the density of this color from paneling to architraves, reveals, and baseboards is typical. Consider high-level stencils and friezes with simple geometric motifs or motifs based on fruit, flowers, or leaves; grapes, pomegranates, pineapples, willow and oak leaves, and tulips are all authentic.

Floors Wide, stripped pine floorboards are ideal, but if your house doesn't already have them, modern wood-look floor covering strips make an acceptable alternative. You can use subtle paint effects, perhaps even a stencil around the edge to mimic a rug. Hooked, crocheted, knitted, or braided rugs, and embroidered needlepoint rugs, or

Berlinwork with rose motifs, look perfect and make walking barefoot comfortable. Plain or striped, inexpensive cotton, hand-woven rag rugs can work equally well. Although not strictly authentic, wall-to-wall carpets in near white or neutral tones won't detract from the look, provided they aren't too sumptuous or shaggy.

Windows As the look depends on plenty of natural light, make the most of windows. Outline small windows in the same color as baseboards and picture rails; you can paint wooden window frames, reveals, and sills, or simply apply a band of color to the wall surrounding the window. White-painted internal louvers, wooden Venetian blinds, and plain, checked or striped fabric shades are fine for the look. If privacy is a problem, or the view is far from leafy and rural, hang simple white net or muslin curtains. A little swag made from patchwork fabric adds a pretty finishing touch on its own or with another window treatment.

Lighting For practicality, have several light sources: low-level, sited near to the bed for night reading, plus wall-hung and/or ceiling-hung for general illumination. Candles in sconces, freestanding or wall-hung, add to the mood; electric lights mimicking candles are useful as well as attractive. Table lamps with simple shades in checked, striped, or plain fabrics, and earthenware bases, such as old jugs, are ideal. Victorian-style brass table and floor lamps with translucent glass shades, or plain, small contemporary lights, also suit the look.

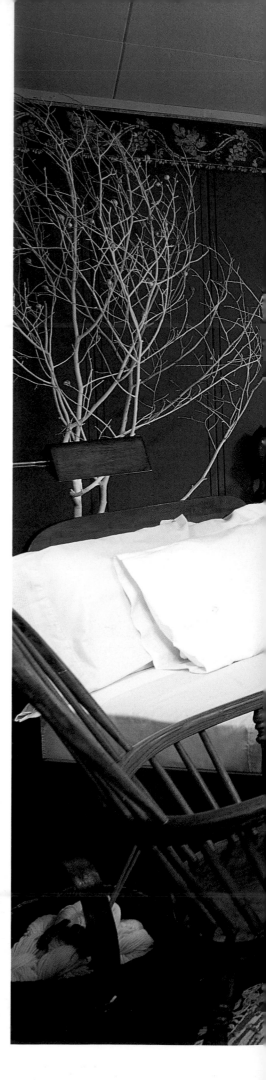

ELEMENTS OF THE STYLE

Natural materials, practical furnishings, and restrained but rich color schemes typify country style. Note the features pinpointed here to help you recreate the look.

ACCESSORIES
Traditional touches include an old cradle housing dolls and a Shaker-style peg rail.

WINDOWS
Roman blinds in unbleached cotton and off-white painted window frames and reveals add to the sense of natural light.

FURNITURE
An antique mahogany bed with turned wood posts and acorn-shaped finials is comfortably dressed with crisp cotton bed linen, a checked blanket, and traditional quilt. A Windsor chair and simple wooden bench provide seating.

WALLS
Vertical tongue-and-groove paneling, painted teal blue with a grapevine motif frieze, makes a rich backdrop, lifted by the off-white ceiling and paintwork.

FLOOR
Varnished pine floorboards are softened with simple, plain, and striped throw rugs, echoing the wall and ceiling colors.

FURNISHINGS

The bed This is the focal point of the room. Interestingly, early American antique beds would today be considered too narrow and short, so oldish and reproduction beds are better in terms of both comfort and cost. Four-poster beds with or without canopies, or half-testers with two headposts and a small canopy, in dark, polished old wood such as bird's-eye maple, mahogany, or fruitwood are ideal. Curved, carved headboards and carved finials – fruit and flower motifs are typical – on slender, turned posts add to the look. Simple brass beds are equally suitable. On a budget, decorate plain pine furniture with Pennsylvania Dutch-type stenciling, perhaps repeating stenciled wall motifs.

Other furniture Freestanding, dark, polished wood is best; keep away from built-in units or matching suites. Authentic choices include huge old armoire-type wardrobes, 'high boys' and 'lowboys', which can double as desks or dressing tables. At the foot of the bed, place a stenciled dowry chest, blanket chest, or old sea trunk. Candle stands and washstand cupboards make authentic occasional tables; on a budget, cover an inexpensive table with a floor-length patchwork or white damask cloth.

Accessories Layers of fresh-looking bed linens, topped by a patchwork, appliqué, or plain quilt, a white chenille bedspread, or a woven coverlet can give an anonymous bed a country look. Crisp white piecework, crochet or lacework cushions, runners, and tablecloths add a softening influence. Display simple vases, jugs, and baskets of garden flowers and house plants. On the walls, hang framed needlework samplers, or unsophisticated paintings or prints of fruits and flowers, domestic animals, or country scenes.

▲ *An old wooden chest of drawers, cane-seated bentwood chair and brass bed set the general tone, but a contemporary director's chair fits easily into the look.*

▼ *The slender bedposts and pale wood bedside chest and chairs have a hint of Scandinavian style, but bold blue and white plaids, Shaker-style oval wooden boxes, and a carved wooden bird are firmly American.*

▶ *Shaker-style boxes, hand painted with country scenes in the naive style of American primitive artist Grandma Moses, are charming accessories – and very useful for storage.*

◀ *Lacy cushion covers and an appliquéd quilt featuring a nineteenth-century floral motif transform a plain bed into a focal point. Likewise, a lace tablecloth makes the bedside table fit perfectly into the look.*

▼ *Patchwork quilts in the colors of the American flag display various bold designs, reflecting the informality of the look and the creativity of the quilter.*

DETAILS

For the country look, choose every item, however small – from jugs and wash bowls to vases, clocks, toys, and prints – with an eye for hand-crafted, unpretentious charm.

▲ Old-fashioned rag dolls and fragrant strings of dried herbs hung from Shaker-style peg rails strike the right note.

◀ Checked pillows in red, white, and blue, some bearing a cross-stitched heart motif, reflect the simplicity of the headboard and the richly colored log cabin patchwork quilt.

▶ Well-chosen accessories – a silhouette picture, a painted china animal, decorative boxes, and an impressive clock – demonstrate the eclectic but never cluttered nature of the look.

▼ Provide as much storage space as possible with chests and drawers; in terms of authenticity, much more was folded than hung. Painting a pine chest a typical country color – such as Indian red – makes it instantly right.

APARTMENT BEDROOMS

*Light, airy, and modern, the apartment style features streamlined furnishings,
well-planned storage and bold, bright accent colors — it's a look guaranteed
to make the most of small bedrooms.*

The fresh and functional approach to decorating looks fun in any bedroom, but is especially suited to small bedrooms like those in modern apartments. It's a cost-effective look that relies more on a lively imagination and a confident approach than on a generous budget.

The look draws from many varied sources, which is part of its charm. For example, you can combine office-style, high-tech lighting with Scandinavian-style pale wood furniture and ethnic woven rugs. The aim is to create a lively, comfortable space that's practical, well organized, and easy to keep orderly, but with a youthful sense of fun.

Fresh, pale, solid-toned walls are the starting point for the apartment bedroom. As well as creating a restful ambience, they provide an unobtrusive backdrop for colorful accessories. Inexpensive, simple furniture available from home-decorating stores suits the style's streamlined look. Many pieces come in flat-pack, self-assembly form – practical when negotiating apartment elevators and narrow stairways. Where possible, opt for dual-purpose bedroom furniture, such as a dressing or bedside table, which doubles as a desk, and perhaps a sofa bed – you can then enjoy the room during the day as well as at night.

▲ *The apartment
bedroom is a pared-
down study in contrasts.
Paintbox-bright rugs,
curtains, bedlinen,
posters, and flowers
enliven pale, neutral
walls and floors and
simple, modular
stripped-pine furniture.*

CREATING THE LOOK

Walls and ceiling The smaller the room, the more important it is to use a light-reflective color. White walls are a good starting point and leave your choice of accent colors wide open. Continuing the wall color over the ceiling, especially in an attic bedroom, creates a sense of smooth-flowing space.

Though subtle paint effects such as colorwashing or sponging are suitable, avoid highly contrasting effects and fiercely patterned wallpapers – these can make an already small space seem claustrophobic. Larger bedrooms can take bold, solid but still light-reflective colors, such as rich yellow.

Windows Window treatments continue the pale background theme or introduce bright color. Use streamlined, solid-colored or striped blinds on their own or combined with simple curtains or drapery, in pale or bright tones and plain or patterned, to soften the look.

. Combine shades with net or muslin curtains for daytime privacy and to hide an unattractive view. Venetian blinds, with their razor-sharp, ruler-straight lines, add to the look; their adjustable slats give privacy and shade with a minimum loss of light. Plantation-style louvered shutters are equally suitable and could repeat the theme of louvered

fitted wardrobes. To block out any traffic noises, make or purchase heavy, interlined curtains.

Floors For a sleek, minimalist effect, go for stripped and polished pine floorboards or woodstrip flooring. Add colorful rugs, with bold geometric or otherwise large-scale patterns, for visual interest and comfort, especially near the bed. For safety, put rugs on polished wood floors with non-slip underlays.

If your budget can take it, opt for wall-to-wall carpet for a softer, more comfortable finish underfoot. Choose a solid-toned, neutral-colored one which, like a solid-toned wall, creates a sense of space – especially in a small room. Carpets can be white or a more practical neutral such as beige or gray, perhaps with one or more scatter rugs as focal points. Pale, plain natural-fiber floor covering is a less expensive option, and looks especially attractive combined with unpainted wicker furniture.

Lighting Choose lighting to suit the room's streamlined, functional feel. Discreet, wall-mounted torchères give good overall lighting, and are supplemented with simple, elegant, or chunky bedside lamps or portable office-style lamps that you can move about the room as necessary.

ELEMENTS OF THE STYLE

Copy or adapt some or all of the features shown in this apartment style bedroom, together with those shown on the following pages, to help you recreate the look in your own home.

WALLS AND CEILING

Fresh white walls and ceiling reflect the light and create a spacious atmosphere as well as a neutral backdrop for colorful furnishings and accessories.

ACCESSORIES

Framed posters reinforce the blue and white color theme and break up the wall space. A few well-chosen accessories – vases of flowers, bedside candlelamps, and simple knickknacks – add a personal stamp.

SOFT FURNISHINGS

Blue and white bedlinen in a strong, naive design adds a bold splash of pattern. A blue and white ticking roller blind, softened with voile drapes, provides night-time privacy.

LIGHTING

Slender candlelamps are an elegant choice and provide ample light for bedtime reading. Wall-mounted torchères, in white to match the walls, give restful overall lighting.

STORAGE

Bedside tables provide storage space for books and other items. Clothes may be hung in freestanding or built-in wardrobes or from a screened-off hanging rail.

FURNITURE

A wrought-iron bedstead and wicker bedside tables and chair have a straightforward, contemporary feel and clean outlines which are perfect for the look.

FURNISHINGS

Furniture Apartment-style decorating revolves around maximizing space and minimizing cost, so try to choose furniture that offers plenty of storage space and serves more than one function. A well-lit, clutter-free dressing table, for example, doubles as a desk to make a quiet work place away from the main living area; a low, painted chest makes a perfect bedside table with room inside for bed linen; a platform bed with pull-out drawers or even a second, spare bed underneath is a real bonus; and in an older home, a built-in window seat creates a snug corner for relaxation and provides valuable storage space. If your bedroom is really small, consider installing a sofa bed to free up maximum floor space during the day. Futons have a suitably modern feel and are generally reasonably priced.

In terms of style, keep to functional furniture. Pale, stripped, or stained wood, in white or primary colors, laminate furniture, and polished or painted metal are just right. Avoid cluttering up the bedroom with too much furniture. In addition to the bed and built-in storage (see below), all you need are bedside tables and, if there's room, a comfortable chair and perhaps a basic dressing table or desk. Wicker furniture is inexpensive and adds a friendly touch, especially if other furniture in the room is stark. Glass-topped tables take up little visual space and add emphasis to any ornaments or objects displayed on them – a clock or vase of flowers, for example, seems to float in the air.

The bed Like the other furniture, the bed should be simple and functional in style. Choose a basic wooden bedstead, natural, painted, or stained, or a wrought-iron one for contemporary chic; or opt for a simple daybed and dress it up with boldly patterned and colored bed linen. Set against the walls with a bolster at each end and some scatter cushions along the back, such a bed provides sofa-style seating during the day.

Storage With space at a premium, built-in floor-to-ceiling cupboards and wardrobes make sense, along one wall, filling an alcove or fitted in an arch over and down the sides of the bed. Mirrored doors on storage units double the sense of space and light and, unlike a freestanding mirror, take up no additional floor space. In a very small bedroom, choose built-in furniture to tone and blend in with the walls.

Check out office supply stores for functional filing cabinets and box storage systems, which come in a bright array of colors as well as traditional gray and black. Industrial suppliers are a potential source of clever storage units, such as galvanized metal high-security boxes.

On a limited budget, you can fit a clothes rail across an alcove and screen it with bright fabric curtains or with white or boldly painted medium-density fiberboard panels. For added storage options, build one or more shelves at various levels behind the screen.

▲ *In this well-planned bedroom, a fiberboard desk and shelving are situated at each side of the headboard, where their surfaces provide display and work space during the day, and somewhere to rest a book and drink at night, complete with adjustable lamps for reading.*

▶ *Mirrored wardrobe doors seem to double the size of this bedroom. A formal, symmetrical layout and minimal white, black, and pale wood color scheme add to the serene spaciousness; the glass bedside tables seem almost invisible.*

◀ *A positive approach to color and pattern brings its rewards in the apartment bedroom. As simple and confident as a child's drawing, this curvaceous, black-painted, tubular steel headboard sets off the appliquéd, dotty bed linen and scalloped wainscoting line made of plywood fretwork.*

▼ *An inexpensive stack of swivelling wooden drawers makes a bedside table, and a windowsill doubles as a shelf for books, a bedside lamp, and house plants. Pared-down wooden shelving bracketed from vertical tracks fills an alcove, and galvanized metal security boxes provide dust-free storage.*

DETAILS

Choose bed linen, rugs, and cushions with an eye for color as well as comfort. Limit yourself to a few, carefully selected prints or posters and decorations that reflect your color scheme and personal taste, then give each one the display space it deserves. Introduce one or two house plants for a natural lift. Above all, keep it simple.

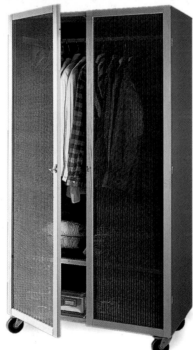

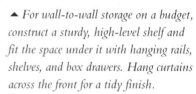

▲ *For wall-to-wall storage on a budget, construct a sturdy, high-level shelf and fit the space under it with hanging rails, shelves, and box drawers. Hang curtains across the front for a tidy finish.*

◀ *This inexpensive fiberboard wardrobe-on-wheels, with its metal mesh door panels and a useful low-level shelf, gives style and practicality on a budget.*

▲ *Make a splash with colorful sheets, pillowcases, and duvet covers. Easycare fabrics in bold, geometric patterns are perfect for the look.*

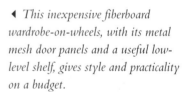

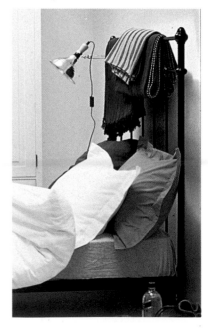

◀ *Rugs are another excellent way of adding a dash of bold pattern and color to an apartment scheme.*

▶ *This modern, portable lamp is ideal for apartment living. You can clamp it to a headboard for bedtime reading and move it from desk to dressing table to armchair as needed during the day.*

SCANDINAVIAN KITCHENS

With its streamlined country elegance, the Scandinavian style is an ideal solution for the heart of the home. Natural finishes and understated decorations combine to create a sense of warmth and hospitality for a family kitchen.

With its emphasis on natural light, clean lines, and painted wood, Scandinavian style is an excellent look for a contemporary kitchen. The innate simplicity and charm of the approach creates a sympathetic background for modern living.

If you find a kitchen built around the latest appliances and fixtures a little too stark and functional, but want to avoid a full-blown rustic look, Scandinavian strikes the perfect balance between tradition and modernity.

The style originated in eighteenth century Sweden as the homespun Nordic version of classicism, copied in humble local materials. Yet while the look has character and distinction, period detailing is restrained.

The style is easy to recreate and need not be expensive. Basic ingredients include simple curtaining and upholstery in ticking and gingham, chalky cool colors featuring on the walls and woodwork and plain tiled or sanded wooden floors. If you don't wish to start from scratch, you can give existing kitchen cabinetry a facelift with a light wash of color, or replace cupboard doors with stock versions in keeping with the look. Homey touches, such as stenciled decoration and folksy artifacts, provide a cheerful lived-in look with the right feel.

▲ *From a medley of traditional furniture, subtle paint effects in pale, muted colors and folk curios emerges a distinctive Scandinavian style for the kitchen.*

CREATING THE LOOK

Walls On the whole, the Scandinavian palette is pale and cool, but never insipid. Paint is the key finish, for walls, ceilings, woodwork, and built-ins. Surfaces are matte and soft-looking, rather than hard-edged and glossy.

Color influences are toward the cool end of the spectrum, favoring gray-greens, blue-grays and blue-greens. If your kitchen needs more warmth, a pale ocher or creamy yellow is a good option. You can paint the shell of the room in a pale version of your chosen color, and highlight woodwork or cabinets in a stronger tone, or simply paint the background white for freshness. Avoid pastels because these lack the depth and luminosity associated with Scandinavian decor.

Tiled areas are always a good idea in the kitchen, particularly behind the sink and stovetop. You can choose plain ceramic tiles in white or pale grays and blues to tone with the decor, make a graphic checkered pattern, or inset decorative or pictorial panels in a plain background.

Woodwork The warmth of the look relies on an extensive use of wood, which is always painted and never left in an unfinished or natural state. Existing doors, wooden moldings, and architraves can be painted in a slightly stronger shade of the main color. Choose eggshell rather than gloss for a soft finish.

Wooden paneling unifies built-in elements and provides a durable, washable surface where walls are likely to be splashed or spattered, behind the main work surface and sink for example. Tongue-and-groove boarding taken two-thirds of the way up the wall provides a sense of enclosure and warmth.

Floors Kitchen floors need to be practical, resilient and easy to clean. The classic Scandinavian style flooring consists of pale, sanded boards, bleached to a light tone. Other types of wood flooring, including hardwood strip, would work equally well, provided they are not stained dark. Tiled floors of various descriptions are also suitable. Keep the effect, light and simple.

If your kitchen also serves as a place to eat, you may wish to mark the distinction between the two areas of activity with a change in floor covering. Natural fiber carpeting in sisal, seagrass, or coir makes a sympathetic treatment for an eating area, if you can keep spills to a minimum.

Lighting Combine discreet, serviceable modern fixtures such as recessed ceiling lights or spots for working areas with contemporary pendant fittings over the dining table. Glass or plain pleated paper shades or period style lanterns strike the right note. A simple chandelier in dull metal rather than crystal makes an attractive focal point.

ELEMENTS OF THE STYLE

Welcoming and lived in, traditional rather than high-tech yet cool and spacious, this kitchen exhibits many hallmarks of the classic Scandinavian style in its content and layout. When recreating the look in your own home, there are plenty of features and details to inspire you in this picture and those on the following pages.

WALLS

Partial paneling, to wainscoting or high-shelf level, is a popular way of treating walls. The wood is painted in a typical shade of blue to set the color theme for the room. The wooden tongue-and-groove boards and the plate shelf above make good display surfaces for kitchen utensils and ceramics. The wall above the paneling and the rest of the woodwork is kept a crisp white.

ACCESSORIES

Accessories spell out the roots of the look. In this case, handmade mosaic plates, painted jelly molds and a copper pan hanging on the wall are all traditional gestures towards a bygone, self-sufficient age. Hand-crafted wooden and metal models can nod in the same direction.

WINDOWS

Window treatments are kept simple and unobtrusive – sill-length curtains, as here, or shades are most appropriate, usually in plain or checked lightweight cotton.

FLOORS

Well-sealed woodstrip flooring really suits the look. Stripped, bleached and varnished floorboards are also suitable. Otherwise, the smooth, clean finish of vinyl, stone or ceramic tiles is ideal.

FURNITURE

A combination of blue-painted cupboard doors and curtained unit fronts help to define the smartened-up rustic image. Wooden cooktops, dining table, and cane chairs conform with a general bias towards the use of natural materials. Here a huge stove holds center stage, but a solid-fuel range or built-in oven and cooktop can fit in just as well. Other kitchen apparatus is conspicuous by its absence or is carefully concealed.

FURNISHINGS

Built-in fittings Scandinavian-style base and wall units are available from major home furnishings stores. Unit fronts should be made of wood, either with simple moldings or in tongue-and-groove paneling. The wood is usually painted in traditional blue, gray, or green colors. A subtle paint effect, such as stenciling or whitewashing, may be applied according to personal taste. Solid wood or granite countertops are traditional, but simulated wood or stone finishes on synthetic countertops are reliable substitutes.

You can revamp old units simply by replacing the doors and painting all cabinets in a suitable color. Otherwise commission a carpenter to make new doors in tongue-and-groove, or, if your units are standard, you may be able to change the door style from stock supplies. It is even less expensive to hang curtains over unit fronts, using gingham or ticking tightly gathered along a covered wire.

Furniture If your kitchen is large enough to include an eating area, furnish it with a plain wooden table and chairs. There are a range of contemporary and traditional styles from which to choose. Look for clean lines, natural or painted finishes, and classic proportions. Old farmhouse chairs can be painted to match the woodwork; add small touches of freehand or stenciled decoration for a pretty effect. Benches or settles are also in keeping with the look. Neat seat tie-on cushions or bolsters covered in ticking, gingham, or stripes provide comfort.

Window treatments Let in plenty of light with flimsy, unlined curtains in checked or plain cotton. Café curtains, with or without matching fabric tiebacks, are suitably modest. A soft fabric valance adds a simple flourish.

▲ *From a traditionally Scandinavian point of view, the golden cream and coral pink color scheme of this kitchen is somewhat unconventional but makes a soft, cozy antidote for the cool hardness of a gray stone floor. In any case, a characteristic L-shaped settle confirms the authentic Scandinavian credentials of the approach.*

◀ *A genuine, old-fashioned Scandinavian kitchen, with multi-shaded white tiles and delft panels on the walls, plus blue-green painted paneling and cupboard doors, stands the test of time well enough to serve as a reliable role model for modern-day versions of the look.*

▲ *An open-plan combination of gray-green units, granite countertops and cream wall tiles are the perfect recipe for a cool, clean Scandinavian-looking kitchen.*

▼ *An eye for classic Scandinavian features, such as the pale green-painted paneling and darker window frame, painted chairs, and red checked curtains, makes this corner of the kitchen a cozy place in which to eat.*

Aim to preserve the streamlined country atmosphere of the Scandinavian style – blue and white china and an orderly array of utensils, for example, help to generate an unpretentious feel.

▶ *Grouped together, a crisp linen café curtain, rustic pottery, an informal arrangement of summer flowers, and a wooden goose girl emphasize the country affinity of the look.*

◀ *With their attractive hand-embroidered motifs, these linen tea towels are very much in the Scandinavian mold and are worth putting on display in the kitchen.*

▼ *Delicate stenciled floral and leafy motifs on the table and chairs are typical of the individual hand-crafted approach to this style of decorating in Scandinavian mode.*

◀ *Rustic artifacts such as this wheat decoration have a folksy appeal that helps to enhance the self-sufficient image of the look. Carved figures or animals and painted tinware are equally appropriate.*

BEACH-HOUSE BATHROOMS

*Bring a breath of fresh air to town bathrooms with a
breezy beach-house theme, or create a soothing mood inspired by
the natural colors and textures of the seashore.*

The beach-house bathroom is full of gentle contrasts. Clean lines and a restricted color palette create a fresh, uncluttered look. The colors of sun, sea, and sand are naturally an influence. The style is low key, romantically rustic, and simple, and the way you put the colors together should reflect these qualities.

Take the cool blues – deepest marine to palest aqua – for inspiration, and choose from the yellows – vibrant sunshine yellow and sand-gold to cream – to provide a contrast. Using white as a foil, you can blend colors to express quite different moods. Opt for a bright and summery seaside atmosphere with

▲ *Tongue-and-groove paneling captures the simplicity of beach-house style, complemented by fresh blue combined with sunlit cream and white. Add to the theme with marine-inspired accessories and beachcombed treasures.*

strong color brights – use deckchair stripes on furnishings and tiles. Alternatively, choose the sun-bleached looks of a beach cabin – soft whites, muted blues, light sandy-grays, and pale yellows – and echo the weathered tones of driftwood and pebbles with limed and color-washed wood and stone effects.

CREATING THE LOOK

For a fresh, airy, coastal mood, paint walls and ceiling white, or in a pale to mid-tone matte latex. A change of texture – tongue-and-groove paneling or plain tiles – will add interest below wainscoting level. A darker color will "ground" the scheme and suggest sea and sky. Choose strong contrasts such as marine blue and white, or go for a subtle distressed or color-washed finish. Pale colors and close harmonies will create a gentle, ethereal look.

Beach-house style has a period feel but it is easy to integrate modern features. Select a simple bathroom suite in white or cream, or a clean-lined retro-style design. Panel the bathtub to complement the wainscoting area, or with natural or whitewashed pine. Otherwise install a freestanding, curtained bathtub. Site a shower cubicle behind a divider "wall" – this can be tiled on the inside and paneled on the other – or screen the shower area with a marine pattern shower curtain or a plain or striped glass panel.

If stripped, limed, or painted floorboards are not available, choose vinyl flooring in a coastal color, or cover existing flooring with wooden decking. Natural fiber matting and cork tiles also work well. Stone tiles, quarry tiles, and mosaics enhance the rustic look – make them warm with cotton rugs.

STYLE POINTERS

 WALLS Atmospheric color: soft white, neutrals/aqua/blue latex/tiles/ tongue-and-groove paneling; stenciled marine motifs; aqua color mosaic details.

 WINDOWS Curtains/simple: pale/white semi sheers; tab-headed, cased, basic gathered styles; eyelet/laced calico panels; improvised driftwood/painted wood curtain rod. **Blinds/shutters:** natural wood slatted blinds; roll-up cane; painted/distressed wooden shutters.

 FABRICS Naturals/stripes: rough/smooth/loose weave linens; muslin; waffle cottons; toweling; striped cottons; marine prints.

 FLOORING Natural/rustic: stripped/painted/limed boards; wooden decking; stone/quarry tiles; cork. **Rugs:** woven grass/rush mats; nubby cotton weave/rag rugs; wooden boardwalks/cork mats.

 BATHROOM FITTINGS Period style/white: simple, wood paneled bathtub; old-fashioned freestanding bathtub; matching basin; low-key modern styles; traditional cross head brass or chrome taps; see-through shower panels/marine motif/striped shower curtain.

 FURNITURE Weathered wood: country-style cupboards/chest/chair/shelves in limed, distressed, color-rubbed wood, iron frame/wicker.

 LIGHTING Simple/period: glass/metal fishermen's brass lantern; turned wood sconce candelabrum/candles.

 ACCESSORIES Marine/weathered: shell or driftwood mirror frame; porthole shaped mirror; rustic shelves; wooden bath rack; rustic style/period glass containers; cane/wicker laundry basket; color coordinated/striped towels; sea sponges; natural objects – pebbles, shells, starfish; model boats; carved wooden seabirds.

▶ *A deep blue and white color scheme captures the mood and its fresh simplicity, while marine stencil motifs add a jaunty nautical touch.*
Tongue-and-groove paneling is a typical style feature, as is the shelving, which provides storage and display space.
The simple white bathroom suite with traditional fixtures flatters the marine color scheme, and has a suitably restrained look.
Wooden window shutters subtly suggest the proximity of the elements – painted to match the rest of the scheme they help to create a coordinated look.
Color-matched accessories and displays of beachcombed shells underline the style theme.

▶ *The simple, definitive looks of Shaker style – the practical peg rail, natural wood features, and signature blue – translate easily to a beach-house theme. Balanced with white and cream the mood is restful and relaxing.*

FURNISHINGS

The textures and patterns of the seashore – as well as its subtle colors – should be reflected in the furnishings of the beach-house bathroom. Learn from nature and balance smooth and rough surfaces: tiles, porcelain, and painted wood with crunchy sisal and seagrass matting, containers and wicker baskets. Use towels to introduce an accent color or pattern – choose harmonious blends of sandy yellows, ochers and browns, or blues, turquoise, and aquas – or introduce a nautical note with navy and white.

Curtains and window blinds are an ideal way of introducing a splash of a theme color or pattern, or emphasizing a mood. They can be part of a coordinated scheme – based on marine motifs and stripes, for example – or you can create a romantic mood with billowing muslin or voile.

Atmospheric lighting is a must; choose a bulkhead-style fixture in white or metal, or a traditional fisherman's lantern. Add distressed wood wall sconces and introduce the smell of the sea with scented candles.

▼ *Clear coastal light seems to infuse this romantic setting. The inspiration comes from weathered driftwood and the gentle neutrals of rocks and pebbles. The distressed armoire makes a charming focal point – and a showcase for towels and linens.*

▶ *Create a tactile display on a coastal theme with a rustic dish of marine-inspired treasures. Among these sea urchins and shells lie everyday bathroom requisites such as the pebble-colored soap balls, sponges, and wooden combs.*

▲ *Soft naturals and neutrals with a dash of navy blue color this period-style bathroom. The sandy-beige wall covering with seashell motifs flatters the white painted wainscoting and the delicate Victorian-style details and accessories.*

If space permits, choose simple items of furniture – a chest of drawers, cupboard, or cabinet will provide extra storage, while a small chair is always useful. Mellowed pine, a color-wash, or a distressed paint finish will conjure up driftwood, weathered fishing boats, and storm-aged beach huts. A wooden crate is easily transformed into makeshift "beach-combed" shelves – ideal for displays of seashore treasures. Use shells, driftwood, and sea-smoothed pebbles to trim shelf edges or to embellish a plain mirror frame – with a hot glue gun these projects are quick and easy.

▲ *Nature and the elements are celebrated in this serene scheme where white sand, sun-bleached wood, seashells, and pebbles are an evocative influence. Smooth, soft white acts as a sympathetic foil for the wonderfully diverse textures and the golds, creams, and browns of the fixtures and accessories.*

▶ *Give a beach-house look to a bathroom scheme with a collection of themed accessories. Take your lead from seaside print fabrics, distressed wood and rope-trimmed frames, nautical motifs, and a plethora of aqua-colored or neutral containers.*

DETAILS

The seashore theme is rich and popular, so there is plenty of choice when it comes to the finishing flourishes. Look for objects and details that combine beauty with practicality.

Small touches can provide visual clues to your decorating inspiration – little wooden boats, starfish, and seashells, for example. Look in toy shops, gift shops, and even the toiletry departments of big stores for objects with a seashore theme.

You can also improvise. Driftwood may have a pleasing sculptural quality – display it with the same care you would give a work of art, or select specimens to create a driftwood towel bar, curtain rod, or mirror frame. Collect small smooth-patterned pebbles to make a mosaic-style table top, or to insert between rows of tiles. Add rope trims, cork floats, and shells to curtain headings or tie backs, and take every opportunity to create a sensual, marine atmosphere featuring aqua-colored bath salts and scented oils.

▶ *Simple wooden box frames flatter collectors' displays of nautical ephemera. Here, in a plain white frame with a touch of navy blue, a little model lighthouse provides a visual clue to a coastal theme.*

▲ *Innovative ideas abound when you adopt a beachcomber approach to creating bathroom accessories. Simplicity itself, this shower curtain is fastened to a painted driftwood branch with twine and embellished with seashore trims.*

▲ *An old-fashioned wooden bath rack is invaluable to a coastal theme. This one's weathered color and texture flatters a collection of soaps and bathing accessories.*

▶ *Paint a tongue-and-groove paneled cupboard or shelf unit to match your scheme and to create a suitably rustic setting for a themed collection of marine treasures. Make the most of the shelf space by adding bathroom toiletries to the display.*

APARTMENT BATHROOMS

*Sleek and functional, an apartment bathroom is designed
to cope with limited space and busy lives. Choose simple shapes
and gleaming plain surfaces for a modern look.*

Creating a stylish, easy-care bathroom in a small space is a common problem for many people, and particularly for city dwellers, where space is at a premium. The newest bathroom designs are focused entirely on using the most up-to-date technology to meet these needs, with high-tech steel appliances, streamlined ceramics, and tough, durable surfaces. Decorative details are an unnecessary luxury – texture is more important; accentuate the differences between matte and shiny, and rough and smooth surfaces. The contrasts of steel, granite, wood, tiles, and glass create interest enough, combined with tough, industrial materials such as concrete, glass bricks, and studded rubber flooring.

▲ *This restful all-white scheme depends on a subtle harmony of repeated shapes for its interest. The square windows are echoed in two different sizes of tile; a circular mirror repeats the curve of the round bowl, with its matching curved countertop, and the rounded vase. Add brightly colored towels for sharp contrast.*

The apartment bathroom is a good place to experiment with color, as the areas to be covered are never huge, and are generally seen for short periods only. Try unusual color combinations used in flat blocks rather than decorative patterns; or keep to cool, clinical white and steel, with small pools of concentrated color provided by towels and accessories.

CREATING THE LOOK

Aim for a simple, functional look, with sharp, straight edges contrasted with streamlined curves. If you are starting from scratch, plan the layout carefully for maximum space. You may even consider dispensing with a bath in favor of a roomy showering area with a folding seat.

Door and window frames are ideally plain and boxy, with a flush door and sleek fixtures. If you have a window, consider fitting frosted glass to avoid the necessity for any other window treatment.

Walls are best either tiled or painted in a flat vinyl latex or eggshell finish. Plain white or colored ceramic tiles are inexpensive and suit the look perfectly, as do small mosaic tiles. For a bolder look, use plain tiles in an unusual color

– perhaps lilac or lemon. Granite, marble, sandstone, or slate tiles have a suitably apartment-style look, and set up satisfying contrasts with gleaming steel and fluffy soft towels.

For a seriously industrial look, cover the bath panel or cupboard doors in galvanized tin or aluminum; or experiment with metallic paint on woodwork for a similar look – a gunmetal, bronze, or silvery color would change the look of built-in louvered cupboards or an existing vanity unit.

For the floor, choose ceramic tiles, or sealed woodstrip or cork for a warmer feel on bare feet; linoleum or vinyl in plain or marbled effect would suit the look, or investigate tough rubber-studded flooring, which is available in a wide range of colors.

STYLE POINTERS

 WALLS Neutral or strong: latex paint in flat colors – either subtle stone, stark white, or bold combinations.
Wallpapers: imitation stone, paint lookalikes, or strong contemporary designs on limited areas.
Tiles: plain glazed ceramic tiles, white or strongly colored; sheet mosaic tiles in ceramic or glass; granite, sandstone, slate; sealed cork.

 WINDOWS Frosted glass: replace plain glass with milky white, reeded, or other effects.
Blinds: narrow Venetians in metal or wood; plain roller, Roman, or pleated blind; simple eyeletted panel.

 FLOORING Smooth: pale woodstrip; large, plain white or black tiles, stone tiling; linoleum, vinyl, or rubber in plain or semi-plain designs.
Rugs: short pile cotton bathmat, wood-slat bathmat.

 PLUMBING FIXTURES Contemporary: simple sculpted shapes in white ceramic or steel; bathtub with granite or wood surround and tiled, flush wood, or sheet metal panel.
Faucets: space-age, chrome, or nickel-plated.

 FURNITURE Metal or wood: spindly metal chair or small stool; tub-shaped stool doubling as laundry basket, with a reinforced lid that you can sit on.

 LIGHTING High-tech: recessed ceiling spotlights or simple modern central light fixture; plaster or metal wall torchères; halogen lights in recesses.

 ACCESSORIES Modern: gleaming, shiny, or satin steel for towel bars, toilet roll, and toothbrush holders; glass, metallic, or sleek blond wood shelves; simple mirror, unframed or with steel/wooden frame; plain white or colored towels.

◀ *A confident use of color distinguishes this spacious shower stall, which is created by screening off an area with a wall of glass bricks. Mosaic tiling continues the grid-like effect, with a huge, functional shower head.*

▲ *The concept of form and function is highlighted by simple streamlined fixtures and minimal styling. Bold color contrasts of blue and white define the room shape with a dramatic simplicity. Smooth metallic surfaces, gleaming glass, and pale woodwork help create a sense of calm and space. A small square window creates a well-balanced focal point, and the warm-toned frame creates a visual link with other wood details.*

FURNISHINGS

If you are choosing new plumbing fixtures, you can take advantage of lots of new ideas and innovations for a sleek, up-to-the-minute look. Modern ceramics are designed to fit effortlessly into small spaces, with smoothly rounded corners and flowing lines. Bathtubs are often molded around the body to narrow at each end, saving a vital few inches. Corner sinks, semi-inset sinks that can be set into a shelf, or inset sinks to drop into a countertop all offer clever design options. For extra floor space, choose a free-standing sink on a narrow pedestal, or a wall-mounted unit that leaves the floor free. Explore industrial and catering suppliers for high-tech steel sinks to set into a countertop or vanity unit.

Granite-effect kitchen countertops supplied by the yard or meter are perfect for apartment bathrooms. Fit a simple cupboard under the sink to stack away all your toiletries, and paint or stain it. Catering suppliers may have steel cupboards, too. If you need more storage space, slot glass or steel mesh shelves into an alcove, but keep the contents tidy and color-coordinated with the room.

Faucets and shower fixtures should be steel or chrome, rather than brass or gilt, and in contemporary, streamlined shapes; some sinks and bath faucets can be mounted on the wall, with a long, elegant spout to splash gracefully into a round basin below.

Close-coupled toilets have a neat, compact look. Alternatively, you could completely conceal a toilet tank behind a false wall, which you can top with a useful shelf. Many toilets have a seat and cover molded as part of the design.

▼ *Separate planes of bold black and white mosaic tiling give this simple shower enclosure a strong sense of style – reinforced dazzlingly by a black and white patterned towel.*

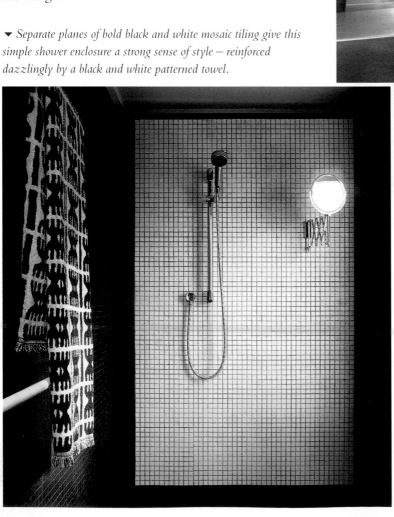

Fit a heated towel rack instead of a standard radiator – choose stainless steel or white – so you can have a comfortable room plus warm, dry towels. Site a square or circle of mirror glass above the basin, or choose a mirror with a built-in magnifier or shaving point and light.

If you fit shower doors rather than a curtain, look for plain, clear, or smoked glass; shower curtains can be clear plastic, or the brilliantly colored nylon used for yacht sails, eyeletted and threaded on a tension wire or curtain rod across the bathroom.

▲ *Simple curvy white sanitaryware is echoed by plain white walls and a filmy white shower curtain on a circular rail. Mosaic tiles in gray are echoed by charcoal gray towels on a steel towel bar.*

◀ *This ultra high-tech scheme relies on the contrast between the gleaming steel, used for all the fittings and cupboards, and the softly burnished natural effect of the plaster wall. Touches of black create an air of sophistication.*

▼ *In a pristine all-white scheme, color-splash towels create a bold graphic statement.*

Curtains and fabric shades have too soft a look for an apartment bathroom; if you need to provide extra privacy, choose a simple roller blind in a plain color, a pleated blind, or narrow slatted Venetian blind in metal or wood.

Lighting should be discreet but effective. Low-voltage halogen spotlights in the ceiling are ideal, or paint simply shaped modern wall torchères to match the walls, siting one on either side of the mirror; contemporary tracking spotlights are good for flexible lighting where you most want it, and look suitably high-tech.

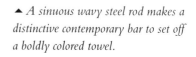

DETAILS

Details and accessories in an apartment-style bathroom are kept strictly to a minimum, and carefully chosen to flatter the style. Door handles and knobs have crisp, functional lines, or are ergonomically designed in sleek tapering shapes to fit your hand.

There is a wide range of accessories, ranging from towel bars and toilet-roll holders to soap dishes and tooth mugs, available in large home supply and specialty stores; these items add essential character to the room. Gleaming stainless steel or nickel looks sharp and clinical, contrasting well with frosted glass dishes and bowls in fresh citrus colors.

Pick up the color accents in towels, facecloths, and bathmats, or go for pure white fluffy towels contrasted with linen in taupe and gray for a neutral scheme.

◀ *Mundane bathroom tumblers become strikingly stylish when placed in curly chrome holders.*

▲ *A sinuous wavy steel rod makes a distinctive contemporary bar to set off a boldly colored towel.*

▼ *Good-looking and practical, a wire stack of shelves is topped with a handle, so you can easily take all your toiletries from basin to bath or shower as you need them.*

▲ *In a black and white scheme, chrome and aluminum accessories are a sleek choice. Color-matched toiletries accentuate their simplicity.*

TOWN-HOUSE HALLS

*A beautful home deserves a grand entrance that lives up
to the promise inside. The refinement of the town-house style provides
just such an elegant introduction to gracious living.*

First impressions count. However small, the area immediately inside the front door is more than merely a place to hurry through on your way in or out; it sets the tone for what follows in the rest of the house. The classic elements of the town-house look add character and distinction to any hallway.

The essence of the style is tradition and formality. Characteristic features include timeless elements such as black and white tiled floors, fine architectural and decorative detail, and a symmetry of arrangement. It is a sophisticated look, but need not be expensive to recreate. While the effect is elegant, practical requirements are well served.

Halls are connecting spaces, which means that decorative choices must be made very carefully to avoid abrupt clashes of color, pattern, and style in the transition to other rooms. This does not mean that bold and striking effects must be ruled out, but it is best to plan the look of the hall in the context of your overall decorating scheme.

Every hall takes a certain amount of battering from the daily comings and goings of household members, so surfaces must be able to withstand a fair degree of wear and tear. Town-house style has the practicalities covered. The look incorporates many time honored elements, such as floor tiling and paneled wainscoting areas, which provide tough and easily maintained surfaces. Other nods towards practicality involve equipping the hall with a mirror, a small table for leaving keys, messages, and mail, and maybe a clock.

Above all, as the initial encounter with your home, halls must be welcoming to visitors. Stylish finishing touches, in the form of fresh flowers and decorative objects set the right mood.

▲ *Decorated in true town-house tradition, an elegant hallway offers an hospitable welcome to all comers. A strong, warm color scheme, period-style furnishings, and practical considerations, such as durable flooring, are well integrated into a sophisticated and serviceable entrance.*

CREATING THE LOOK

Walls Neutral tones may be a safe bet in the hall, but the overall effect tends to be a little bland. A positive color gives an immediate lift that clearly spells out a welcoming message. Try yellow for a bright, warm feel, particularly in a hall that receives direct sunlight. Warmer tones, such as cerise, are also effective if the hall is dark, while soft greens are soothing.

Wainscoting is a traditional feature that earns its keep in the hall. The convention is to cover the lower third of the wall space with a hardy surface, such as a textured paper, that can withstand greater abuse than the rest of the wall treatment. You can achieve a similar effect using a coordinating border in place of the wainscoting rail. The visual distinction between the upper and lower portions of the wall effectively lowers a high ceiling. For a classic town-house effect, set off the walls with crisp white woodwork and moldings. Eggshell or satin finishes are more elegant than high gloss ones.

Many hallways in period houses have architectural flourishes in the form of brackets, cornicing, and corbels. In a featureless modern hall, apply strips of curved coving to the junction between walls and ceiling to lend a note of distinction.

Floors The classic town-house solution is some form of graphic black and white tiling – in marble slabs, ceramic tiling, or linoleum – that looks crisp in entrances.

Alternatively, carpet the hallway, provided you supply some additional protection for the areas of heaviest traffic. Natural fiber flooring in sisal or seagrass is a good, traditional option for an understated look.

A buffer zone by the front door, where shoes can be wiped clean, helps to keep the rest of the floor in good condition. The neatest solution is to stop the main covering about a yard (meter) short of the front door and cover the remainder in coir matting, sunk to the same level and running across the full width of the hall.

Lighting Halls should be well lit, for safety and security. The main hall light can be an eyecatching feature in its own right. In many hallways, such fixtures are viewed from above as you descend the stairs, so pendant lights and lanterns that enclose the bulb are more attractive than those which leave it exposed. Regency-style coach lanterns or a chandelier are in keeping with the look. If you wish, you can install wall sconces or table lamps, but these should not be the sole sources of light.

The front door To make the hallway seem more spacious, it is a good idea to paint the inside of the front door the same color as the interior woodwork, leaving darker, glossier shades for the exterior of the door only. Glazing in or around the door increases the sense of openness, provided security is not jeopardized. If your existing front door lacks character, replace it with a period-style paneled door, with or without glazing, to add an element of architectural distinction.

ELEMENTS OF THE STYLE

The key decorative and practical features arranged in this sophisticated town-house entrance, and in those illustrated on the following pages, give you plenty of style pointers to copy in your own hallway.

WALLS

Golden yellow is a favorite town-house color, especially for creating a perpetually sunny hallway. Instead of genuine wainscoting, gray-striped wallpaper absorbs the brunt of the day-to-day scuffs. White-painted woodwork is typical of the town-house style.

FLOOR

Traditional black and white checkerboard tiles are virtually indestructible and easy to clean. A large coir doormat spares the floor from the full onslaught of dirty feet entering the house.

STORAGE

'A place for everything and everything in its place' is a useful motto for keeping an open path through the hall. An umbrella stand keeps wayward walking sticks and umbrellas under control. A coat stand or boot rack organizes hats, coats, and footwear in an equally efficient and stylish manner.

ACCESSORIES

Certain practical accessories are a necessity in a well-equipped hall. A large mirror, for example, has the dual advantage of making a narrow hallway seem wider and providing a last chance for a quick check on your appearance before going out. Plaster plaques hanging on wide black ribbons or a gallery of framed prints look suitably elegant. Flower arrangements are attractive and welcoming.

FURNITURE

To maintain free access through the hall, furniture is kept to a minimum. Here, a discreet semi-circular console table, useful for leaving keys and mail, is fixed unobtrusively to the wall. A small chair may be useful when answering the telephone or changing shoes.

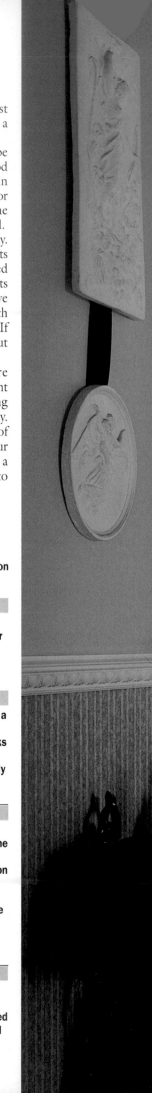

FURNISHINGS

Furnishings In the average household, the hall often ends up as a repository for items waiting to be moved elsewhere – everything from mail to discarded boots. Make a clean sweep of the clutter and find other places to keep essential gear stowed out of sight. This leaves space for a few well-chosen pieces to convey the sophistication of the town-house look and transform the hall from a passageway into a room with its own character and purpose.

Most halls are narrow, so hall furniture should be relatively compact and pushed back against the wall to allow free movement. A console table, fixed to the wall with just a pair of supporting legs at the front edge, provides an elegant punctuation point.

A pair of hall chairs is an added refinement. If the hall is wide enough, a small chest of drawers makes an effective substitute for a console table, with the bonus of providing a place to keep gloves, hats, and other items ready at hand.

Fittings Radiators are a feature of many hallways, but although the warmth may be welcome, they are not particularly attractive to look at. By encasing a radiator in a boxed housing with a front grill or fretwork panel, you can hide the eyesore and gain a useful display surface.

Details A fine mirror is an indispensable accessory for the town-house hall – the larger the better. Victorian overmantel mirrors or plain gilt frames are ideal for siting over a console table. If you position the mirror opposite the entrance to the main living areas, you set up internal views and create a good sense of spaciousness. Other traditional town-house features include brass umbrella stands, antique or reproduction barometers, and grandfather clocks.

Hall walls are excellent places for a display. You can treat the hall as a miniature picture gallery with framed prints, paintings, and drawings, massed in rows or groups. For a supremely stylish look, create your own print-room effect using cut-out photocopies of engravings applied directly to the wall.

For a final flourish, make good use of flower arrangements. Nothing looks more hospitable as you walk through the front door than a vase of fresh flowers.

▸ *Most halls offer a gallery's worth of wall space for hanging pictures and prints. Treating a narrow hallway as a nineteenth-century print room like this makes it look amazingly spacious. While the woodwork is characteristically white, the wainscoting area is painted in a scratch-resistant traditional color.*

◂ *Grand floral displays always create a good first impression. They needn't be extravagant; this one uses a few roses arranged among a mass of foliage and berries. It is placed on a slender sideboard that fits neatly into the confines of a narrow hallway.*

▲ Stained-glass panels are a cheering way of raising the tone of the front door and brightening up the hallway. To copy the colorful effect, you can buy inexpensive plastic sheets of mock stained glass that you simply lay over dampened plain glass.

◀ Draftiness is one authentic town-house feature you won't want to duplicate. To solve the problem in this hallway, a span of floor-to-ceiling curtains pulls across the front door to exclude drafts. They also contribute rich color and pattern to complement the authentically town-house colored deep green walls.

DETAILS

Keep space and practicality as well as town-house elegance in mind when selecting accessories for the hall. Period-style mirrors, small chairs, and compact console tables are all useful and enhance the setting at the same time. As tidiness is paramount for safe access to and from the house, hunt for neat storage ideas like an umbrella stand and a coat rack.

▲ *A small dark wood telephone table with a built-in seat anticipates the inevitability of lengthy phone conversations. There is even a drawer for keeping your telephone directory and address book neatly out of the way.*

▲ *An easily accessible row of coat hooks or a free-standing coat rack in the hallway is invaluable for keeping outdoor clothes neatly together. Here a table lamp casts a mellow glow, ensuring that the hall and stairway are always welcoming.*

▶ *Monitoring the ups and downs of atmospheric pressure can save you from a drenching. Before leaving the house, a quick glance at a barometer, strategically positioned by the front door, will tell you whether it is prudent to leave your umbrella behind in its stand or not.*

APARTMENT HALLS

Sophisticated simplicity sums up the look in apartment-style halls. Space may be at a premium, or the hall double as a living area, so features are both decorative and practical.

The apartment-style hallway offers a first glimpse of a home where a busy urban lifestyle is reflected in its pared-down, stylish decoration. Planned with creative flair, the furniture is streamlined, the storage practical, and the color scheme distinctive. Utilizing space in a visually pleasing and innovative way is a priority. Hallways can be small and narrow, or airy and open plan, with boundaries between the hall and the living or work areas not traditionally defined.

Color, shape, and texture create an essentially upbeat mood. Space-enhancing neutrals are balanced with vibrant color accents and simple furniture and accessories. These have sleek organic or geometric lines, in pale wood, metal, glass, or plastic, perhaps counter-balanced with high-tech industrial-look pieces, or flattered by textured natural fibers. Simple accessories, such as a plain table lamp, are in keeping with the pared-down look.

▲ Neutrals, naturals, and a strong sense of shape and texture underline the minimal styling in this hall.

CREATING THE LOOK

Visual streamlining creates a sense of space, and minimizes less than perfect features. Use pale color or white to create a sense of light and space, and consider how the color choice will affect adjoining rooms – aim for a good tonal balance, using either color harmonies or contrasts. Use stronger color or interesting texture such as rough-cast plaster, and glossy finishes, to accentuate structural features such as pillars, posts, alcoves, prominent walls, or sloping ceilings. In a narrow hall you can use mirrors or mirror tiles to open up the space or front a built-in cupboard.

In a larger space such as an open-plan hall/living room, create a visual break with a screen wall of glass bricks, or use a free-standing shelving unit as a divider between the entrance and the living area.

Counteract the effect of too many doors – or any other unwelcome details – by painting them a color to blend with the walls. Woodwork should match the wall color, or be painted a slightly lighter or darker shade in a matte finish. To suit the style, doors should be plain and flush with a wood veneer finish, glass paneled (with wired glass for a high-tech look), or painted as a color accent feature. Door furniture and handles should have a contemporary twist – in matte metallics or quirky resin shapes.

▶ Brilliant blue and yellow color blocks – the accent walls and narrow chest – are dramatically framed by whites and subtle metallic neutrals. The limed-effect flooring leads the eye through the hall to the end white wall, while the innovative door surround, chair, and accessories develop the quirky metal theme.

STYLE POINTERS

 WALLS Plain/color block: white, neutral, space/light-enhancing walls and ceilings: controlled contrast color areas, textural, rough-cast/mirrored/metallic/glass brick areas. **Wall coverings:** graphic images, bold colorwash effects.

 WINDOWS Simple blinds/curtains: natural or colored wood slatted Venetians, white, neutral, color accent Roman, or roller blinds; rod pocket/tab, eyelet-headed/tension wire curtains, panels; metal curtain rods.

 FABRICS Neutrals/striking color: natural heavy cotton/linen weaves; bold checks; stripes; bold, stylized abstract florals/graphic prints.

 FLOORING Sleek/space-defining: blond woodstrip/colored floorboards; natural fiber matting; linoleum/rubber flooring; contrast color tiles; plain wall-to-wall carpet; bold abstract/designer rugs.

 FURNITURE Streamlined/space saving: clean lines, designer/architectural pieces, dual purpose, blond wood, steel/aluminum, console table/chest of drawers/desk, neutral/mirror fronted built-in cupboards; modular/free-standing shelf unit; color-accent occasional chair/seating.

 LIGHTING Atmospheric/high-tech: wire tracking/halogen spotlights; sculptural effect pendant/avant-garde/quirky, designer chandelier; versatile task/atmospheric lamps; wall-mounted or free-standing torchères, natural finish, metallic, glass; table lamps in molded plastic, metallics, glass, parchment.

 ACCESSORIES Color accent/sculptural: designer-style, avant-garde, bold, organic form/streamlined looks for: clothes/hat stand/hooks, umbrella stand in pale wood/brushed steel; sleek wood/metallic picture frames, graphic/modern art/photographic prints; plain/colored glass/plastic or brushed steel vases/containers, modern clock; specimen flowers/large plant/cacti; over-sized urns/twisted willow twigs.

▲ *A light and airy color scheme is enhanced by simple styling and mirror tiles, which add to the feeling of space. Imaginatively placed lighting suggests an avant-garde approach; rows of spotlights each side of the mirrors are in the style of theatrical dressing room lights. Elegant dark wood furniture creates pleasingly graphic silhouettes against the light, contrasting background. A neutral color carpet continues the pale theme – a typical apartment-style foil for displaying interesting shapes and textures.*

FURNISHINGS

Floors Smooth, hard floors are the elegant, practical choice for the apartment-style hall. Pale and modern woodstrip flooring is light and space-defining, and looks good on its own or with a vibrant abstract design rug or two. A smooth sweep of plain floor acts as a foil for light and bold areas of color, and acts as a flattering background for the clean lines of streamlined furniture and furnishings. Alternatively, a boldly colored floor – tiles or a customized linoleum design – can work equally well as a focal point in a low-key setting.

Lighting This is more than functional – use it to create an inviting mood and use vibrant lampshades to create color accents. Position spots or torchères to emphasize architectural details or color features, and place table lamps to illuminate plants, flowers, or other accessories. Take the opportunity to make a feature of a central fixture with a futuristic design or quirky chandelier in metal, glass, or plastic; or opt for a minimalist, gallery effect with wire tracking and adjustable halogen spots; or just choose the simplicity of a paper shade.

Windows Emphasize the functional aspect of a hall window – if it has colored glass take that as a color lead for other accents – and make the most of the light. Simplicity is the key, with plain white or color accent blinds, or cotton or linen fabric panels to tone with the walls. Lace these through metal eyelets onto tension wires, or fit simple tab-headed or clip-topped curtains, hung from wrought-iron or steel rods.

▲ *A natural woodstrip floor suits the streamlined look of the apartment-style hall, where an absence of clutter is a key factor. In this hall, light, mid-tone, and darker wood finishes create a good tonal balance, while cool blue-green woodwork adds contrast color interest.*

◀ *Checkered tiles lead the eye through from the hall to the adjoining room – a useful visual ploy to create a feeling of space. The shared, restricted color scheme also adds to a calm and orderly feel.*

◀ *The silvery look of aluminum or brushed steel is a flattering foil for the warming tones of natural wood. These contrasting materials create an exciting textural balance; a feature that is developed to the full in this stylish apartment hall.*

Furniture Choose furniture which blends with the pieces in adjoining rooms, provides useful storage or display potential, and looks light, airy, and uncluttered. Shelf units, a console table, a chest of drawers, or a desk can all be found in a range of attractive designs and are above all functional. Finishes can include pale, blond wood with steel; contrasting black ash with honey-tone wood detailing; glass with wrought iron, and lacquered white or colored laminate surfaces. Hat, umbrella stands and coat hooks should match or blend with your furniture finishes. Choose chair or seating shapes for their sleek silhouettes – curvy organic forms or strikingly sculptural looks – and upholstery in vibrant colors. Powerful acid green, deep turquoise, scarlet, and ultramarine as well as neutrals, black, cream, or charcoal, are all colours that are in keeping with the contemporary style.

▶ *This coat and hat stand would be at home in any apartment-style hall, where functional looks are essential.*

▶ *Disguised as a stylish chest, a shoe cabinet is a practical storage solution in a modern hall. Color-matched pieces help to create a cohesive look, while the yellow and white scheme looks fresh and airy.*

DETAILS

Colorful plastics and molded resins come of age when they are used for innovative accessories in the apartment-style hall. Lamps, frames, and containers, in quirky shapes and jewel-bright colors, have the stamp of modernity and, as sleek examples of contemporary chic, can be clever or practical. Metals – brushed steel, aluminum, sand-blasted finishes, and industrial-style sheet metals such as zinc – are also appropriate for details. Use them for surfaces, containers, and elegant lamps, and for fittings such as handles and hooks.

For a white or neutral setting, choose one or two eyecatching color pieces to add dramatic impact. A brightly covered chair, an impressive table lamp, or the details in a pair of framed prints are good subjects. Alternatively, focus on shape and texture contrasts. Add to the graphic quality of black aluminum frames, and display the group in a tight formation; or place a curvy, floor-standing iron jardiniere or coat stand where its silhouette makes a dramatic contrast with the background. Otherwise, arrange a group of the same-color objects together, as on the shelf unit on the left below, so that they create a low-key pattern and textural interest.

◀ *Clean lines and curvy shapes are characteristic of sophisticated apartment style. The wavy green drawers on this birch-veneered chest would make a focal point in any neutral, understated setting.*

◀ *Freestanding shelf units take up little space. They can be used as room dividers, and are a useful background for stylish collectibles. Here, the monotone color theme is carefully considered for effect.*

▼ *Apartment-style accessories have stylishly simple lines and provide bold color accents when required. These designs would work well with white, blond woods and cool, silvery metallics.*

3
COLORS AND PATTERNS

LIVING WITH COLOR

With the help of a color wheel, you can assess color relationships and discover why a particular arrangement of colors works – or not – so that you can mix and match colors successfully and with confidence.

We live in a brilliantly colorful world, surrounded by a kaleidoscope of vibrant and subtle colors in nature, on films and television, in pictures, books, and magazines. Why shouldn't the colors of the paints, papers, carpets, and fabrics you use for decorating your home be equally joyful and stimulating?

Color is certainly the most important factor in setting the domestic scene. Different combinations influence and create moods, seem to alter the proportions of a room, and establish a specific period feel. On the whole, vivid, bold colors give a room a lively, youthful image while paler ones create a more restful setting.

When you start to put together a color scheme, the choice of fabrics, paints, wall coverings, flooring, and accessories is vast. Take a deep breath and please yourself first. Remember that the use of all color is based on a few simple rules which are clearly explained by the color wheel.

▼ *All other colors are ultimately derived from the three bold primary colors, blue, yellow, and red, together with black and white.*

THE COLOR WHEEL

The color wheel is a traditional diagram of the relationship between various families of colors and throws light on the best ways of using your favorite colors.

The colors used in decorating come from the pigments and dyes which color paints, stains, and inks for printing wall coverings, and dyes for coloring fibers that are woven into patterned fabrics.

These start out as a pure color, or hue, on the color wheel:

The three primary colors are red, blue, and yellow. All other colors can be produced by combinations of these, plus black or white.

Three secondary colors are obtained by mixing equal amounts of two primary colors: blue and yellow give green; yellow and red produce orange; red and blue result in purple.

SETTING THE MOOD

When you look at the color wheel, you will see that the colors naturally fall into two sides: warm colors – the reds, yellows, and oranges and their various shades, tints, and tones – and cool colors – blues, greens, and violets.

Two colors come on the cusps – yellowy green and violet. Some yellow-greens are warm, some are cool, depending on how close the color is to yellow or green. Similarly, some violets are warm, if they have a high percentage of red in their makeup; others can be cool as they veer towards blue.

▼ *The cool colors on the blue-green side of the color wheel appear to go away from you, making an area look more spacious. The darker shades and tones are less space-making, so use pale values if you are trying to enlarge a small space. They can also be used to fade an unattractive feature into the background. As these colors can make a place feel decidedly chilly, it is best to reserve them for a sunny bedroom like this.*

▲ The reds, oranges, and yellows from the warm side of the color wheel seem to advance toward you, making a space look smaller and more intimate. They can also be used to draw attention to an attractive feature, but if overdone this can be overpowering. In a small space like this bedroom, use the pale tints of these colors if you want to warm it up without making it feel too enclosed.

Decorating a room is similar to coloring a sketch of the layout on a sheet of white paper. In reality, when it comes to choosing color schemes, most people favor either paler tints — achieved by mixing bright primary colors into white — or muted and pastel shades and tones, obtained by combining primaries and secondaries together with each other and with various proportions of black and white.

HARMONIOUS SCHEMES

Color schemes based on a single color, or a limited range of colors adjacent to one another on the color wheel, are fundamentally safe and comfortable to live with. The ease with which they can be put together more than makes up for their lack of contrast.

Monochromatic schemes are the simplest kind of harmony, relying on arrangements based on shades and tones of one color in a room.

These are virtually foolproof color schemes which share many of the restful qualities of a neutral scheme because the colors blend so well together.

To make them work successfully, you must make sure they come from the same basic hue. One of the easiest ways of building up such a scheme is to pick your colors from paint color charts or tinted systems of mixing paints, where colors are arranged in strips of different tones and shades of the same color.

Adjacent or **related harmonies** are made up from groups of colors that lie next to each other on the color wheel. Look, for example, at the colors between blue and yellow and you will find a smooth transition from blue-greens and green-blues that is naturally easy on the eye. You can combine two, three, or four neighboring sections – all warm, all cool, or a mixture of both – to compose color harmonies that are very relaxing. You can see this cool-warm harmonizing put into practice very successfully in the yellow-green color scheme of the living room below.

CONTRASTING SCHEMES

These are the dynamic color schemes to go for when you want plenty of visual excitement in your surroundings. Calmness is all very well in a bedroom or living room, but a dining room, hallway, playroom, or kitchen can sometimes benefit from a more energetic look.

If you use the two colors diagonally opposite each other on the color wheel together – red versus green, yellow against violet, blue with orange – you end up with highly stimulating schemes. By mixing warm, advancing and cool, receding colors, the association is never dull.

Their special relationship means that when used together, they bring out the best in one another. Red used with green, for instance, has more punch than it has when used with more harmonious partners.

For a vivid, high-contrast scheme, blend the brightest shades. Some enjoyable schemes can be made around the less strident contrast pairs, like the olive green working so boldly with the deep magenta in the bathroom on the right.

NEUTRAL COLORS

Neutral colors don't appear on the color wheel. But these non-colors are very useful either as an uncompetitive background for other strong colors in a wall covering or fabric, or as a trim to define a specific design feature, such as the woodwork in a room or on a frame around a picture.

True neutrals Strictly speaking there are only three true neutrals – black, white, and gray, made by mixing black and white together.

Accepted neutrals Colors such as the beiges, creams, mushrooms, and tinted grays are commonly referred to and treated as neutral shades in decorating. They all relate back to an original hue on the color wheel via the addition of some white and/or some black.

Other accepted neutrals are the very pale tinted or natural whites, which feature prominently in paint ranges. Again these always stem from a pure color on the color wheel.

Contrary to common expectation, all true and accepted neutrals require extremely careful color matching.

▲ Paradoxically, without black and white it would be a far less colorful world. In combination with pure colors, they are responsible for producing a bonanza of the subtle and delicate shades, tints, and tones that are so popular and familiar in home decorating.

In their own right, too, black and white are important decorating colors. Used separately or in exclusive partnership, black and white are responsible for some of the most extreme and stirring of contrast schemes.

◀ Natural colors such as these creams, beiges, and honey tones are commonly regarded as neutrals. Here they are used in a similar way to the black and white above, to provide a restrained background and warm detailing definition.

DESIGNING WITH COLOR

If you plan your room schemes so that the colors relate to those in adjacent areas, your home will have a unified and harmonious feel.

Your home is like a huge blank canvas, and just as an artist considers his canvas as a whole rather than section by section, so you need to think about the way the colors in one area relate to, and are affected by, those in the rooms that lead off it. Each room should have a distinctive character that reflects its shape, size, function, and aspect. But if every room is treated as a separate entity, the house will lack a sense of coherence.

Ideally, the progress from one space to another should not be visually jarring, but there is always a place for colorful surprises. If you plan carefully you can use color to provide visual links, and to lead the eye from room to room so that the house acquires a sense of continuity, spaciousness, and completeness, regardless of its size.

Start by walking around your house, making a note of those areas that pose potential problems. The entrance hall is important because it is where visitors gain their first impression of your home. Throw all the doors open and survey the house as though you are a stranger. Notice the way the walls of the hall, and the architraves of the doors act as frames for the rooms beyond. Go into the rooms that lead off, and look back into the hallway. Doors pose an interesting problem because when they open into a room, the color on the outside becomes part of the room.

Providing logical progressions of color is most important in open plan homes, and in any part of the house where one space leads on from another – in rooms leading off a hallway, in bedrooms with an attached bathroom, and in kitchens with a dining area, for example.

▼ *A large area of bright cornflower blue is set off by a small area of intense yellow, while in the adjacent room a dense, matte green provides a contrast of hue. White architraves, baseboards, and cornicing provide a framework for the main blocks of color. A mellow wood floor carried from one area to another creates a sense of space and continuity.*

WALLS

The walls are the most obvious place to start your decorative scheme. Think about the main planes of color on walls, floors, ceilings, doors, and furniture, and the points at which they will butt up to each other. Apply test color to large sheets of card and stand them against walls and alongside each other to assess their impact. The simplest color schemes are based on different shades of the same color. In the rooms off a hallway, for example, you could use shades of rose, pale terra cotta, and crimson, with white or sage green woodwork and architraves, providing a unifying link. Harmonious colors – colors from the same sector of the color wheel – also provide a ready-made unity. So blues, greens, and blue-greens used in adjacent spaces will allow the eye to flow effortlessly from one space to the other. Pleasing effects can be achieved by teaming harmonious or neutral colors with a carefully chosen contrast color. Balance dramatic wall colors with neutral floors and natural materials. Another approach is to use a range of related neutrals on walls and floors, with accent colors to create impact and mood in the different rooms.

▼ *In this casually atmospheric home, the bedroom, living room, and dining room open on to each other. The walls are painted from an harmonious palette of sage greens and muted yellows, the broken, mottled, and glazed textures on the wall providing the unifying link. Color, shimmering light, texture, and the solid wood floor (left and bottom right) help to create a satisfying sense of unity.*

▲ *The view from the living room into the dining room shows the contrast between the greenish appearance of the walls in shadow and the way sunlight plays up the yellow component. Paintings are a useful way of introducing visual links and splashes of accent colors – the still life cleverly combines the basic palette of colors, and introduces a cool, contrast blue.*

▲ This bright and light-filled corridor combines lemon yellow with blue-greens and greeny-blues which have yellow in their make-up. The pinky-reds of the stained boards lead the eye inevitably to the pale terra-cotta walls in the bedroom at the end and the richly carved armoire. The checked fabrics on the soft furnishings skillfully draw all these colors together.

◀ Light changes the appearance and character of colors, especially complex colors built up from broken colors and layers of glazes. In the living room, light floods in from French windows looking on to a flower-filled balcony. Bright sunshine plays up the yellow on the mottled green walls, while the pale green pots on the mantel emphasize the flecks of green in the walls.

OVERALL LOOK

There are many ways of achieving a sense of completeness in your home. Walls, floors, architectural details, furniture, and soft furnishings are all important components which can be adjusted to harmonize or provide a splash of contrast color. Everything has a part to play in the overall look, from walls to paintings and small decorations.

Using the same or similar flooring throughout your home is an easy way to impose a sense of continuity – it also creates a feeling of spaciousness. You could, for example, choose natural sisal or a light honey-colored carpet for halls and stairs, vinyl tiles or woodblock in similar colors in the kitchen, with stripped and polished floorboards in the main reception rooms and bedrooms. Rugs can be used to vary the look of each room, and to pick up color from the rest of the room.

Pattern is a good way of creating a color sequence through your home. Fabrics and wallpapers featuring different patterns in related colors, or similar patterns at different scales can be played off against each other. You can pick up an important color from one room and incorporate it as a minor color in the next room. A patterned wallpaper in a hallway can be used to provide the palette for the adjoining rooms.

Architectural details such as baseboards, wainscoting, and picture rails can be used to provide a visual thread that carries color along corridors, through rooms, and even up stairs. White or off-white applied to architraves and other architectural features provides a crisp framing for blocks of color on walls, floors, and ceilings.

Accessories, pictures, rugs, curtains, and other soft furnishings can be used to provide splashes of related or contrast color which underline a predominant scheme, echo the color in an adjoining space, or provide a touch of visual drama.

▲ *In this colorful sequence of rooms, a range of blues and blue-greens is used in spaces that open into one another. The splash of yellow in the nursery draws the eye, providing a colorful climax. The repeated verticals of the wood paneling are a linking theme, and the pale, neutral carpeting provides a restful foil for the bright colors and emphatic textures.*

▲ *Floor tiles, which provide a good visual link in room schemes, are available in an exciting range of colors.*

▶ *This splendid suite of rooms provides a riot of glorious color: aquamarine, lilac, dark blue, and the startling cerise and gold of the theatrical chairs. This explosion of color is held in check by large areas of white on doors and architraves and on the splendid bookcases. However, by far the largest area of color is the golden oak floor which flows from one space into the next.*

Blue and white is a combination that never loses its appeal. In this elegantly understated dining area, a country-style table, chairs, and a magnificent hutch have been washed with chalky white paint and distressed to give a gently aged appearance. White walls provide a soothing background. The blue and white floor provides a splash of restrained color which links to the adjoining kitchen area (below).

◄ In this serene kitchen, simple wideboard cabinets and a chest of drawers have been painted a chalky white. Tiles and ceramics introduce blue and white throughout — but it is the bold checkerboard of white and gray-blue tiles which draws the eye from one space to the next.

BRIGHT AND BOLD

Relatively small areas of color become important in certain contexts. In a predominantly pale room, a piece of bright blue glass at a window will draw the eye and have an impact which is disproportionate to its size. Introducing a new color into a room can entirely alter the existing color relationships. And because the eye looks for the similarities, you can use touches of the same color to set up connections which will draw the eye around a series of rooms so that they are experienced as a single entity. Texture, tone, and even repeated shapes can also be used to suggest unity and harmony.

▶ *A vibrant blue teamed with bronze and terra cotta gives a North African flavor to this dramatic hallway. The staircase is often neglected in decorative schemes, but in this case its bold geometry and central location lends itself to a strong treatment.*

▼ *In this gorgeous scheme the violets, lilacs, and blues ricochet around the spaces, while neutral walls and floors and white baseboard and architrave hold it together. A violet blind, bright lilac cushion, braid, and a throw, all reinforce the dominant theme.*

▲ *Pretty plates in lilac, white, and gold neatly echo the decor.*

▼ *Dainty porcelain and table linen are a clever way of underlining the lilac and gold scheme.*

PREPARING A SAMPLE BOARD

*The real decorating fun begins when you collect swatches
of fabric, paper, paint, and carpet to arrange around a sketch of the room-to-be
for a preview of how your design ideas will work out in practice.*

Armed with your decorating check-list and mood board as inspiration for the look you want, you are ready to translate your ideas into the raw materials of decorating. Samples and magazine cuttings of fabrics, wall finishes, paints, and floor coverings you like are fine tuned onto a sample board to arrive at the final selection of materials and an accurate impression of your scheme.

A sample board is a marvelous opportunity to confirm that you are thinking along the right lines in your choice of colors, patterns, textures, and accessories. For example, you may have seen a picture of the cottage living room of your dreams carried out in a rusty red, when you would prefer it in yellow. So look for samples in the shade of yellow you want to reassure yourself that it would look as good. By following your sample board, there are no nasty shocks or expensive mistakes in store and you should end up with a room that satisfies all your likes, hopes, and requirements.

The sample board approach to anticipating the final look of a room is infinitely adaptable. You can put together a board for any room or look you choose, as demonstrated on the following pages.

▲ *A tastefully decorated bedroom is fair reward for all the careful scheming that goes into preparing a personal checklist and compiling mood and sample boards.*

COLLECTING SAMPLES

Try to gather as broad a selection of swatches as possible, without editing your choices at this stage. It's a good idea to keep a careful note of potential manufacturers with the samples, so that you know where to find a good supply of the materials you want to use.

Most retail shops are prepared to cut samples for you, but they are generally narrow strips which give only a hint of the colors and no real impression of the pattern, especially if the design has a large motif and repeat. If you can't get a piece at least 3in (75mm) square, make a note of the company that produces the fabric or wallpaper (often printed on the selvedge of the fabric on the roll or on the back pages of wallpaper books) and telephone the manufacturer directly to ask for samples. Some companies will supply a free or returnable sample, possibly 20in (50cm) square. It's not common but it's worth asking about.

It's not always easy to get carpet samples, but there may be a promotional leaflet showing colors and patterns that you can take home. Once again, if you see an example that you really set your heart on, try to phone the company directly and ask them to send a sample to you.

Clippings from magazine articles, advertisements, and brochures also help to build a detailed picture of the sort of furniture and the all-important accessories that fit into the scheme.

▼ Aided by an atmospheric mood board, you can put together a sample board of decorating materials that gives a clear impression of how the room will look when you have redecorated it (see above). The warm pinks versus the fresh blues and greens in the floral and check fabrics in this bedroom, for example, are reminiscent of roses and clematis clambering over a trellis arch — imagery that is carried through to the overhanging bed canopy.

tie curtain fabric back bow to with pecan match bedhead border

brass curtain rings

edge bed canopy and bedhead with peach border

lace over paint swatch for wall

woodstrip floor

▼ *By juggling with ordinary fabrics, wallpapers, and furniture, and adding a few designer tricks plus unusual groupings, you can arrive at a scheme that looks refined and exclusive. Here a medley of patterns in mustards, grays, and black charts an alternative, more sophisticated townhouse image for the romantic-look bedroom shown on the previous page.*

tie up bed drapes
and swags and
tails with black cord

cushions
trimmed with
black cord

1010 - Y10R GINGER COOLER
1020 - Y10R CORNICE
1030 - Y10R SPRING FAYRE
1040 - Y10R TEA FOR TWO•

wallpaper
border

bed cover, border
and valance

carpet

PATTERNS AND PLAINS

It is perfectly possible to use a number of patterns together in the same room, but many people are rather timid about this aspect of planning a room. If you are nervous, it is generally safer to pick one strong, larger pattern to take center stage in the scheme; then you can choose other, smaller, less powerful patterns to complement this, in colors that echo the main one. Employing small quantities of fabrics for impact in this way means you can probably afford to schedule a few extravagant but gorgeous patterns in your plans.

Look at the main pattern carefully and isolate the individual colors in it. Then look for a tiny print, for example, which picks up on one or two of those colors. You may use another color in a check or stripe. You can introduce a range of colors in snippets of different patterns in this way, to keep the overall impression lively and more spontaneous than if you stick too rigidly to two or three precise colors.

You can pull plain colors out to use on the walls and woodwork, as accents in cushions and other soft furnishings, or even as buffers between two different patterns that share that color in common. Apparently insignificant details, such as trimmings and buttons, play a significant part in pulling the disparate elements of the scheme together.

Certainly, accessories such as lampshades, mirror frames, and pictures are far too important to underestimate. Each contributes interesting profiles, reflective surfaces, and potential patterns to the scheme so you have to give serious consideration to their roles in your plans.

PREPARING THE SAMPLES AND SKETCH

Spend some time sorting through and whittling down your collection of samples to a few compatible favorites. Start by just laying them side by side, but eventually it is more effective to pin them in their approximate positions so that you can see the impact of different light during the day in that particular spot. For plain walls, paint a piece of card in the required color and stick that to the board, together with any samples of wallpaper or borders to go with it.

Include pictures of any items of furniture, lighting or accessories you intend to use. Such three-dimensional elements ensure that your sample board conveys as realistic and complete an impression of your future room scheme as possible. Remember to attach a small piece of carpet or alternative floor covering as well.

The central feature of the sample board is a drawing of the room, colored in to show the effect of the various colors and finishes in relation to one another. Your drawing can be as realistic or as sketchy as you want – it is just meant to give you an overall idea of how the colors and patterns blend together.

When sketching the room, position yourself in one corner so that you have a good view of the main elements in it – for instance, in a bedroom include the window and the bed. Draw in the ceiling, floor, and walls, then fill in the larger items, keeping everything roughly in proportion. Add in smaller details like tables, pictures, and mirrors at this stage too.

Then, referring to your selected samples, use crayons, felt tips, or paints to fill in the colors and patterns you plan to incorporate into your scheme. Don't worry about indicating too much detail of any patterns – it's more useful to pick out trimmings such as borders and tassels since they are crucial to the finished effect.

square yellow buttons for cushion trim

button up for bedhead cover

cushion cover

satin curtain

trim main bedhead fabric with yellow border to tie in with curtains

wall hanging behind bed

flooring

bedcover

◀ *Assembling the materials for a powerful look that bombards you with strong colors, boisterous patterns, lively textures, and joie de vivre galore, calls for especially careful forethought. More than ever, you need to work out in advance how well all the potentially dominant elements will hang together in reality, to steer clear of design overload. On the sample board for a bedroom, for instance, a multi-colored check, proposed as the binding for the bed canopy and the cushion cover on the bedside chair, visibly establishes an essential rapport between the two forceful patterns on the curtains and bed canopy.*

▲ *A sizzling color scheme for styling a happy-go-lucky apartment bedroom can take your breath away. Such zany colors take some handling and getting used to – which is where a sample board comes into its own as a trial run for the look. It's a timely opportunity to find out whether you love or loathe the effect you visualized at mood board stage before you invest time and money in getting all the materials.*

Paying attention to details also helps to distinguish a room that has been designed from one that has been merely decorated. Here, for example, big buttons echo the dotty effects in the two dominant patterns of the scheme and offer color continuity at the same time.

ASSEMBLING A SAMPLE BOARD

To assemble a sample board, you need a piece of card that is large enough to accommodate your sketch plus all the swatches and cuttings of any details. When you are cutting out your sample pieces, bear in mind the relative proportions of the respective fabrics, papers, paints, and trims and size them up accordingly.

Mount the sketch of the room in the center of the board and arrange samples around it. Overlap items which are close together, perhaps showing a trim peeping out from behind the fabric it is to partner. Vary the surface by mounting some upholstery samples on pieces of card so that they stand out from the background; pleat curtain fabric at the top so that it flares out at the bottom for a realistic, draped effect. If you want, you can draw arrows to key in the samples to their positions in your drawing, and add little notes to remind yourself of particular associations – remember that this is a working plan, not a work of art.

When you have decided that you are happy with the arrangement, stick all the samples and cuttings down with double-sided tape. Let some overlap the sketch and slip others underneath, much as they will fall in real life.

Position the finished board where you can see it easily when you enter the room. After a week or so, you should be able to visualize in your mind's eye the way that the room will look when it's decorated. If ideas spring to mind, you can amend the sample board at any time. The board becomes your constant reference for what item goes where as you decorate.

▼ *When the time comes to put your decorating ideas to the test on a sample board, spread all your swatches and equipment, such as scissors and adhesives, around you on a large flat surface before you start arranging anything on the board.*

COORDINATED COLLECTIONS

Coordinated collections of fabrics, wallpapers, and accessories are the perfect solution for foolproof color scheming and lively pattern mixing, leaving you to add those important final touches of personal sparkle.

Coordinated interior design collections are available in patterns and color schemes to suit every room in the house, from the living room to the nursery. Some consist of a closely related selection of designs that vary only in scale and shade; others are expanded collections that include a variety of patterns on fabrics, wall coverings, floor and wall tiles, rugs, bed linens, and paints. Some manufacturers offer an all-around decorating service so that you can have chairs covered, blinds and curtains made, and bedcovers quilted to order.

Many manufacturers also suggest ways to use their products by supplying brochures full of photographs showing inspirational room settings; or they may provide user-friendly sample books which illustrate

swatches of curtain and upholstery fabrics, wallpapers and borders, and carpet in a single color scheme, all put together so that you can see at a glance how the patterns work with one another.

With so much guidance and the nitty-gritty of color and pattern matching already done for you, it's almost impossible to go wrong. And don't worry about duplication – with so many pattern and color options available in each group of designs, you are unlikely to go for exactly the same permutation as anyone else, or use it in exactly the same way, even though you may arrive at a similar style. But to avoid any hint of a store-bought look, inject a personal touch by including some of your favorite possessions and pieces of furniture as part of the plan.

▲ *Bed linen is often a good starting point around which to build a coordinated look. Many product lines have ready-made curtains, blinds, tiebacks, and borders to complement the colors and patterns on the sheets, pillowcases, and duvet cover.*

PLANNING A COORDINATED LOOK

A good fabric or wallpaper design can often hold the key to the entire color plan of a room. Look at the pattern closely and you can discover how the component colors relate to each other tonally, in what proportion they are used, which are the background colors, and which the accents. You can then pick out other coordinating elements that you need for decorating and furnishing your room.

Collect samples of fabrics, wallpaper, friezes and borders, paints, and trimmings from a number of color ranges. In theory you can be as adventurous as you want and set up a room scheme incorporating elements from different manufacturers and product lines. In practice, however, it's wise to be cautious as there are almost bound to be subtle shifts in tone and shade between the colors that just miss the mark.

When you are selecting the patterns that suit your room best, consider their scale. Save large patterns for broad areas, such as full-length curtains, a huge sofa, or vast expanses of walls. Smaller designs usually work better for cushions and blinds, although you may like to center a large pattern on a cushion to add impact to the room.

▶ *By offering a choice of wallpapers and fabrics, plus complementary borders, cushions, lampshades, and ceramics, a coordinated design takes the guesswork out of color and pattern matching, leaving you free to devise a room with charm like this.*

▲ *Many coordinated combinations rely on enlarging or reducing and rearranging the motifs of one pattern to create another, allied design. Here the nursery rhyme scenes on the fabric are rearranged to make a border. Note how the starry background of the fabric becomes the overall background of the room – but this time on white.*

▶ *When the various fabrics and wallpapers of a design range are just loosely linked by color and pattern, some refreshing schemes emerge. Here a tiny motif from the pattern in the fabric covering the chaise longue is picked out on the wallpaper and lining of the curtains and incorporated into a far more elaborate pattern in the main fabric at the window.*

▲ *A fully coordinated range of fabrics and wallpaper offers a wide selection of patterns – floral, check, stripe, and mini-print – in the same colors. You can combine any or all of them, confident that they will look good together.*

As a general rule you are often advised to restrict yourself to one large pattern per room to avoid a power struggle between large designs. But if you want to use a wall covering with a large design next to curtains with a related large-scale pattern, try it.

PLAIN SUPPORT

Some manufacturers supply or suggest paint colors and plain fabrics as part of their coordinated packages. Others offer a selection of fabrics and wall coverings that mimic paint effects, such as sponging and ragging, or are printed with a single-color, all-over design, which reads almost like a solid color when viewed from a distance. These subtle effects are known as plains, and play an important integrating and accenting role in any color coordinated scheme. Plain colors are an excellent foil for patterns, especially in

a small room, where too rich a mix could overwhelm the space. Used generously, they give a scheme breathing space and allow individual fabric and wallpaper designs to be appreciated.

Plain colors are effective in other ways, too. Used in small amounts in a highly patterned design, they act in the same way as an accent color, providing touches of potent contrast or continuity. By picking out a secondary color in a wallpaper pattern to use as the color for the paint on the woodwork, for example, you can tilt the whole balance of the scheme.

THE DESIGNER LOOK

When you have settled on the color scheme and designs, the next step is to look at your samples in their intended surroundings. This is particularly important because you may find that when you see the shades and patterns in your room's natural light, they look completely different. Making changes to your selection could involve nothing more than a minor adjustment, swapping one pattern for another perhaps, or you may find you have to re-think the entire color scheme.

If you feel that the patterns work well together but the colors just don't gel, consider another color scheme from the same design. Alternatively, if you love the colors but feel the designs don't do anything for each other after all, look at other product lines from the same manufacturer. Often a designer or manufacturer works with the same palette of colors for several collections and one of them may well provide you with the ideal combination of color and design.

MIXING AND MATCHING

Although some designers believe that you should never mix more than four different designs in one plan, you can use a larger selection if they are totally compatible. To get the best mix, aim to include one large-scale pattern with one or two smaller patterns that are related in color and style: geometric designs such as stripes, checks or trellis, stars or spots are a good choice of smaller pattern.

If the main pattern is a traditional floral, blend it with an all-over leaf design or a sprig pattern. If it is a bold oriental print, a small paisley or French country pattern works as a more subtle contrast.

The opportunities for using different patterns side by side are enormous. In a living room, for example, a wing chair covered in a checked fabric contrasts well with a floral sofa, while matching curtains could be lined with a toning sprig or stripe. The wainscoting region offers scope for teaming one or two complementary wallpaper designs with a decorative border. Cushions, armcovers, and tiebacks open up further scope for building the complexity of the coordinated plan.

Sometimes, you can add pattern in less obvious ways to give an individual look. One method favored by some designers is to repeat a design motif throughout the scheme. For example, a trellis wallpaper could be echoed in a textured fabric with a diamond weave and again in the sculptured texture of a rug. Used sparingly, this device can make a room seem perfectly integrated. Repeating the motif in a stenciled border, using a reversible jacquard fabric, or hanging printed, sheer curtains at the window reinforces the look.

The art of mixing and matching lies in knowing when to stop. Avoid becoming a slave to coordination at all costs. Once you have set up the pattern and color linkages, you can start including some of your own accessories and decorations, not identical to the other designs but carefully chosen to go well with the rest of the plan.

▲ *This classically coordinated bedroom works because the variety of exuberant patterns on the fabrics, wallpapers, and border are so evidently interrelated. There is a good distribution of scale – from a mini-print on the wainscoting area that reads as a plain, to a geometric pattern above, separated by a large paisley motif along the border.*

IN THE BEDROOM

If any one room is an ideal testing ground for coordinating designs, it must be the bedroom. Ready-made curtains and matching bed linen proliferate in every possible color and style. Then if you want to carry your chosen pattern further, some designs also offer wallpapers, borders, and fabrics by the yard or meter for making your own accessories.

When you choose bedroom coordinates from a design that includes fabric, the scope for originality increases enormously. You can make a focal point of the bed by covering a padded headboard, or create bed drapes for a canopy, half-tester, or coronet. On a less ambitious scale, you can make a customized window treatment with valance or pelmet, tiebacks or blinds to go with the curtains, or pile cushions on the bed or chair.

▲ *Sometimes, one pattern is incorporated as the basis of a separate design. In this case, the interwoven trellises on the tablecloth and blind are neatly integrated into the floral pattern of the curtains, providing an eye-catching link between the two.*

◄ *Color reversal is a good way to create compatible patterns. Here, the contrasting tones of a fabric design form a striking partnership as blinds and curtains at this large window*

NEVER-HAVE-GUESSED COMBOS

Probably the supreme examples of coordinating design schemes are those that look least coordinated. Instead they give the impression of being a carefully selected assortment of fabrics and wall coverings that go very well together, sharing a common color theme. This leaves you as the designer to take all the credit for your well-researched and skillful choice of materials.

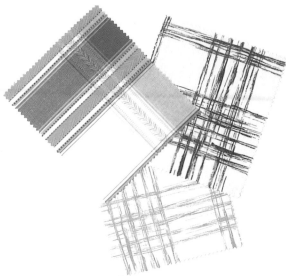

▼ *Related colors in dissimilar patterns produce an original combination. Here the outrageous floral used for the curtains is the perfect response to the checks in the upholstery. Cushions unite all the patterns and introduce a further one, in the form of a stripe.*

▲ *All the fabrics on this bed work well together, even though at first glance, it seems that all they have in common is their color scheme. In fact, if you look closely, you can see subtle but deliberate links between the designs. The small diamond-shaped motif on the red fabric, for example, is carried through in the stripe on the bed linen, bolster, and valance. A similar motif is used on the ribbon threading through the floral duvet cover, another version of which appears on the bed canopy.*

NEUTRAL COLOR SCHEMES

*You can put the quiet tones, subtle hues, and melting
contrasts of flexible neutral shades to good use in designing rooms
that reflect your lifestyle rather than dictate it.*

Often thought of as the colors without color, the range of neutrals is vast. Strictly speaking, they span from black to white through all the grays, yet are also taken to include shades of cream, beige, and brown, such as taupe, ecru, fawn, and stone, and off-whites. These neutral shades are infinitely versatile, forming the basis of many restful interior schemes, from restrained soft modern to high-powered glamour.

Many people shy away from a purely neutral scheme for fear it may be dull or austere. Nothing could be further from the truth. A fresh confidence and interest abounds in the unadorned good looks of neutral finishes. As well as being quite capable of holding center stage in their own right, neutrals play an important part as an unassuming background for bolder accent colors.

The successful execution of a neutral scheme probably involves more initial thought and planning than a layout where colors reign supreme. You need to ensure that every element, from paint and fabric to ornaments and trims, pulls its weight. But once the scheme is established, it is very easy to live with, and leaves you free to insert further items without fear of color conflict.

*▶ Cool, fresh white and cream
fabrics and paint create a
harmonious, restful setting.
Natural wood and fiber mats
supply the background the
neutral color scheme needs,
while shafts of sunlight create
patches of significant brightness.*

PURE WHITE

White is the absolutely colorless neutral. But for all its neutrality, you should not expect white to play a totally passive part in a scheme. As paint, it can dazzle with its brightness on walls and woodwork, while as sheer fabric, it forms a misty screen in front of windows and over beds.

Completely white schemes are the accepted, hygienic norm in a kitchen or bathroom. White walls refresh a living or dining room and a bedroom, too, reflecting the maximum amount of light during the day, even in a shadowy room. Indirect artifical lighting softens any tendency to harshness in the evening.

SUBTLE GRAYS

There are grays from every part of the color wheel; warm grays with hints of pink or heather in them, cool blue-grays or fascinating greeny grays that defy description by changing color throughout the day. In all its hundreds of variations, gray is a delight to use, either as a foil to black and/or white, or as a blend with other soft and subtle colors.

If black and white is too blunt a contrast for your taste, setting different shades of gray off against white is an elegant compromise. For a cool, romantic bedroom, for instance, white walls decorated with a gray stenciled border, gray damask upholstery, and gleaming gray silk curtains held back with ropes of pearls complement a bed dressed in snowy white cotton.

▶ *A simple black and white layout has to be the height of living-room chic. Delightful little touches, such as the black piping on the sofas and the striped cushion covers, add all the detailing required.*

BLACK AND WHITE

Monochromatic schemes based on the extremes of black and white are really most dramatic. This is an old yet always up-to-the-minute decorating device, exploiting the attraction of opposites. Black is dark and receding, while white is light and advancing, so they provide a powerful visual contrast. Combined with the clean-cut lines of contemporary furniture and high-tech lighting, black and white is a good choice for creating stylish, modern interiors.

◀ *Gray and white together are the toned-down version of the black versus white contrast. Here, the lightest of gray walls sets a restful bedroom scene, with the crisp white bed linen giving a bright lift and deeper gray picture mounts blending superbly.*

▶ *Cream walls, a white bedspread, and pale wood sounds like a formula for blandness. But in practice the mellowness of the paintwork, the texture in the quilt, and the honey-colored wooden dressing table create an extremely attractive country bedroom.*

CREAMS AND BEIGES

Creamy colors – the slightly yellowed whites – are the mellow version of pure white. They are generally substituted for white in country and traditional-style decor, to create elegant, restful rooms. Cream is also a good color for suggesting a slightly aged appearance.

For many years beige has been the ultimate safe choice for decorating – the color scheme you choose for want of any other particular preference, or to provide a universal, neutral sort of background. There are many shades of beige, from the creamy to the pinkish and slightly olive. By playing off various colors, such as a rich mushroom beige, on the wall against paler versions on the ceiling and woodwork, you can build color schemes of amazing complexity.

▶ *Smart cream upholstery against a rich beige background is a recipe for creating an extremely elegant room.*

NEUTRAL HARMONIES

The great charm of neutrals is their effortless compatability, so you are bound to find color combinations that please you. Used in imaginative ways, these easygoing colors create satisfying and harmonious schemes of endless fascination. Next time you go to the beach, take a close look at an assortment of pebbles, stones, and shells. You can use their blends of colors as a reference point for your decorating schemes by studying the subtle interchange between dark slate gray, the sandy gold of flint pebbles, and the veins of white marbling in chunks of granite.

Mixing gray and cream, as shown on the left for example, forges a refined combination that looks quietly understated yet smartly adult. Start by sponging the walls in two shades of cream and painting the ceiling in ivory. Then introduce storm-cloud gray as an accent on door and window architraves, with the doors painted in a paler tone. The pale gold of sisal or jute natural flooring makes a textural contrast on the floor, with richly textured fabrics in cream colors outlined and tied back with gray cord at the windows.

Far from being harsh, the contrast between the darkness of black and the paleness of cream is intriguing. Together, they are responsible for creating some very handsome room schemes with a thoroughly modern edge, like the one shown right.

▲ *In this living room, various shades of gray and cream more than live up to their reputations for being the ultimate in understated style. The broken-color paint effects on the wall and furniture and the mixture of simple patterns suggest a Scandinavian style of decorating.*

▶ *Regardless of room style, neutral colors always work best in unfussy, streamlined layouts. The low-key blend of beige and cream in this soft modern living room is spontaneous and spacious. Notice how slightly darker neutral shades are strategically positioned around the room as accent features.*

◀ A strong sense of design emphasizes the thrilling contrast between black and cream in this stylish bedroom. The bold, straight outlines of the four-poster bed, the picture frames, and the border in the carpet form a defined structure for a host of abstract and geometric patterns.

IN FAVOR OF NEUTRALS

There are many plus points when you opt for a scheme based on neutral tones.

• Muted, quiet tones such as creams and grays provide a restful backdrop for a hectic lifestyle.

• Neutrals are perfect for open-plan living areas where different parts of the room have various functions; coordinating the separate areas is far easier with soft tones that blend easily with each other and with other natural surfaces such as wood or brick.

• For a hardworking family room, brownish gray or charcoal colors which don't show dirt and wear and tear are a boon. Choose mottled, knubbly carpets and heavily textured upholstery fabrics, saving lighter tones for items that are easily cleaned, such as cushion covers.

• Eliminating powerful colors casts the spotlight on the shape of the room itself and on the items in it. Play up any interesting architectural features with lighting, and go for contrasts by placing a spindly metal table in front of the plump curves of a sofa.

• Exciting textural details really come to the fore in a neutral scheme. Look for surfaces with different textures – wallpaper with a raised, ribbed surface instead of a printed stripe, natural stone or wood flooring, cane or bamboo furniture, and textiles with patterns in the weave.

• Accessorize neutral color schemes with natural materials that rely on their texture and shape for maximum effect – wicker baskets stacked with pine cones, a terra-cotta urn filled with seedheads, or a panel of antique cotton lace over a headboard all fit the bill.

▲ A striking room like this puts to rest for once and all any suggestion that neutral schemes are boring. Mid and charcoal tones of gray look wonderful with pale beige walls.

NEARLY WHITES

As anyone who has tried to match white with white can testify, even this most neutral of neutrals can have a tinge of color, which does not become evident until it is contrasted with purer white. Whites with the merest suspicion of another color are most popular and widely used as neutrals, even though they are more accurately described as the palest of pastels.

You can buy ready-mixed, tinted white paints with a hint of color, such as apricot, rose, or green, that take the hard edge off a brilliant white. The tint tilts the room toward a color theme, without committing you to a definite scheme. Use tinted whites to create light, airy rooms, with a warm touch of apricot or a romantic hint of pink, for example.

◀ *Neutrals and naturals are often treated as one and the same thing. Hence a coarse linen cover for the sofa in ecru — a stone shade of beige — set against a pale blue-gray wall, looks at home in a country setting.*

▲ *A yellowy shade of cream paneling looks like the top of the milk above the white-tiled countertop in a country pantry.*

▼ *A delicate pale apricot on the walls is the perfect warming foil for cool, dove gray upholstery and a marble fireplace.*

BLACK AND WHITE

*Black and white turn up everywhere together –
on china, fabrics, and wallpaper – so it's impossible to
ignore their stylish and charismatic effect.*

The ultimate contrast between pure black and white is renowned for creating dramatic minimalist schemes, but it has an equally important part to play in softer, more traditional rooms as well. Throughout the centuries, black and white, probably more than any other colors, have remained popular.

At opposite ends of the tonal scale, black and white make a strong combination. When the two ends of the scale are brought together, they set up a visual seesaw that is both satisfying and fascinating: maximum visual contrast. The close juxtaposition of the colors works particularly strikingly in geometric designs and also throws into focus the lines of furniture and accessories.

Although black and white is often associated with severe, hard-edged interiors, you'll find it fits in to numerous situations. A profusion of fabrics, wallpapers, ceramics, and decorative objects are available to create a totally mono-chromatic scheme, or to add a dash of verve to other colors. Whether you are planning a whole room, or looking for a single article, there is bound to be a look that you like.

▲ *There's a place for a black and white color theme in both traditional and modern surroundings. Traditional plaid and houndstooth checked cushion covers help integrate the look.*

BLACK WITH WHITE WITH BLACK

A black and white scheme is open to infinite interpretations, especially in the proportions used. On the one hand, you can favor the lightness of a mainly white room with dashes of black accents; on the other, you can focus on the drama of a largely black room with specks of white; not to mention the many, more balanced combinations in between.

While stark white and pure jet black give the strongest contrast, you can get a softer effect and the same elegance by using variations of the two shades. There are lots of broken whites, from just off white through ivory to rich creams and oatmeals. Charcoal gray, gunmetal, and dark-stained woods offer a variety of blackish tones. A range of these colors, combined with an assortment of textures, ensures a room retains warmth and character without sacrificing the startling simplicity of the effect.

GRAPHIC BACKGROUNDS

There are plenty of ways to set the stage for a symphony in black and white, besides a tin of white latex and a can of black gloss. Subtle white-on-white striped papers, fine graph-paper squares, or sponged-effect, nearly white wallpapers all give the right, cool sort of harmony. You can adopt quite a different tack and go for a clearer statement with jazzy checks, powerful black on white stripes, or scribbly designs.

On the floor, the elegance of a gleaming expanse of black and white marble is an extravagance, but it's easy to create a similar effect by alternating less expensive vinyl, linoleum, or ceramic tiles. You can even paint bare floorboards with a black and white checkerboard pattern. These effects would be perfect for a hall, kitchen, or bathroom.

MINIMALIST LOOK

Eliminating color from a room can induce an atmosphere of calm and tranquillity. Modern minimalist furniture designs feature clean, functional lines, uncluttered by decorative elements. You can accentuate these qualities with the simplicity of pure white walls, screening windows with black Venetian blinds, and laying shiny marble-effect vinyl or black-studded rubber tiles on the floor.

The minimalist style is practical for hardworking areas such as bathrooms and kitchens where space is limited; inexpensive white tiling provides the perfect backdrop for black steel mesh accessories, black wooden or melamine doors, and stainless steel pans or white appliances. Brisk and businesslike, the look has a hygienic, squeaky-clean feel to it.

▶ *Black details are the perfect complement to a pure white scheme. In this bathroom, slit tiles at baseboard, wainscoting, and ceiling height supply valuable definition. Black towels and black-edged floor tiles reiterate the theme.*

▸ *Occasionally, a shock of color can heighten the modernistic drama of purely black and white decor. With its white walls and china plus black furniture and etchings in black frames, this dining room is strictly monochromatic. The cobalt blue wine glasses are an excellent way of adding an apt and instant dash of vibrant color to the scene.*

◂ *Contrary to expectation, a black tiled bathroom turns out to be positively upbeat, thanks to an abundance of shiny and reflecting surfaces and a dazzling white bath.*

◂ *The counterplay of black and white in this hallway embodies the racy glamour of the Art Deco period. The white walls, sleek black gloss paint, and basic black and white patterns and prints are further dramatized by the large mirrors and polished metal fittings and furniture.*

▾ *The spare outlines of Japanese design pre-date high-tech by centuries, but the reliance on black and white gives a similar effect.*

RELIEVING THE STARKNESS

The absence of any alternative color in a black and white room can be too much of a shock to some systems. At least one colored accent feature, on the floor or as a painting, for example, helps relieve a monotone. You can make it a neutral shade, a bright splash, or rich wood, as long as you use enough of it to ensure that the impact isn't eclipsed by the drama of the overall theme.

To create a sense of period, turn to French eighteenth-century scenic wallpaper designs of coy shepherdesses or picturesque mandolins in black or gray on a cream or white background, with a matching fabric for the comprehensive look. For a completely different effect, cover the walls with sheets of newsprint and seal the surface with a matte varnish.

◀ *The use of strong color contrasts is always a dramatic design device. Certainly it works in this elegant living room, where black and chestnut brown cushions supply effective contrast to the white walls and upholstered furniture.*

◀ A plump cushion with bands of golden tan in a black and white pattern provides the perfect accessory to grace a scene set by a finely drawn traditional wallpaper design.

▼ Here the natural warmth of the wooden floorboards, fireplace, and furniture helps to counter the severity of a black and white layout very effectively. The hexagonal tiled strip of flooring demonstrates the classical use of strong geometric patterns.

NATURAL WARMTH

The black and white theme acts as an excellent foil for the glow of wood and other natural finishes. You can think of mahogany, oak, or limed ash as colors in their own right. The purity of white walls and stark black paintwork is also good for accentuating the delicate tones in basketwork, rush matting, natural linen, stoneware, and terra cotta, and calls for little in the way of extra color; glass and metallic finishes, such as copper, bronze, and gilt, add a vital touch of glitter.

ADDING COLOR

Black and white accents the glowing tints of other colors very well. Setting one or two strong colors, perhaps a sofa in rich burnt orange, against the calm monochrome allows the true flamboyance of the colors to shine. Even a small touch of subtle color, a bowl of delicate pink tulips, for instance, comes into sharp focus. The huge advantage is that you can vary the whole look of the room by the addition of quite small, mobile items. You can swap a bright framed print for a pair of electric blue glass vases, for example, or have a new cushion cover every few months.

◀ In a predominantly black and white color scheme, selected items of bright turquoise bed linen provide relief from their sparse surroundings.

USE IN COLOR SCHEMES

▲ Laid in a traditional checkerboard manner, black and white floor tiles can be relied upon to give a colorful room, such as this Mediterranean-style kitchen, a snappy finish.

Using the mix of black and white as accents in another color scheme produces an exciting range of options. Pick one strong color for a background – say a flat Greek Island blue on all the walls – and then set black and white against it – a black iron four-poster bed with white curtains and lots of black and white photos in narrow black frames, for example. The blue accentuates the detail of the black and white very clearly; add a few rustic textures like an old pine wardrobe and natural jute matting to soften the effect, and a huge bunch of cornflowers in a white pot.

Most schemes benefit from a touch of black and white somewhere in the room. Small decorative articles – ivory and ebony inlaid tables and jewelry boxes from India, for example, a collection of black and white photographs in silver frames, a neat black and white piped edge on a deep green sofa, or an eye-catching appliqué cushion or wallhanging – add liveliness to the most traditional of schemes. Imagine an elegant sitting room in soft yellow and gray: yellow silk curtains, gray leather upholstery, and butter-and-cream striped wallpaper. The addition of a series of black and white botanical prints, neatly framed in black and hung on black and white striped ribbons, adds just the right spark.

▶ A colored background shows black and white off in a new light. Here, pale blue walls set a cool stage on which to play off black and white upholstery and stenciled details. Deeper blue cushions serve as accents on the black and white sofa.

GLORIOUSLY RED

As a rich basis for a wall color or an invigorating accent, red adds life and vivacity to a room. Though bold, it's a warm and welcoming color, companionable at close quarters with a wide variety of shades.

Impressive and regal, bold and brave, red is the color of kings, but also of rebels; a color of formal tradition, but also the flag of change and renewal. Being the color of fire, red has instant warmth and draws the eye irresistibly. As a color to live with, you may love it or hate it, but few people will be indifferent to it. Used in quantity it makes a bold, confident statement but it takes courage to use it this way. As a partner to other colors, red makes a lively contrast, bringing a fizz and resonance to quieter combinations – and you can add it in splashes as an accent to give a spark of welcome.

In the color wheel, red is at the heart of the warm section of the spectrum, the hottest shades being pure vermilion or scarlet. Around them range a whole selection of gentler shades which are often easier to use and make delightful partners for many other hues.

Moving towards the orange section of the spectrum, red attains a rusty tinge, giving the antique look of Chinese lacquer and fading to the softer tones of terra cotta and coral – all wonderful to enliven schemes of jade green, turquoise, or deep aquamarine. Sliding around the wheel towards the cool blues, you find the elegant jewel tones of crimson, plum, and burgundy, which make an attractive glowing foil for gold and silver, or subtle partners for bottle green, lime, or sage. Even alarm-box red has a cool tinge to it, being on the bluer side of true scarlet; it is often difficult to discriminate between these fiery shades, but worthwhile in order to use them to their best advantage.

If you want to give this color its head as star of the show, set it against any number of cool neutrals such as dove gray, cream, fawn, beige, or ivory, where its brilliant vitality can shine undisputed.

▲ The vibrant glow of alarm-box red sets the scene for dramatic occasions in this dining room. Chinese brocade in the same tone adds an exotic theme, echoed in cooler contrast by the classic blue and white platters mounted on the wall.

ALL-OVER RED

Interior decorators of antiquity were far bolder with strong colors than is generally supposed. The walls of Roman, Greek, and Etruscan villas were covered with panels of glowing red, ocher, and green; Chinese palaces were lined with scarlet and gold and these were copied with enthusiasm in Regency chinoiserie drawing rooms; the Victorians used newly synthesized versions of costly crimson pigments to create rich, glowing backdrops for sumptuous entertaining.

Using a strong red as a basis for a wall color is a bold step but can be immensely successful in giving character to a room. Used with traditional furnishings, touches of gilt and dark wood, and richly patterned fabrics, the impression red gives is one of coziness and comfort.

Red is traditionally used in dining rooms – the Victorians believed it aided the digestion. It makes a wonderful backdrop for sparkling silver and glass, sets off the rich tones of dark wood furniture, and casts a romantic glow in candlelight. This is a room used generally in the evenings and for short periods so it avoids the danger of becoming oppressive, and you can afford to be lavish with color.

For a sitting room which gets more regular use, you can sponge the walls in two or three tones of red for a softer effect, and add strong elements in cooler tones – as in the picture on the right, where calm deep blue patterned drapes, tablecloths, and cushions, combined with pale cream upholstery, cool and lighten the tone and offset the strength of the crimson walls. It's important when working with such powerful contrasts to interweave the different elements of the scheme well – if you half-close your eyes the colors should appear well distributed throughout the room in varying proportions.

As an expression of warmth and welcome you can't do better than to use lots of red in a hall. It makes a good background for the restrained elegance of engravings, and using black as a contrast gives a subtle oriental tone which is surprisingly restful. Red with a slightly orange tinge also has a Chinese feel to it; terra-cotta shades give the same warm glow to a hall and show an interesting range of hues as the light changes, from rosy pink and coral to rust.

Smaller rooms such as bathrooms and powder rooms may be a surprising setting for the rampant glory of red, but you can afford to experiment here where materials are a minimum outlay and the room is used for short spells only. Offset a chilly white or cream bathroom suite or cool ceramic tiles with coral red walls to create a warm and luxurious room in which to linger; play along with the theme by adding towels in deeper corals and rich cream, or warm coral pink lampshades. In the smallest room, indulge yourself with vibrantly dancing patterns of reds and greens, or plains of singing color balanced with natural wood and stainless steel accessories for a modern approach. This works well in a kitchen, too.

◀ *Soft subtle coral makes a bathroom to linger in. Detail is kept to a minimum to allow the warm soothing color to flood the room unhindered, giving a clean, contemporary look. Cream porcelain, a white shower curtain, and a honey colored wood floor provide gentle contrasts without breaking the calm mood.*

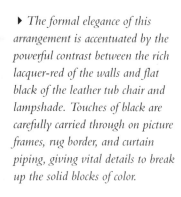

▶ *The formal elegance of this arrangement is accentuated by the powerful contrast between the rich lacquer-red of the walls and flat black of the leather tub chair and lampshade. Touches of black are carefully carried through on picture frames, rug border, and curtain piping, giving vital details to break up the solid blocks of color.*

◀ *Confident use of rich tones pays dividends in a room full of character and style. A sponged finish diminishes the dominating effect of such a mass of red on the walls, and deep blue and cream provide a lively contrast. Again, details feather the edges of the solid blocks of color – here the red is echoed in sofa cushions and a deep curtain fringe.*

▼ *Carefully balanced coordinating patterns can give an overall impression of one color without the overpowering dominance of solid color. Here a rich rusty red is the background for a small sprig pattern, and crops up again partnered with green in a stripe.*

PATTERN POWER

Red is a favorite choice for patterns precisely because of the strength of its impact, which contrasts so well with other color groups. Regal red and gold has covered the walls and furnishings of opulent households for centuries; exotic cultures delight in the fiery combination of hot red with spicy yellow and orange in their dress and environment; nature juxtaposes vibrant red blooms with cool green foliage to create the perfect balance; the fresh, sporty combination of red and white has a strong nautical flavor.

For such a powerful color, red is surprisingly companionable at close quarters with other warm-toned shades. You can jumble together a series of patterns in reds, warm burnt sienna, ocher, and golden yellows, perhaps in a pile of cushions, or in a collection of pottery and ceramics. Take inspiration from traditional, spice-colored Madras checked cottons, or the singing colors in a bunch of red, yellow, and orange anemones – when you see how effectively they catch the eye and lift the spirit, you won't be able to resist making bold color moves in your home.

A flick through decorating magazines or a stroll around a fabric store reveals red has long been a favorite choice for many well-tried traditional patterns. The hot, sun-baked countryside of southern France is reflected in the cheerful color combinations of Provençal fabrics; from France again come elegant and romantic eighteenth-century designs, frequently printed in red or deep pink on white cotton; and the multi-colored tartans of Scotland are spiked with brilliant lines of red that seem to vibrate against the soft rich greens and purples of the designs.

▸ *Cushions are the obvious way of adding a splash of color to brighten an austere room. They are particularly good when strong tones are needed to provide life and vigor for a dull color scheme. A jumble of checks and stripes achieves cohesion with a dominant color, adding textural interest along with the cheerful effect of a range of warm colors.*

◀ *A timeless combination, red patterned with gold has an unmistakable aura of wealth and grandeur – an interesting and unusual choice for a bathroom. These stunning Chinese lacquer-style panels give a sense of glamour and elegance to the room, balanced cleverly with an austerely pinstriped window shade and a pure white bath suite.*

▼ *Floral designs provide a soft, gentle way to use brilliant hues in this restful bedroom scheme. Pale creams and white in the background of the fabric, bed linen, and tieback offer no conflict to the flashes of strong color, so the overall effect is dreamy but warm.*

BOLDLY DETAILED

Whether you want a grand or understated effect, red is remarkably effective in small quantities; a splash here and there in a blandly neutral decor gives instant life and vivacity, changing the whole tone of the room. Try a fine line of red around cream or beige painted architraves and moldings, a couple of richly patterned red tapestry cushions, and maybe a huge red wool tassel or two to tie back plain curtains, to achieve an immediate makeover. Spice up a pristine white kitchen with lively touches of bright red – a collection of shiny scarlet apples and peppers, a classic enamelled coffee pot, red-handled cutlery on a stand, and red and white checked dishtowels will be enough to lift the tone.

Alternatively, you can echo the graceful style of old Scandinavia by adding tiny touches of red and white check to the cool blues, grays, and turquoise typical of the northern landscape. Minute checks on ribbon picture bows, neat red hearts on napkin rings, and fine red rims on pure white china are all typical of the restraint of this look, and add a warm and cheerful note without disturbing the refined character of the style.

Florals blend red in natural sequences with other colors, imitating the effortless contrasts of nature. This is a painless and gentle way to introduce warmth into a bedroom, set against the pale tones of white and cream linen. The wealth of floral patterns in chintzes give plenty of scope for imaginative schemes using warm reds without the overpowering effect of solid color; pick out colors from the floral design and use them around the room to tilt the scheme in whatever direction you prefer.

For a bolder splash, you can try painting a single piece of furniture in a rich red and filling it with accessories and pictures that play around the whole red spectrum. Mexico is famous for its jubilant use of clashing pinks, reds, golds, and oranges – once you lose your fear of using these exciting contrasts, you will relish the rich glow of color in your home.

▲ *The cool, elegant style of old Scandinavia uses sparks of red in tiny details to warm this scheme. Red and white checks appear in picture ribbons, tablecloth, and lampshades, while fine red lines edge the plates on the wall; all are carefully balanced against a cool turquoise blue.*

▼ *Painting a large piece of furniture in a bold color calls for conviction, but it's a great way to introduce color as an accessory. Soften the effect with accessories in other tones, but from the same side of the spectrum – oranges and pinks make an arresting blend of warmth and detail.*

▲ *A glowing amber red upholstery fabric complements the inviting curves of this wing chair. The graceful filigree of the woven design softens the strength of the color so that it tones perfectly with the linen throw and wood floor.*

PLUM AND DAMSON

From jewel-bright reds to deep, dark purples, the plum palette is rich, gorgeous, and eye-catching, adding a sense of luxury to all interiors from the classic to the ultramodern.

If you yearn to use strong colors but are wary of the primary reds, the luscious plum palette will certainly find a place in your home. The plums are a complex family of muted reds, ranging from deep maroons which verge on brown, through crimson, dark fuchsia, and purplish reds to the redder shades of violet.

The names given to this glorious range of colors are a clue to their seductive appeal. If you want to conjure them up in your mind's eye, think of the scintillating crimson of claret or burgundy seen against the light, or imagine the dark, purplish bloom of grapes, bilberries, and damsons, and the dark crimson red of plums. The splendor of these gorgeous colors is also seen in semi-precious gemstones such as purple amethysts, and the reds of rubies and garnets.

The plummy reds and purples are strong, rich and intense, but unlike the hotter, orange-reds such as scarlet, they are never flagrant or shrill. They bring warmth and richness into the home, but with great finesse and elegance. Where the primary reds must be controlled and balanced, these reds take their place in such an unassuming way that even the most faint-hearted colorist soon feels quite comfortable with them.

The plums are regal colors, traditionally associated with display and magnificence. They cry out for luxurious materials – brocades, velvets, and silks – glossy textures, gleaming antique woods, and gilded details. They are theatrical but tasteful, gorgeous but never vulgar, and incredibly easy to live with. Use them in bold, flat passages in a modern interior, or choose dusty colors and distressed paintwork for an aged look which is timeless.

▲ *The plum colors will delight and fascinate you with their ability to form unexpectedly successful partnerships with myriad other shades – such as the greens and golds of the needlepoint foliage and the wicker basket, and the metallic gleam of the brass jug.*

175

IN THE PURPLE

The purplish plums combine easily with a wide range of colors. They work particularly well with any shade of yellow from bright lemon to earthy yellow ochers and antique golds. A particularly striking pairing combines damson with lime green. For more harmonious schemes, combine the purply shades with related colors such as blues and reds.

Used boldly and as solid areas of color, damson is grand without being overwhelming. It is ideal for rooms used for entertaining, a formal living room or drawing room, for example, or a dining room. If you shop around you may find good-quality, secondhand velvet curtains at a fraction of the cost of new ones. Hang them on gleaming brass rods with an elaborate finial, and tie them back with gold cord and big gold tassels, or use a fixed brass hook.

Use brocades and velvets for upholstery, trimming it with gold braid, fringes, and brass pins. The floor covering should be patterned – a rug or a wall-to-wall carpet with a small motif. Good color combinations are gold or yellow with touches of blue-green and gray.

In a darker or small room, use slightly lighter versions of these colors and choose patterned fabrics with a pale background. Try a traditional eighteenth-century French scenic wallpaper, a Victorian sprig design, or an elegant Regency stripe. A gilded overmantel mirror, a brass fender and fireplace set, and brass or carved and gilded wood wall sconces will introduce a metallic gleam and suggest the right degree of opulence. Existing wall lights can be gilded with metallic gold paint.

If you prefer a relaxed and less formal look, use aging and distressing techniques combined with secondhand furniture and textiles to create the lived-in splendor of an old country house.

A striking bathroom can be constructed around a checkerboard of tiles in shiny, fruit-bright colors. Combine purple reds with hot reds, mauves, cool cobalt blues, dark green, bright yellow, and sky blue to produce a feast of color. A white washbasin, a plain unframed mirror, and a chrome towel rack will provide a utilitarian contrast.

Fruity and sensuous, damson is a lovely choice for bedroom schemes. It is pretty in an elegant way and makes a pleasant change from pastels. Provide relief with crisp white or cream, and introduce colors such as green, pink, and yellow in patterned textiles and wall coverings. Don't be afraid to combine patterns – stripes, florals, and checks can work very well together as long as there are two or three colors that provide a linking theme. A few items in the accent damson will hold the scheme together.

◀ In times past, people weren't afraid of strong, bold colors. Here painting the woodwork in a Georgian house in a deep damson color gives the room a studious atmosphere.

◀ *For a striking look, use flat areas of strong, bright color. Cover a plain sofa in an intense shade of amethyst. Set this against matte aquamarine walls and a light wood floor. For a unified look, pick up the blue-greens of the walls in cushions.*

▼ *It takes conviction to use strong colors on your walls, but you can soften the effect with methods such as color-washing, sponging, or ragging which break up the color. Here a bright violet wash provides a delightful foil for a bowl of colorful flowers.*

◀ *Patterned wallpapers and fabrics are a good way of introducing rich plum colors without overwhelming a room. Here a delicate lilac eighteenth-century French scenic wallpaper provides an elegant background for the more solid pattern on the armchair.*

▼ *Whether in the form of plains, florals, or checks – or the genuine article – the purple plums bring warmth and richness into the home.*

RED PLUM

These are the wine red shades like claret and burgundy – cooler, bluer and more relaxing than scarlet but more defiantly red than the purple plums.

Plum and gray are a chic combination, ideal for a cool but elegant and thoroughly modern living room. The particular shade of gray is important – it should be a blue-gray, perhaps with a hint of lilac, and not a dull, dark steely gray. The cool gray provides a marvelous foil against which warm plums really sizzle. Apply a flat, matte gray to the wall, with a darker version on baseboards and architraves. The plum should be introduced in small, subtle touches. You could, for example, use it to paint the interior of bookshelves and glass-fronted cabinets. To complete the look, find a rug with a lot of crimson or fuchsia in it – the geometric pattern of a kelim in red and black would add an emphatic touch.

For a stunning traditional bathroom, look for an old clawfoot bath and paint the outside a deep, dull burgundy red. On the wall use a delicate robin's-egg blue – matte and pale on the walls, darker and glossy on the architraves of windows and doors and on baseboards. Instead of tiles use tongue-and-groove paneling to wainscoting height and gloss paint it in blue. Team this with metal shelving and freestanding metal tables painted the same deep, dried-blood color.

A strong red might sound too intense for a bedroom, but the joy of these plummy reds is their soothing quality and the warm and welcoming glow they give to the room. They are also kind and forgiving colors, giving you a flattering glow last thing at night and first thing in the morning no matter how you are feeling.

Plum and brilliant white is a stunning combination, ideal for an inviting yet striking hallway. On the walls use a flat, matte shade of burgundy. Divide the wall into rectangles, using plain wood moldings painted glossy white. Paint squared garden trellis with bright white gloss and fix it to the wainscoting area. For a really zany effect, find an elaborate chandelier-style light fixture and paint it brilliant white. The result is bright, sunny, and modern without being clinical.

◀ *The wine-red of plums makes for sophisticated schemes whether classic or modern. Team the plum colors with blue-gray, hints of gold, or brilliant white to explore the range of effects they have to offer.*

▲ *These stained cherrywood boxes are a practical way of storing items that don't have an obvious home. Rather than hide such a handsome collection, they could be displayed so that the luscious colors catch the eye.*

◀ *This airy living room exudes understated style. The formula is simple – pale walls, lots of light and bleached pine furniture, contrasted with a mix of plummy shades on furnishings and accessories.*

▼ *Treat yourself to a glamorous bathroom. Here dark, rich claret shades, elaborate patterns and a lavish window treatment create a sense of luxury. The opulence of the color scheme is emphasized by the metallic details, which sparkle in the light.*

▼ *Tartans are often based on color combinations derived from nature. Deep berry reds are a recurrent theme, with the blues of sky and lake, and the blue-greens and heathers of Scottish hillsides.*

TOUCHES OF PURPLE

With these strong, attention-seeking colors, a little goes a long way. A few touches of maroon, burgundy, or mauve enliven and add emphasis to an otherwise cool and restrained setting. Trimmings such as braids and fringes are the most obvious and understated way of introducing these accent colors, but you can sneak them in via door furniture, rugs, picture mats, lamps, and lampshades.

Finding exactly the right accent color takes time. The best way is to make yourself a color board which combines all the predominant colors in the room. Use this to isolate precisely the shade that pulls disparate elements together or makes a scheme really zing. Sometimes the right note is already there, on a favorite ornamental piece or hidden away in a multi-colored pattern. On other occasions you have to impose an accent color – a strong maroon to add impact to delicate lilacs and pale mauves, or touches of violet to lift pinks and terra cottas.

Sometimes the accent is a deliberate contrast, a ruby-red plum or damson breathing life into apple green and turquoise, primrose or cobalt blue. Don't always go for the obvious combinations. Be prepared to surprise yourself and above all trust your own judgment. The oddest combinations can work beautifully, and because the accent is present in controlled amounts you can get away with risky mixes.

▲ *Tall, lean cabinets with their burgundy drawer fronts introduce two columns of dramatic color to this light and airy sitting room.*

▲ *The gorgeous violet of this vase would draw the eye in almost any setting. Here it reveals the character of this versatile color – notice the way the red in the background brings out the blue in the vase, which in turn complements the green and lemon.*

▶ *Here an occasional table has been given a new lease of life with a lick of Georgian red paint. Get to work with your paint brush – you'll find the matte and slightly subdued versions of red and purple blend easily in almost any setting.*

EARTH TONES

*Create harmonious schemes based on the ancient tints of minerals,
rock, and soil – the colors of the earth are part of our natural environment
and make a perfect background to everyday living.*

The restful tones of earth colors are derived from naturally occurring pigments in the ground – varying types of soil, minerals, and rock are part of the earth's structure and their colors vary in shade and intensity. These chestnut browns, terra cottas, and ocher yellows all belong in the same tonal range, however, and so have an in-built harmony which means they blend well together.

Brown is central to the range, firstly as a pure color in its own right, and then as creator of an enormous diversity of subtle hues, tinged with shades of red, yellow, or green – brick red, burnt orange, mustard brown, and khaki all fit into the picture. Add to this all the delicate shades of beige and cream created by mixing in lime or chalk, and the shadowy tones of soot and charcoal, and the strength and usefulness of this color group become clear. These are hues that have formed the basic palette of life for every culture of the world, and were used for sophisticated Roman tempera murals, Aboriginal war paint, and Celtic pottery.

In character, rooms that are decorated with earth tones have a gentle, welcoming feel and a sense of timelessness. These are colors that our eyes recognize as familiar friends, even though they are often – because of their muddy, blended origin – very hard to define. They are as far from the pure, clear primary colors as you can get, and have their origins rooted well back before synthetic dyeing processes made bright, dazzling colors generally available.

For inspiration, look at old Afghan rugs glowing with soft ochers, rusty red, and pinky beige; take a trip to a local museum to soak up color ideas from primitive terra-cotta pots, ancient mineral glazes and glass; and plunder your library for books on African tribal decoration and Aboriginal finger paintings for rich contrasts in burnt umber, earthy pink, and slate.

▲ *A jumble of sturdy rough-glazed pots and bowls harmonize in style with the textured grain of simple stained wooden trays. The warm glow of traditional earth colors is totally at home with natural surfaces and rustic artifacts.*

COOL EARTH TONES

This is the range of tones achieved by mixing white, or pigments from the cool side of the spectrum such as blue and green, with the basic earth colors. Think of cool stone and slate floors, or the washed creams, gray, and pale sand of a seashore on a winter morning, to get the feel of the colors. They create a soothing but elegant ambience of natural beauty.

Beige, putty, cream, and parchment all make perfect background settings, so the range of paints and papers that falls into this category is enormous. If you choose to paint rather than wallpaper, a number of translucent washes of different colors from this range will give a more natural finish than a flat latex; in earlier times these colors were full of natural impurities and so had interesting variations of shade and depth. You can either continue the same tones throughout the room, or use the walls as a canvas against which to set a richer series of colors.

If you're using this palette alone, it's important to avoid bland, featureless expanses. Texture, pattern, and detail are vital factors and occur naturally in many of the items that you may choose to include in this type of scheme. For rustic earthy textures, use greeny gold rush matting, jute webbing, rough sandstone, and textured weave linens and cottons. Stone busts and urns, limed wood, or reclaimed bleached pine furniture all give character and interest.

You can also add interest with strong patterns which don't tend to dominate because the colors are so muted. Look for bold ethnic designs for fabrics and wall hangings, or densely patterned floral or leafy wallpapers in pale olive, straw and mushroom tones. Important details will count for more in this subtle setting – bone buttons, steely gray upholstery studs, a rough twist of raffia around a recycled glass jar all reinforce the picture but break up the sheer planes of color.

For a sophisticated room, add metallic accents such as antique gold picture frames and mirrors, ornate silver, or burnished steel. Shiny textured fabrics such as moiré, taffeta, and silk keep up the interest and add a sense of luxury. Antique furniture glows with particular richness in this setting.

▶ *The earth colors on the cool side of the range give a relaxed, elegant welcome. Here a subtle olive and beige striped fabric is used for the sofa and blinds at the windows behind, giving an airy sense of spaciousness. The gentle color scheme is continued in the coordinating floral stripe of the curtains. Varied pale and golden wood tones blend quietly, while the key colors are delicately accented with pale green and soft rust cushions.*

▶ *Walls in cool cream and bleached terra cotta throw objects of interest into stark relief, as they recede quietly and allow the eye to dwell on stronger tones. Here natural glazed pots and bowls, the curiously shaped wall plaques, and antique shovels are all allowed maximum attention by the quiet colors surrounding them.*

◀ *Patterned wallpaper makes a delightful and undemanding background when the coloring is toned down to soft beige and cream. Wood paneling below is painted in a similar warm buttermilk, so that the impact of strong color is focused in richly embroidered, ethnic-style cushions in rust and indigo.*

▶ *Where better to use back-to-basics earth tones than in a country-style kitchen? Here beige walls and wooden units provide a mellow backdrop, enhanced by the watery green backsplash and granite-effect work surfaces.*

WARM EARTH TONES

These are the hot, spicy colors that glow with warmth and depth in Etruscan wall paintings and cave paintings alike. The names of artists' pigments bring the colors alive – raw sienna from Tuscany, the burnt umber of the fertile Umbrian hills, Naples red, Oxford ocher. They have all acquired their names from their places of origin. Raw sienna is a yellowy brown like ground cinnamon, while burnt sienna has more of an orange tinge; raw umber is a pure golden brown that turns chestnutty when burnt. Yellow ocher is a golden mustard or dirty yellow color.

A mixture of these colors in a scheme will give a vibrant, rich effect without strident clashes. Combine dark, lustrous wood furniture with richly patterned rugs, embroidered cushions, and hand-thrown terra-cotta pots. Walls can take on the same earthy tints; these strong tones make a handsome background for paintings, and in lamplight or sunlight give a wonderful glow. Echo the palette in the tones of any metals in the room: bronze and copper, brass and distressed gold artifacts will add a fiery gleam.

For a broader decorating palette, all these colors may be mixed with white to create a series of warm, mellow shades that are soft and easy to live with. Peachy terra cottas, the pinky beige of old brick, and pale, mustardy gold are all gentle colors that, with their subtle and earthy origins, have an edge of interest about them.

▼ Warm earth tones are a natural choice for bathroom color schemes, which benefit from their soothing glow. Here pale, burnt umber walls are teamed with furnishings in wood, stone, and clay.

▶ Earthy colors may be softened with white to provide gentle colors such as peach and apricot as background tints. Subtle tones allow leeway for contrasting textures – here quilted moiré vies with gilt, brass, and pine for a rich but casual mix.

▼ *Buttery ocher yellow strikes a welcoming note in this airy entrance hall. Warm yet fresh, it balances well with the cool stone floor and teams successfully with the natural elements of wood and bamboo. Touches of rust and olive green in the stenciled border, also earth tones, continue the theme.*

▲ *In this sitting room strong designs blend harmoniously as the tonal range is similar. Kelims and tapestries often feature warm natural earth colors because the pigments have been in use for centuries. Look for fabrics with flowing natural designs of leaves and flowers to complement them.*

CONTRASTS

Touches of contrast always enliven a color scheme and because earth colors are so redolent of the landscape, their natural partners should be taken from the same territory. The green of a cypress tree and a blazing azure sky offset perfectly the baked red-bronze of ploughed earth on a Tuscan hillside; the delicate eggshell blue of an English sky complements the warm red earth of the west of England.

You can use these contrasts to stunning effect in an interior. Lay rich forest green Victorian tiles on pale yellow ocher walls for a vibrant kitchen scheme, complemented by pine furniture and recycled green glass. The patina of pale green verdigris on copper would make the basis for a softer scheme in the same range of colors; wash walls with pale blue-green, and use coppery tones for upholstery and curtains.

Indigo blue was a favorite of ancient civilizations, and beautifully sets off the fiery tones of burnt orange and Tuscan reddish browns. Use these colors to accent each other – a cool slate-blue floor with dark ocher rugs and walls makes an elegant entrance hall. Delicate powder blue provides a subtle contrast for mustard yellows and terra cottas for a sunny scheme to enliven a gloomy corner.

▲ *Aquamarine and indigo blues are age-old partners of the earth pigments, all of them dating back to the decoration of ancient civilizations. This room captures the essence of this vibrant combination, with its terra-cotta floor, blue-painted furniture, and glowing patterned curtains.*

◀ *The enduring elegance of the ancient earth pigments makes a wonderful color scheme for a room with a neoclassical slant, the rich warmth emphasizing the cool lines of sculptures and decorative garlands. Touches of watery blues and greens balance the scheme perfectly.*

▶ *The muted tones of seeds, pods, dried leaves, and fruit allow the satisfying mix of textures in these objects to take center stage. Their natural earthiness is highlighted by the rich golden brown of the table on which they sprawl, and the stenciled wall behind.*

4
OPTIONS

CHOOSING CARPETS

Before buying a new carpet, it's vital to find out as much as you can about the different types – how they're made, what they are made of, and how well they'll wear – to be sure of choosing the right quality for each room.

Ideally, choosing the carpets for your home should take priority over any other decorating decision. As well as providing a warm, hard-working covering for your floors, a carpet contributes a significant area of color, texture, and sometimes pattern to a room.

Whether you are starting from scratch or replacing an old carpet, selecting a new one that suits your lifestyle and meets all your preferences – for color, pattern, texture, warmth, sound insulation, quality, and cost – is one of the most momentous and expensive choices you ever have to make for your home. Reconciling all these factors with the bewildering variety of carpets available can seem daunting for the first-time carpet buyer. To ensure you make a suitable choice and get the best value for money, it pays to do your homework.

▲ *A plain, wall-to-wall carpet provides a comfortable, neutral background against which to arrange your furniture.*

BUYING CARPET

Check through the following points to make sure you have all the information you require to make the right choice for you.

• Do I want a wall-to-wall or an area carpet?

Wall-to-wall carpet is the most popular choice for providing luxurious comfort and style in a room. If you are intending to move soon, or want to feature an attractive floor, an area rug is a more practical solution.

• How much can I afford to spend?

Always buy the best quality carpet you can afford; cheap carpets are a false economy because they wear and stain badly. Bear in mind that you will probably have to buy more carpet than the area of the room to allow for fitting around awkward shapes, such as a chimney breast.

• Will I have to pay for the installation?

It's always wise to have a carpet installed professionally to get it stretched properly so that it wears well. Many suppliers offer free installation.

• Where do I buy carpet?

Carpet is available from large department stores, furniture or carpet showrooms, and local flooring specialists.

• How do I buy carpet?

New carpet is sold in one of four ways:

Bodywidth is usually 2¼, 3, or 3¼ft wide, to minimize waste on stairs and in hallways.

Broadloom comes in a range of widths over 3¼ft – 12ft and 15ft are the most common sizes – for fitting wall to wall.

Carpet squares or **rectangles** are room-sized rugs with tightly bound or fringed edges.

Carpet tiles are small squares of carpet that are laid and lifted individually.

Book a time for installation when you place your order, allowing a few days for delivery.

• How much carpet will I need?

Some suppliers will bring samples to your home and measure before quoting a price. When visiting showrooms, measure the room first and take along a sketch plan giving the dimensions to discuss with the sales staff; they will advise on how to arrange widths for minimum waste, and where to position any seams inconspicuously and to avoid wear.

• What type of carpet do I need?

Jot down any questions you want to ask the sales assistant about wearing qualities, soil, stain, fire resistance, pile fiber, and density. When appropriate, check whether the carpet is suitable for installation in a bathroom or kitchen.

• What color carpet do I want?

Take samples of wall coverings, paints, and fabrics you want to match to the shop. Then take a swatch of carpet home to check it in daylight and under artificial lighting. At the same time, think about any special effects you want to achieve, such as warming a cold room or lightening a dark one, making a large room look cozier, or adding a pattern.

• Can the carpet be fitted on my floor?

For even wear, the floor must be perfectly clean and smooth. Make sure that all loose floorboards are fixed, planed, or covered with plywood, and solid floors are level and dry. When you have any doubts, ask your carpet retailer for advice.

PILE EFFECTS

As you can see from the carpet samples below, the main difference in the pile effects is between cut pile, where the fibers are in strands, and loop pile, where they remain uncut, passing in and out of the backing to give a more textured look. Cut, loop, and cut and loop pile effects can be achieved in both woven and tufted carpet types.

TWIST	VELVET	BERBER	CORD
The yarn of the cut pile is tightly twisted and heat set to give a firm tuft. The plain blue carpet below has a slightly roughened texture which hides footmarks.	The short, dense cut pile has a smooth, rich finish. *Shag pile* has long, thick strands; *saxony* is a cut pile midway between velvet and shag pile.	The characteristic knobbly looped pile is exceptionally hardwearing. It is often worked in a variety of flecked colors for a slightly tweedy effect.	The tight looped pile arranged in ribs is tough and economical and is particularly well suited to busy areas such as hallways.

CARPET TYPES

The texture and quality of a carpet is determined by the way it is made, or constructed, and the finish applied to the fiber tufts or pile. Test the pile density in the shop by bending the carpet sample back, pile side toward you. The less backing you can see, the better the carpet.

WOVEN CARPETS

Traditionally, the strongest and most expensive carpets have always been woven on looms. The term broadloom refers to any carpets over 3ft wide. The fibers are woven into the backing to form a dense, strong pile. There are two types of weave commonly used for broadloom carpets:

In Axminster carpets, pile is woven into the backing material, a row of U-shaped tufts at a time. This weaving method allows a wide range of colors to be used to create quite elaborate patterns, although plain and simpler designs are more popular. The pile is always cut; it can be short and smooth or long and shaggy.

In Wilton carpets, the pile is woven from continuous yarn, so that the fibers are buried in the backing to make a high density, hardwearing carpet. It is available with a cut, loop, and cut and loop pile.

TUFTED CARPETS

In modern tufted carpets, the yarn is inserted into the backing material, bonded in place with latex and then backed again with foam or fabric for extra strength. The loops of tufted carpets may be either cut or uncut, or a combination of cut and loop. They are quicker and more economical to make than woven carpets, so are generally cheaper, but can be as high in quality.

BONDED CARPETS

These are made by bonding the pile fiber to a woven or foam backing, rather than tufted through it. This gives a smooth finish, but is usually limited to plain colors.

CARPET TILES

These are squares of sealed edged carpet backed with PVC or rubber. They come in many colors and several finishes, from corded for heavy wear to soft pile for use in bedrooms and bathrooms.

Fitted wall-to-wall, they marry the luxury of a carpet with the practicality of a tiled floor. Not only can the tiles be laid more simply than a carpet and in attractive patterns, but they can also be lifted again separately when they need cleaning. Individual squares can be turned or moved to distribute wear evenly, prolonging the life of the flooring.

▲ *Carpet tiles are a sensible choice for laying under a dining table. They can be lifted separately for cleaning when necessary.*

SCULPTURED

Cut and looped piles are combined, or pile is cut to different depths, to form a range of textured and patterned effects that hides wear and marks.

BRUSSELS WEAVE

The tightly twisted loop pile is woven using the Wilton method, so simple patterns incorporating a few colors are possible, as in the one shown below.

WHICH CARPET?

Every room in your home has a different type of carpet requirement, depending on its location and your lifestyle. A household with children needs hardwearing carpets, able to withstand the spills and wear and tear of family life. For a single person setting up home for the first time or a retired couple, cost may be a more important consideration.

Carpet durability depends on the pile formation and the fiber used. Assess the activity level in the room or area you are planning to carpet, designating it heavy, medium, or light, and match that up to the information on the carpet label. If in doubt, ask your carpet retailer.

LOCATION	RECOMMENDED CARPET
Hall, stairs, and landing	**Heavy domestic** Patterns, darker colors, and/or hard twist pile or cord help disguise dirty footprints. An 80/20 mix of wool/nylon wears well and keeps its appearance without being too extravagant.
Living room *For family use*	**General domestic** Patterns and darker shades disguise soiling. Synthetic fiber twist or a loop pile with a stain-resistant finish will stand up to spills.
For adult use	**Medium domestic** Velvet pile looks luxurious in plain, light colors. Lay 80/20 wool/nylon mix for long-lasting good looks.
Dining room/ study	**Medium domestic** For rooms subject to less wear, look for colors or patterns to coordinate with adjacent hall carpet to create an illusion of spaciousness. Carpet tiles are an ideal floor covering for family dining areas.
Bedroom *For adults*	**Medium domestic** For a luxurious feel, choose velvet pile in 80/20 wool/nylon, or 60/40 wool/polypropylene for economy, in a plain color or textured pattern.
For children	**Medium domestic** Choose a stain-resistant wool/synthetic mix, or all-synthetic type, in a cheerful color.
For guests	**Light domestic** Fit a 50/50 or 30/70 wool/synthetic mixture for economy.
Bathroom	Special rubber-backed nylon pile carpets are available for bathrooms which are rot-resistant and completely washable.
Kitchen	Lay carpets especially designed to stand up to rigorous kitchen activities. Carpet tiles are often a more practical choice if you want a soft floor finish.

TYPES OF FIBER

There are two main categories of fiber used in carpet manufacture – natural and manmade; their brand names and trademarks appear on carpet labels and price tags:

NATURAL FIBERS

Wool is the ideal carpet fiber, being naturally warm, soft, and resilient with a good crimp (the ability of the pile to spring back after being crushed). It is easy to keep clean, naturally fire retardant, and dyes readily, but it is expensive.

Cotton is hardwearing, but lacks resilience and tends to flatten. Small cotton rugs for bathrooms and bedrooms are usually machine washable.

MANMADE FIBERS

Modern synthetic fibers are extremely hardwearing and stain resistant, although they still lack the resilience, crimp, and fire-resistant qualities of wool. Their greatest advantage is that they are not as expensive as natural fibers.

Nylon is one of the toughest manmade fibers, but in its untreated form attracts dirt and is prone to static electricity. Fibers can be treated with a stainblocking system to prevent liquid penetration, so spills can be wiped up.

Acrylic is closest to wool in feel and appearance. Most have anti-soiling and anti-static features. Blends with wool or nylon are increasingly popular for use in areas of light wear.

Polyester is a waterproof, easy-to-clean fiber with a good soft feel but it is less hardwearing than other synthetic fibers and is not used widely in carpet making.

Polypropylene (Olefin) is a tough, hard-working fiber with a very high level of stain and dirt resistance. On its own, it tends to flatten, so works best mixed with wool.

Viscose rayon is a cheap fiber that is not very hardwearing, resilient, or fire resistant.

MIXED FIBER

Carpets made from a mixture of fibers combine the resilience, look and feel of wool with the toughness and economy of manmade fibers. The higher the percentage of wool, the better the performance; a popular choice is a blend of 80 per cent wool with 20 per cent nylon.

Other animal hair, from goats, cows, horses, or pigs, is also combined with synthetic fibers to form hardwearing carpets that do not attract dirt and are fire resistant.

▲ *A dark, patterned carpet is an ideal choice for a hall and stairway, where it will absorb the heavy traffic and stay clean.*

◀ *The same colored carpet laid between rooms gives the impression of space.*

▶ *A soft carpet is always welcome underfoot in a bedroom. Here, the carpet's trellis design introduces pattern into an otherwise plain scheme.*

CARPET LAYING TERMS

You are quite likely to hear the following expressions when buying a carpet:

• **Fluffing** refers to loose fibers left on the surface of the carpet. They appear during manufacture and continue to work their way to the surface during the first few months of wear. They disappear with regular vacuuming.

• **Pilling** describes small balls of fiber left on the surface of nylon or nylon mix carpet. It is usually a manufacturer's fault.

• **Grinning** is what happens when you bend a carpet back over your hand and the backing shows through the pile. This is a sure sign of a low-density pile, particularly on Axminster carpets. Do not use carpets which grin on stairs.

• **Sprouting** is the term applied when strands of thin woven backing material, such as jute, appear or "sprout" through the pile. This is no cause for concern – simply trim away the loose ends with sharp scissors.

• **Shading** refers to the light and dark patches that may appear on cut-pile carpets, particularly plain-colored velvets with synthetic fibers. It does not affect the life of the carpet and has the benefit of disguising dirt and stains.

PADDING

It is worth spending money on a good padding to prolong the life of the carpet, increase comfort and warmth, and provide sound insulation.

Padding is always laid beneath a carpet, unless it is foam backed. Buy new padding to use with a new carpet. Several types are available: be sure to match the type to the kind of carpet you are laying. The carpet showroom will advise on the most suitable one to use in each case.

Some installers line the floor before putting padding down on floorboards. This prevents vacuuming from drawing dirt up into the pile. On foam-backed carpets, the lining stops the backing from sticking to the floor. Lining sheets come in paper or nylon, usually in 78in widths.

RUBBER

Flat rubber is the most hardwearing and resilient of the rubber padding, but is not soft to walk on.
Foam rubber (below) has a waffle, or ridged, finish which makes it soft and easy to handle. It is springier but less tough than flat rubber, and is unsuitable for solid floors with underfloor central heating.

FELT

Felt is the traditional padding material, available in several thicknesses, and is still the best choice to use on stairs, under seamed carpets, and for soundproofing.
Rubberized felt (below) is not as hardwearing or long lasting as felt or the better rubber paddings, but it combines the advantages of both.

▲ *Waterproof, rubber-backed carpets are suitable for use in a bathroom. Although you don't need to put down padding, some installers put lining sheets underneath to prevent the rubber backing from sticking to the floor.*

Choosing Wood Flooring

The natural appearance and feel of a real wood floor can be very attractive. Warm and mellow to look at, practical, and hardwearing, it can considerably enhance any home.

There are two ways to have a wooden floor in your home. You can lay a wood floor covering over your existing floor, whatever it is made of – floorboards, chipboard, plywood, quarry tiles, or concrete; or, if you already have natural wooden flooring, you can strip, sand, repair, and seal the floorboards.

With either method, the result is a hardwearing floor that is beautiful to look at and easy to keep clean. The wood may be enhanced by staining, with special paint effects such as stenciling or by adding colorful rugs, preferably on non-slip mats, for which the smooth wood is a natural backdrop.

You can buy wood flooring and the adhesives and tools you need for installing it in do-it-yourself stores, in department stores with a large flooring department, or in specialist flooring shops. Apart from parquet flooring, which is difficult to buy and even more difficult to lay, all types of plank floor covering come with installation instructions.

▲ *Natural plank flooring works in complete harmony with the rest of the room – from the picture frames to the spicy palette of the upholstery.*

WOOD FLOOR COVERINGS

There are four main types of wood floor covering: strip flooring, block flooring, mosaic flooring, and cork/wood flooring.

STRIP FLOORING

This looks like very smooth, tightly packed floorboards. It comes in a wide range of wood, including both softwood (pine, spruce, and birch) and colorful hardwoods (cherry, oak, ash, beech, and maple). Each board has a tongue and groove to ensure a tight fit with its neighbor.

The thickness of the flooring can vary from around ⅜in (9mm) up to ⅞in (22mm). Some woodstrip flooring is solid, like floorboards; some is laminated, with a thin surface-wear layer on top of a thicker softwood or plastic base layer. This makes the flooring more stable than it would otherwise be, less likely to expand and contract. Woodstrip flooring also comes with a hardwearing melamine surface layer.

You can install all types and thicknesses over an existing floor. Generally the boards are laid on a special cushioned, damp-proof sub-floor and secured to one another with clips or adhesive; they are never stuck or screwed down to the floor below. This is known as a floating floor. It is essential that you leave expansion gaps, covered with molding, all around the edges of the floor.

The thickest types can be used to replace existing floorboards. Carefully nail each plank through the tongue to the floor joists so that none of the nail heads show.

BLOCK FLOORING

Often known as parquet, this type of floor covering is generally used over an existing solid floor. The individual rectangular wood blocks are between 1in (25mm) and 2in (50mm) thick, and laid in a herringbone pattern, bedded into mastic adhesive. Laying new block flooring is a job for a professional, but you can sand down existing thick block flooring and reseal it in the same way as old floorboards.

MOSAIC FLOORING

This type of flooring, which confusingly is also known as parquet, consists of tongue-and-grooved tiles made up of narrow strips of wood. A typical tile is divided into four squares composed of four or five strips joined together with wire or adhesive and mounted on a mesh backing. The strips in adjacent squares lie at right angles to one another, so when laid across the floor they form a basketweave pattern.

Glue mosaic flooring to the sub-floor with special adhesive; the construction of the flooring allows a degree of flexibility so that it can cope with slightly uneven surfaces. Some makes are self-adhesive.

CORK/WOOD FLOORING

This is a different type of woodstrip flooring. It consists of cork over a plastic sub-layer topped with a thin wood veneer which in turn is covered with a hardwearing clear plastic. The visual appearance is that of a wood floor, but it is quieter, softer, and warmer underfoot because of the cork. Cork/wood flooring is held in place with adhesive.

▼ *The basketweave pattern of mosaic flooring makes a distinctive entrance way.*

▲ *The ever-popular herringbone pattern for woodblock flooring becomes a sensational focal point in this room. The strong natural light streaming in from two sources helps to bring out the beautiful, subtle shading in the floor.*

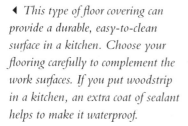

◄ *This type of floor covering can provide a durable, easy-to-clean surface in a kitchen. Choose your flooring carefully to complement the work surfaces. If you put woodstrip in a kitchen, an extra coat of sealant helps to make it waterproof.*

PREPARING SUB-FLOORS

When laying wood floor coverings, the underlying floor surface must be dry, flat, and level. Examine your existing floor and consider what you need to do to it before you can put down new wood flooring.

Solid concrete, stone, or tile floors with a damp problem need to be treated with a damp-proofing compound. If the trouble is serious, you must dig up the floor and re-lay it.

You can smooth out uneven solid floors by spreading a leveling compound over the top. However, this raises the floor surface and may involve rehanging doors. For the neatest effect, remove the baseboards, and replace them once the new floor covering is down.

Suspended floors – floorboards or plywood sheets in modern houses – should not have a damp problem, but they may be uneven. You can usually solve this by pinning sheets of hardboard over the existing floor before laying the new wood floor covering.

If the floor is very uneven, consider using sheets of chipboard or plywood, rather than hardboard. Again, this affects the flooring level at doorways, although you can usually leave baseboards in place.

STRIPPED FLOORBOARDS

If you already have natural softwood floorboards, why look further when you want the beauty of a natural wood floor in your home? Unfortunately, the answer often lies in the condition of the floorboards themselves. There may be gaps between the boards which trap dirt and can let in drafts. The boards may be split, warped, or rotten, or have deep nail holes in them. Sometimes the supporting joists may have weakened, or they may be suffering from woodworm or dry rot.

In the case of woodworm and/or dry rot, remedial work including chemical spraying and replacement of damaged wood is essential, whatever type of flooring you are installing. If you want floorboards as your floor covering, all of the existing boards that are rotted or worm-eaten must be replaced. There are ways to cure most other floorboard defects.

Gaps Small individual gaps between floorboards need to be filled with wood filler, stained papier mâché, or slivers of wood, glued in place and planed down to the level of the surrounding boards.

Large gaps or gaps between all the boards are more difficult. Often it's best to lift the whole floor and re-lay it. A floorboard clamp or wooden wedges force the boards together until they are nailed in place. This leaves a big gap at the end which must be filled with an extra floorboard.

Warped boards In time, floorboards can cup – curl up along the long edges. An industrial floor sander is ideal for getting rid of this. Working diagonally across the floor with coarse abrasive paper quickly removes the raised edges.

Damaged boards Individual boards can be replaced, the only problem being that modern boards may be slightly different in size from older boards, which may mean some adjustment or cutting away of the board and/or joist.

Loose boards Where the nails holding a board have become loose, the answer is to replace them with screws, which secure the board and stop it squeaking. Protruding nail heads should be hammered down with a nail punch, and nail and screw holes must be filled, before sanding.

Painted/waxed boards Where floorboards have several years' worth of paint, grime, or wax on them, it's best to clean them before stripping them. Steel wool and mineral spirits remove a build-up of wax polish and grime. An industrial floor sander, fitted with a medium abrasive paper followed by a fine paper and worked along the length of the boards, smooths off the surface. Finishing around the edges requires a hand-held sander.

Protective varnish With the gaps filled, the floor repaired and its surface sanded, the wooden boards need at least three coats of polyurethane floor sealer. Water-based types have less odor and are quicker drying than solvent-based ones.

▶ *It would be a crime to cover up these fine wide floorboards. Sanding and sealing them with a satin finish creates the character of the room and provides a welcome contrast to the matte homespun texture of the upholstery and drapes.*

◀ *The rich glow of the stripped floorboards adds an inviting warmth to the hallway. A mat in the doorway and the durable high gloss protects the floorboards from excessive wear.*

WOOD-FLOORING CARE

All types of wood flooring, from parquet to floorboards, tend to darken as they age, especially in natural daylight. After a while, the once shiny flooring takes on a matte appearance. To maintain your floor at its best, keep it properly sealed and cleaned regularly:

• Seal bare floorboards and unsealed wood with polyurethane floor varnish. Even when sealed, wood flooring is not the best choice for bathrooms where it often gets wet, nor for entrance halls where dirt gets trodden into it. In a kitchen, give an extra coat of sealant to prevent water getting into the cracks.

• Sweep wood flooring daily.

• Mop up spills at once with a damp cloth.

• Glue felt pads under table and chair legs.

• Provide mats to prevent outdoor dirt from getting into the flooring.

▶ *A large rug softens an expanse of bare stripped pine floorboards and creates a focal point for grouping furniture.*

PAINTED EFFECT

Stripped boards with a simple coating of clear varnish are an attractive sight on their own; but if after you've been through all the trouble and hard work of sanding the boards, you still have the energy and inclination to further embellish them, why not stencil a motif around the edges of the stripped boards to create to a border? A colorful pattern in the middle of the floor, painted to mimic a rug, makes an instant focal point, while simple strips of color to match the decor add interest.

If your floor is less than perfect, a coat of paint in a contrasting or toning shade hides rather than highlights any defects, but you still need to repair them before you apply the paint. Once the floor has been painted, it is advisable to treat it to one or two coats of varnish for a truly hardwearing finish.

◀ *Before being varnished this floor was stained in a bold checkerboard pattern diagonally across the wooden strips.*

▼ *The boldest of blue makes a highly dramatic floor color. The deep shade would help hide any imperfections in the boards that might mar the overall effect.*

VINYL, LINOLEUM, AND CORK

With their sleek good looks, vinyl, linoleum, and cork floor coverings have much to recommend them. Attractive, easy to clean, hardwearing, and long-lasting, they are also a competitively priced option.

As a significant surface area in a room, a floor has a great bearing on its overall appearance. Smooth floor coverings are a versatile option – the range of vinyl and cork available today is so vast that you should have little difficulty in finding something to suit your taste as well as your budget. Indeed, there is a pattern and texture of smooth floor covering to suit every room in the home, from a classical parquet appearance for a living room to marbled effects for kitchens or bathrooms.

On the practical side, smooth floor coverings cope well with the wear and tear of everyday family life. They are ideally suited to heavy traffic areas such as the kitchen and hall, where other floor coverings quickly become worn. In bathrooms and kitchens where the floors are liable to get wet and have messy things spilt on them, a floor covering that's waterproof and easy to clean is a must.

In a bedroom or a living room, you'll find smooth floor coverings surprisingly warm and comfortable underfoot. They can also add interesting color, texture, and pattern that can either complement other furnishings or become a focal point in their own right. Alternatively, you can choose a plain, restrained shade to create a mellow, neutral background for attractive rugs.

▲ *A checkerboard linoleum floor with star inlays is a great way to jazz up a room.*

VINYLS

Vinyl flooring is generally available in different grades to suit various rooms. It comes in sheet form on the roll in 79, 118, and 157in (2, 3, and 4m) widths, so you can buy a single piece to fit most rooms. Unlike natural wood, it has no tendency to warp in extremes of damp or heat.

Most types of vinyl also come in tile form – a convenient way of buying it. Packs of standard grades of vinyl are readily available and come in plain colors and patterned with marble and tile effects. The least expensive types have a faint flecking, but as the complexity of the designs increases, so does the price. Many are self-adhesive – you just strip off the backing paper and stick them in place.

When buying vinyl tiles, always check that the code number on each pack is the same, or you may find that the colors don't quite match.

Standard vinyl flooring is flexible and fairly thin. It can be cold to walk on and hard underfoot. However, it is inexpensive and easy to clean.

Cushioned vinyl flooring is attractive and capable of withstanding the rough and tumble under a family's feet. Soft and thick, it's made with a layer of padding sandwiched between a wipe-clean surface and a flexible backing. A $\frac{1}{16}$in (1.5mm) thickness is suitable for light domestic use, while a $\frac{1}{8}$in (3mm) thickness is ideal for a kitchen or busy hallway. Its padded filling provides a high degree of comfort that is ideal in a kitchen or utility area where you stand for long periods of time. Cushioned vinyl also feels warm underfoot, so it's a good choice of floor covering in bedrooms and bathrooms.

Look for a *lay-flat* vinyl, which molds itself to the contours of the floor, so there is no need to stick it down at all, not even at the edges.

Rigid vinyl flooring is the most expensive form of vinyl flooring, but it is very hardwearing. It is made to imitate natural surfaces such as marble, terrazzo, stone, ceramic tiles, and wood. Unlike many of the materials it mimics, it is easy to clean and warm to walk on. Rigid vinyl should always be laid by a professional flooring installer because the surface must be absolutely level.

Rigid vinyl is available in sheet or tile form, in a wide range of elaborate designs, including matching borders, corner pieces, and narrow insert strips. Tiles also come in different shapes for a realistic tiled-floor finish.

◀ *The terra-cotta-effect vinyl tiles in this bedroom give the room a warm feel. Each tile is marked into four smaller quarry tile shapes, shaded to give a convincingly realistic look.*

◀ *A sheet vinyl, terra-cotta tile-effect floor is difficult to distinguish from real tiles, with the advantage that it's not nearly as hard on dropped crockery.*

▲ *In some ranges of rigid vinyl, sophisticated designs and cutting technology offer complete styling flexibility. For a luxurious and durable floor in this kitchen, variegated green tiles are laid with narrow gold inserts and contained by a border of three gold bands.*

◀ *Installed by specialists, an elaborate vinyl floor contributes an extra dimension to a room. Here, an abstract seascape design forms the basis of a bathroom design.*

LINOLEUM

Linoleum is made from a mixture of natural materials – linseed oil, pine tree resin, sawdust, and cork, mixed with clay and chalk – pressed onto a fabric backing. Exceptionally hardwearing, linoleum gets tougher as it gets older. It is warm underfoot and water resistant. It is easy to clean with water and detergent – you can remove any scuffs or marks by rubbing the surface gently with fine steel wool. Unfortunately, this traditional flooring has been almost entirely replaced by sheet vinyl, but it is available as an imported speciality item.

◀ *Vinyl tiles inset with green marble-effect squares enhance the feeling of space in the bathroom and coordinate with the colors of the bath linen, curtains, and fixtures. A matching border adds a touch of formality.*

▼ *Warm and quiet to walk on, cork is a comfortable choice of flooring in this kitchen. Buy pre-sealed cork tiles for kitchen floors because these withstand heavy traffic better than tiles you seal yourself.*

CORK

Supplied in tile form, cork is a natural, lightweight flooring that's warm, hardwearing and also an excellent insulator. You can use it to add warmth to a cold bathroom or to take the chill off a solid concrete kitchen floor. It is also suitable for children's bedrooms, halls, and living rooms.

The tiles are available pre-sealed with a coating of clear varnish or vinyl, or unsealed. Once laid, unsealed cork tiles must be given at least three coats of polyurethane varnish for a stain-resistant, watertight surface.

However, although inexpensive to buy, unsealed tiles can prove to be a false economy, as heavy traffic areas need regularly revarnishing. Many cork tiles are self-adhesive, making them easy to lay. When you buy cork tiles, make sure you have a flooring-grade type rather than the less expensive wall tiles because these won't withstand hard wear on the floor.

Cork may also fade in direct sunlight and is easily damaged by sharp objects, cigarettes, and strong household chemicals, such as bleach and ammonia.

▲ *Linoleum has a beautiful marbled texture whatever its shade because of the way it is made.*

▼ *Linoleum tiles in cream and two shades of blue make an attractive gingham pattern that works well in a child's room.*

▲ *Cushioned vinyl sheeting like this is a luxurious choice in a kitchen. It wipes clean and its extra thickness underfoot makes it warm and comfortable if you are standing for long periods.*

▶ *The pale cork flooring in this sun room has a tough top layer of vinyl to make it extra hardwearing.*

BUYING AND LAYING

Before buying any smooth floor covering, draw up a floor plan of the room and mark in the maximum length and width, taking the measure right into any alcoves or nooks. For sheet floor covering decide whether it is more economical to lay it across the width or down the length of the room. If you need to join pieces, remember that the pattern must lie in the same direction on each piece. The easiest types of design to match up are those with light colors and small patterns.

All smooth floor coverings must be laid over a sound, dry, and level floor or they are likely to lift or wear unevenly. You can fill cracks and hollows on concrete floors with a cement mix, but on a very uneven floor you need to apply a self-leveling compound. On a wood floor, secure loose boards and make sure that protruding nails are firmly punched below the surface. For a perfectly flat finish, nail sheets of plywood to the floorboards before laying the floor covering.

DESIGN IDEAS

• Vinyl tiles come in a vast range of plain and patterned finishes, which you can use to create your own designs. For instance, you can use plain tiles with patterned ones, or plain tiles of different colors in a simple yet classic checkerboard arrangement.

• You can buy linoleum tiles as well as sheets, pre-cut into a range of different shapes to form either simple or extremely elaborate inlaid designs. You can pick out a border or create an eye-catching single, central motif.

• As well as printed designs, some vinyl product lines come with optional pre-cut border strips and corners which provide an easy way to add a distinctive effect to a plain floor. You can also buy a range of pre-cut and assembled central motif designs.

• You can stain cork tiles any color. Make sure you buy untreated tiles, then apply a colored stain and seal over the top with several coats of

▶ *A black and white border adds interest to a plain vinyl floor.*

◀ *A stylish inset central motif and matching border design provide interest on a linoleum floor in this dining room.*

▼ *Alternating cream and charcoal gray linoleum tiles is a strong but practical choice of design, particularly in a hallway.*

SOFAS AND SUITES

Buying a sofa or furniture suite is a major investment, so take more than just looks into account. Give size, comfort, construction, and the type of covering careful consideration, too.

The discomfort of sitting on a worn or badly made sofa or armchair is all too familiar. A sofa with broken springs or seat cushions that have so little padding you feel as if you are sitting directly on the base is uncomfortable and, if you sit in it for any length of time, can lead to troublesome aches and pains.

Comfortable and adequate living-room seating is therefore an essential purchase for your home. If your sofa and chairs are worn or uncomfortable, buying new ones should be high on your list of priorities. As with most purchases, cost reflects quality and it is worth allocating as much money as you can afford.

Your reward is a sofa or suite that will give you many years of relaxing service.

One of the main considerations is whether to buy a suite, a unit system or sofas and armchairs separately. The advantage of buying a suite – consisting of a sofa and two matching armchairs – is that you can make considerable savings. Furniture retailers are usually able to offer suites at more competitive prices than buying the items individually. However, a suite may not offer the flexibility that you are looking for or suit the room, so it is worth taking the time to plan what arrangement and size of furniture best fits the space before making the final decision.

▲ *The key to selecting the right sofa for your home lies in choosing one that's well suited in terms of size and design. This three-seater sofa in a simple cotton check is perfectly in keeping with the style and proportions of this informal living room.*

SIZE WISE

Before you even start looking for a sofa, you need to decide on the size. Sofas tend to look smaller in a large showroom, so it is easy to make a mistake and be misled into thinking a large sofa will fit in your living room at home and, just as importantly, through your doorways.

To avoid this, measure your room and the relevant doorways and draw up a scale plan, including major items of furniture. Use the plan to determine what size and configuration of chairs and sofas best suits the room.

Consider the proportions of the room in relation to the height and depth of the sofa. There is a lot of variation in the height of different sofas according to their style, and if the ceilings are low, a high-backed sofa may dwarf the space just as much as a sofa that is too large.

Also use the simple rule that dark colors advance and pale ones recede – a light sofa makes a room look larger than a darker one. Always take a tape measure with you when you shop to doublecheck measurements.

▶ *A rattan sofa with loose cotton-covered cushions is the perfect addition to an understated room scheme.*

WHAT MAKES A WELL-MADE SOFA?

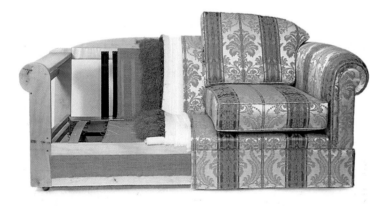

▲ *A cross-section of an upholstered sofa shows what you don't normally see – exactly what goes on under the cushions and covers. A beechwood frame and springs are covered with a canvas overlay. Layers of upholstery follow – fiber, coir, felt, and lastly foam to give the seat a smooth finish – before the damask cover is fitted.*

When you look through a brochure or walk through a showroom, you see sofas and armchairs in their finished state, their frames and upholstery hidden beneath attractive fabric covers. What goes on underneath the covers is just as important as their surface appearance, though, so don't be afraid to ask how particular models are made when making your choice. Upholstered furniture is generally made up of four parts: the frame, suspension, filling, and covering (sofa covers are dealt with on page 210).

FRAME

Traditional, fully covered furniture has a strong and springy hardwood frame – often in beechwood – joined by dowels, screws, and glue. Modern frames may use staples rather than dowels. Cheaper softwood frames do exist, but they have to be solidly built to take the weight. On sofas and chairs where part or all of the frame is on show – known as showwood – the frame is usually a hardwood because softwood dents too easily. Metal and plastic frames are sometimes used, but are not as hardwearing.

SUSPENSION

The suspension is what makes the sofa or armchair comfortable. Traditionally, sofas had large coil springs fastened to a webbing support, but these have largely been replaced by flat zigzag springs, used along with rubber webbing or diaphragms. In some designs rubber webbing completely replaces the springs, while some inexpensive types just have blocks of foam laid on a solid chipboard base.

◀ *You don't have to buy a matching suite. Sofas and chairs in contrasting styles and colors add interest to a room design.*

FILLING

Top-quality furniture uses natural fillings such as horsehair and wool, but the majority of sofas are filled with foam. Regulations insist that fireproof foam be used, so check that this is the case. Make sure that the foam is high density, as low-grade foam does not hold its shape as well. Cushions may also be stuffed with feathers. Make sure these cushions are channeled so the feathers do not settle at the bottom. Plumping feather cushions every now and then ensures that they always look their best.

QUALITY CHECKLIST

Regardless of the cost, make sure the furniture is well made. There are certain points to look out for:
• If the frame is visible, check for knots, splits, and cracks in the wood and that the joints are well made.
• Look underneath the sofa or chair for any signs of poor workmanship in the parts that don't show.
• Feel the padding. You shouldn't be able to feel the springs through the fabric, or the frame through the seat, back, or arms. On foam sofas, look for dome-shaped seats, as foam settles with use.
• Pull the arms and back to see how secure they are. They shouldn't have too much give.
• After you get up, check whether the seat resumes its shape quickly. Sagging seats worsen over time.
• Loose cushions should be reversible to even out wear, and loose covers should have generous seam allowances so they won't pull apart in the wash.
• Check the finish. Loose threads, poor-quality zippers, and rough edges are typical indications of poor manufacture.

▲ *Leather has a unique appeal with some practical advantages as well – it shrugs off spills and dust and only looks better with age.*

▼ *A traditional three-seater and loveseat sofa are paired with a matching armchair with show-wood legs to make up an attractive suite.*

COVER CHOICE

A family with children and pets inevitably gives a sofa a harder time than a single person or a couple, so choose the sofa fabric accordingly. Many upholstery fabrics undergo a "rub" test where they are scoured by a machine until they disintegrate. The higher the number of "rubs," the more wear-resistant the fabric. Ask a sales assistant about this. Acrylics, heavy cotton, wool, and linen mixed with nylon all wear extremely well. Lighter fabrics such as cotton and chintz aren't as hardwearing; they may lose color and start to look shabby over time.

For heavy wear, it's worth buying a sofa in a patterned fabric which shows dirt and stains less than a plain one. Look for a fabric with a stain repellent finish which helps to protect it. Armcaps protect the most vulnerable part of the sofa or chair from wear and tear. If the service is available, it is worth ordering extra covers for the arms and back to extend the life of the cover. Permanent covers on sofas come in for a lot of wear and tear, so it is often a good idea to choose a sofa with removable covers that you can take off for cleaning.

Bear in mind that fabric on rounded sofas tends to last longer than fabric on boxy designs because it isn't pulled over sharp edges. Baggy covers crease and get dirty more easily than tight ones and therefore wear out more quickly.

Sofa covers should be flame-retardant, so make sure that any fabric on your sofa has a flame-retardant backing or is used above a flame-retardant interliner.

When choosing a patterned cover fabric, remember bold patterns can be overpowering in small rooms, while a tiny floral print looks lost on a large sofa or in a big room. For a coordinated style, choose a fabric to match your curtains, but if you have a heavily patterned carpet or curtains, opt for plain upholstery instead, in a blending color. Some manufacturers offer a basic sofa which they cover for you in your choice of fabric.

If a fabric-covered sofa is not for you, think about leather. It's attractive, hardwearing, and needs little upkeep, but on the minus side leather suites are expensive and cold to sit on.

▲ *A fixed-seat sofa, upholstered in blue and white, is the focal point in this room. Wicker armchairs provide an informal contrast and, blending with the pine coffee table, pull the seating area together.*

▼ *This low-backed three-seater is stylishly simple in design. Sofas with straight rather than scrolled arms often have a more understated feel.*

COMFORT AND PRACTICALITY

There are many different aspects to consider when choosing a sofa or suite. If you can, take the whole family along to the showroom, so everyone can try out the various designs for comfort. Bear the following pointers in mind.

- Only shop when you've plenty of time so you can try out a number of different designs. Never shop when you're tired – anything will feel comfortable.
- Take off your coat, sit down, and make yourself comfortable. Bounce up and down on the sofa or chair and check that you can't feel the frame or the springs through the cushions.
- Make sure your feet touch the floor when you are sitting and the front edge of the seat is comfortable.

- Is the seat easy to get out of? This is an important consideration for older people.
- Do you want a high or low back? High backs give plenty of support to the head and neck and are better for tall people; low-back sofas may encourage slouching.
- Check whether the furniture has castors. These make moving it for vacuuming and other tasks much easier.

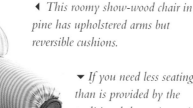

◄ *This roomy show-wood chair in pine has upholstered arms but reversible cushions.*

▲ *Perfect for watching television or relaxing, this armchair reclines, while the front panel extends to provide a comfortable foot rest.*

▼ *If you need less seating than is provided by the traditional three-piece suite, why not choose an upholstered stool instead of a second armchair? The sofa and chair have deep seat cushions and scroll arms, while the stool opens up to provide useful storage space.*

ORDERING YOUR SOFA

Only in very large furniture stores and at sale time is it possible to buy furniture that's ready to go. Most stores don't have the space to keep large upholstered items in stock. Usually the retailer takes your order and passes it to the manufacturer. They then make the furniture, which is delivered 6-12 weeks later.

USING YOUR OWN FABRIC

Most upholstery is offered in a range of fabrics, chosen by the manufacturer as being suitable for that style. The fabrics are tested for strength, durability, and safety, so as well as having a sofa that coordinates with your room design, you can be certain it will continue to look good for years to come. However, if you don't like any of the upholstery fabrics on offer, many manufacturers also offer a service where you can specify a fabric. This allows you to combine the shape and style of sofa you like with the fabric you want. Bear in mind, though, that most manufacturers refuse to take responsibility for any wear that may occur with your chosen fabric.

▲ *This loveseat comes in a range of different fabrics. As illustrated here, different fabrics give a sofa a completely different look – the lush floral suggests a cottage style, the red design exhibits a universal quality, while the two-color pattern has an air of pure elegance. To test the appearance of a fabric, whether it is your own choice or one suggested by the manufacturer, it is worth draping a large piece on the chosen sofa and standing back to see the effect before making a final decision.*

CHOOSING A DINING-ROOM SUITE

*Shop around and you'll find dining-room
furniture to suit not only the space you have available
but the style of your home and your budget.*

Dining-room furniture often outlasts other furniture in a home – a sofa and armchairs may show the strain of the rough and tumble of family life, but a sturdy table and chairs can go on looking good year after year. So work out your needs carefully before you buy a dining suite.

There's an excellent choice of robust, well-made contemporary furniture available to suit all tastes and budgets, from the elegance of Georgian reproduction through sturdy farmhouse to modern steel and glass. Folding or extending tables are a good choice if space is limited or to seat extra guests.

▼ *A separate extension leaf turns this round pedestal table into a more accommodating oval. The elegant chairs complement the table.*

A TOUCH OF THE TRADITIONAL

Traditional dining-room furniture such as a period style suite in solid wood or with a veneered finish is well suited to elegant formal meals. Before you buy it's a good idea to decide how versatile you want your table and chairs to be. Most dining-room furniture has to be sturdy enough to meet different needs. During the course of a day the table may be called on to do duty as a play surface for children's games and painting sessions, a desk for homework, and a worktop for a sewing machine as well as being used for an informal family breakfast, lunch, and tea. Yet it still has to be flexible enough to be dressed up for those more elegant evening occasions.

Consider this multi-functional aspect of the room when you shop for the furniture, and remember it's easier to use attractive table linen to dress up a tough surface like solid wood for formal dining than it is to protect a delicate veneer from everyday knocks and spills. If you do choose a table with a finish that needs protection, buy a table pad you can cover with an easily laundered tablecloth for everyday use. For more formal occasions, take away the pad and use a fancy tablecloth and placemats.

Most modern upholstered dining chairs have been treated to resist stains but for additional protection, use tie-on chair covers, or make covers to slip over upholstered seats.

▼ *A rectangular table with matching chairs is a timeless choice.*

▲ *Wood finishes such as this handsome beech veneer are a popular, affordable option for traditional dining rooms.*

▼ *High-backed upholstered chairs have tremendous comfort appeal. In natural cotton, they blend easily with other upholstery and drapes.*

▶ *A white lacquer finish lends a modern air to traditionally styled furniture. The table is designed to be extended to accommodate extra diners.*

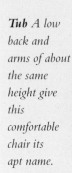

Tub A low back and arms of about the same height give this comfortable chair its apt name.

Bentwood A graceful, curved wooden back and round seat typify this style of chair.

Buckleback This popular Victorian style has a comfortable upholstered seat.

Ladderback A high wooden back like the rungs of a ladder identifies the style. The seat can be wooden, rush or upholstered.

Windsor The back struts of this chair gently curve for comfort. Styles with armrests are also available.

MODERN MOOD

The key to a modern dining room is simplicity. There is no shortage of clean-lined tables and chairs on the market. Favorites for a contemporary room are materials such as glass, chrome, and steel, but almost anything would suit, as long as the design is streamlined.

A laminate or lacquer which wipes clean and resists scratches and scuffs is a cost effective and practical option – especially if the table is going to be used by young children or if it doubles other ways, as a sewing table or somewhere to study or do homework. A modern style of table is best left uncovered, but you can give a more conventional table a bold new image with a dramatic tablecloth.

Make sure you check out a contemporary suite very carefully for comfort and practicality – a glass-topped table may lose its appeal if you are forever wiping off children's fingermarks. Cast-iron chairs can look dramatic in a modern room but they are often very heavy, which makes them difficult to draw up to and away from the table.

▲ *Colored cane chairs and a sturdy wooden dining table are a charming combination of natural materials with a contemporary twist.*

▶ *Black lacquered tubular steel is an unlikely choice for a dining suite yet, softened by the upholstered seats and pine tabletop, the effect is exciting.*

▲ *A glass tabletop and solid beech legs are perfect partners – the coldness of the glass is balanced by the warmth of the wood. A simple wooden chair is the ideal companion.*

▶ *Glass tables reflect the hard edge of modern styling, with the advantage that they make a room look more spacious. Paired with light metal chairs, the total effect is airy and uncluttered.*

COUNTRY STYLE

In designing a country-style setting you are aiming for a cozy, homey effect, whether the dining area is off the kitchen, part of the living area, or in a separate room. Wood is the only choice of material for the style, and the type of wood and the sort of table you choose dictates how formal or informal the room looks. For a farmhouse-style kitchen-cum-dining room, scrubbed pine or the rustic roughness of natural wood has the right feel. For casual dining, simplicity works best. Pick a pine or beech table with fairly plain chairs in solid wood or wicker. For a main dining area you probably want something slightly more elegant. Pine is still an appropriate wood, but you need to opt for a table design with a light, elegant shape and look for comfortable uphol-stered chairs to go with it.

▲ *Compact and simply styled, light oak effect furniture such as this adds a homey touch to the corner of a living/dining room. The dropflap table is a useful option where space is tight, and cushions help to soften the wooden chairs.*

◄ *This table, with base and legs stained a vibrant green, has Shaker-style overtones. It would be equally at home in a formal or informal setting.*

▶ *Light and refined, this antique stained pine table is at home in a formal dining area. The chairs with padded seats match the table and add the right touch of comfort. Matching cabinets can be added to the basic suite of table and chairs at a later date.*

FUTONS AND SOFA BEDS

Finding room for relatives and friends to stay can be tricky, but having a sofa bed or futon in the living room means you don't need a separate guest room.

Sofa beds and futons are real space savers that allow you to use rooms for more than one purpose. They are probably the most commonly used dual-purpose items of furniture. Refined by manufacturers over the years, modern versions are comfortable to sleep on, as well as to sit on, and they certainly do help with making the most of small-space living.

With a sofa bed or futon, you can turn a child's bedroom into a teenager's study-cum-bedroom, or an under-used guest bedroom into a workroom or sewing room. You can also solve the problem of limited space in studio apartments extremely effectively.

The type of bed you choose depends on who is most likely to sleep on it. While children and teenagers are usually happy to sleep anywhere, older people need a bed that provides more support and comfort. Also, consider whether the bed will be in constant or occasional use.

Futons, which are thick cotton bed rolls with wood or metal bases, are generally a little harder than a sprung or foam sofa bed, so when buying either a sofa bed or a futon, make sure that you lie on it to test it – just as you would with a normal bed. Test it as a sofa, too. It may be that, with certain convertible options, comfort and support are less important than the overall look.

▲ *Open up your sofa bed and effect an instant transformation. Turning a living room into an extra bedroom is that easy. Just pull the bed out from the center of the sofa frame, add bed linen and pillows and you're ready for sleep.*

CHOOSING SOFA BEDS

Sofa beds provide both seating and a bed and they are designed to transform from one to another with the minimum of fuss. Sofa beds can look every bit as stylish as normal sofas. With the top of the range models, it is hard to distinguish between a conventional sofa and a sofa bed. They can also be just as comfortable as normal sofas and come in almost as many different shapes and sizes.

With the large range of choices of modern or traditional styles, including upholstered or show-wood frames and printed, woven, or damask cover fabrics, you can be confident of finding a sofa bed to complement your decor. However, some manufacturers offer customers an "own cover" service if you prefer it.

One point to remember about sofa beds is that they are deeper from front to back than a conventional sofa. You should take this into account when you plan to replace an old sofa with a sofa bed, and want to place it in exactly the same place.

There are basically four types of sofa bed: the fold-out sofa bed, the flip-over or flop-out sofa bed, the A-frame sofa bed, and the drop-end sofa.

FOLD-OUT SOFA BED

Usually top of the range, these sofa beds are the most popular choice for the living room. Some are available as part of a full suite range with matching fixed sofas and chairs. These sofa beds have quality foam or sprung mattresses folded away inside. They have a sophisticated spring-loaded opening mechanism, which usually pulls out from the center of the sofa frame. The bed base is supported on an additional pair of legs. A wire mesh base is the least expensive option, but is not very durable. For regular use, choose a base made from laminated wooden slats because these provide good support while still allowing the air to circulate for freshness.

You cannot put a fold-out sofa bed away with bedding left on it, so they aren't ready for immediate occupation. Check that your existing bed linen fits the sofa bed you buy. This can be a problem because mattresses come in various non-standard sizes. A three-seater sofa, for example, may accommodate a 51½in mattress.

FLIP-OVER SOFA BED

With no separate mattress, this type of sofa bed simply unfolds directly onto the floor, so that the solid foam seat becomes the sleeping area. On some models the back unfolds too. Other versions incorporate a tailored duvet or quilt as a sofa cover, under which your guests can sleep.

Flip-over designs are perfect for children or for overnight guests, as they are easy to operate. However, once opened, they are generally too close to the floor for the elderly; they find them difficult to get into and out of.

▲ *At home in any decorating scheme, with a long-lasting base and a comfortable mattress, this type of fold-out sofa bed comes in almost every color, pattern, and style. Alternatively, you can cover it with your choice of fabric.*

◄ Convert this sofa into a stylish single bed by pushing a lever to lower the sides. You can angle an arm to act as a pillow. This is a good choice for a room where there is no space to pull out a double bed.

A-FRAME SOFA BED

The seat and the back on the A-frame sofa form the bed – either single or double. Some types have a quilted cover that you can use as a duvet; others offer storage underneath in which to stow away bed covers during the day.

DROP-END SOFA BED

This is the perfect option for a studio apartment. By means of a few levers, the sofa converts to a chaise longue, a single, or in some cases, even a small double bed. In many styles, you can fix the sides of the sofa at different angles, from horizontal for sleeping, to slightly angled for reading or watching TV.

OTHER OPTIONS

Many clever variations exist, especially for children's rooms, but check how comfortable and supportive the bed is before you buy.

Sofas are also available that have a single foam bed on sprung legs that pulls out from underneath. This "studio bed" is a useful alternative where singles as well as doubles are needed.

There are also many different sorts of chair available, from flip-over ottomans to fold-out bed chairs.

The table bed is a further ingenious variation. It is a coffee table or stool by day, but its hard outer casing opens out to become a bed by night.

▲ Complete with a sofa cover that doubles as a machine-washable duvet cover, this sofa bed makes everything easy. The basic mechanism is that of the A-frame bed – push down the back until it lies horizontal, forming one half of the mattress.

▶ The red-striped sofa looks extremely elegant in this living room. Unfolded, it provides a futon-like foam double bed.

FUTONS

Futon is the Japanese word for bed roll. It is a lightweight cotton or wool-mix filled mattress. Unrolled at night and used as a mattress on the floor or on a bed base, it gives good, even support to the sleeper and provides a smooth, springy surface to cushion the back. By day, you can roll it up for more room.

There are dozens of ways to use futons. You can sleep on them, sit on them, lay them flat on the floor, or on a variety of bases from tatami mats (the traditional Japanese base made of compacted rice straw) to conventional bed bases. Particularly suitable where space is at a premium, you can roll up the futon completely to store it in a cupboard during the day or convert it into a comfortable low-level sofa. Futons often come with a wooden frame – these are now available in a wide range of styles to suit most decors.

The traditional futon is made up of three thin layers of filling, strategically tufted to ensure that the filling stays in place and doesn't eventually become lumpy. The slim format of the mattress means that air can circulate. Futons made from six layers of filling are also available, but are more difficult to fold up when not in use.

Futons absorb moisture during the night, just like any other type of bed. They need a regular airing to keep fresh and springy. Rolling the futon up and using it as a seat during the day is sufficient to air it thoroughly. Futon bases with narrowly spaced wooden slats let the air circulate at all times.

Futons are quite difficult to clean, so it is well worth buying one with a removable cover. These are available in a tempting range of plain, patterned, and hand-printed fabrics. You can also make a removable, washable cover.

▲ *You can set the arms on this wooden futon base at this angle or drop them down horizontally, turning the sofa into a chaise longue or a bed.*

▼ *Just pull this simple A-frame mechanism from the front and it turns into a bed. You can leave the arms where they are or remove them.*

▼ *Push the back down to convert this stylish modern sofa into an extra bed. The sprung base and thick futon mattress ensure comfort.*

▲ *With the base extended (inset, below) and the futon made up with bedding and pillows, this bed is solid and comfortable enough for you to use every night. With the base folded back on itself again (main picture, above) and the futon in place, the room is transformed for daytime use. Ideal for a studio, a futon and base look their best in contemporary settings.*

CHILDREN'S OPTIONS

A child's bedroom usually lacks the space to accommodate a permanent extra bed, yet it is often your children's friends who need somewhere to stay. A perfect solution to this sleepover problem is a dual-purpose bed that can be used as a seat at other times. The following options do not take up much room when set up as a bed or chair because they are especially scaled down for children. Inexpensive and tough, they can be positioned wherever you want and you can make them up at a moment's notice.

Hardy, small-scale flip-over chairs with or without arms make excellent everyday seating in a child's room and they can be opened as a bed when a friend arrives. Ottoman versions are available. These are simply three or more squares of foam stacked and sewn together so they're easy to fold and unfold with the minimum of fuss.

◀ This chair is the ideal futon for children. You simply lift the futon off the base and lay it on the floor – leaving the frame where it is.

▲ A simple foam block, but once folded out, it becomes the perfect place for a sleeping bag and a tired child.

▼ A fold-out bed like this takes pride of place in a child's bedroom. A sturdy yellow armchair during the day, its colorful seat opens out into a mattress with no hassle.

CHOOSING LIGHTING

*A successful lighting scheme that meets practical needs
and creates atmosphere plays an important part in establishing the
style and character of your home.*

There's more to home lighting than a central ceiling fixture backed up by a couple of wall or table lamps. A well-planned lighting scheme should be both practical and decorative.

On the practical side, the right sort of lighting provides illumination for cooking, cleaning, sewing, reading, and many other day-to-day tasks. Decorative lighting helps to create a relaxed atmosphere, and should complement your color scheme and furnishings. It's quite possible to spend a fortune on carpets, curtains, and furniture, and invest hours of time and a great deal of energy in creating a beautiful home, only to be disappointed because poor lighting gives the end result a flat, two-dimensional look.

A successful home lighting scheme is made up of several different elements. Most rooms will need a carefully thought-out mixture of these effects to work well.

▲ *Recessed down lights positioned in a high shelf frame the edges of the room, adding warmth, while highlighting the pictures on the wall.*

LIGHTING CHOICES

General lighting provides overall or background light and should be used in every room.

A *hanging ceiling light* is a common type of light fitting, offering a variety of shade styles in materials as diverse as fabric, paper, or metal. A ceiling pendant that is the sole source of light in a room is a limiting choice; it provides a bright central space with shadowy edges.

Recessed or *semi-recessed low voltage down lights* spaced across the ceiling will give a good level of clear light. Depending on the type of bulb used, and the housing, a recessed down light can spread light over a wide area or in a narrow beam. Semi-recessed down lights (sometimes called eyeballs) can be swivelled.

Controlling down lights with a dimmer system is a good idea because you can then have some of the lights off while others are on, and can vary brightness.

Task lighting is designed to give concentrated, directional light over a small area and may be used in conjunction with general and accent fixtures. The type of task lighting you choose depends on the activity you have in mind.

A *desk light* with a flexible arm is the perfect example, as it can be adjusted to provide light exactly where it is needed.

A reading lamp should be tall enough to shine onto the pages of the book, but not into your eyes. A *floor lamp* positioned behind the reader is ideal.

Light for writing, sewing, or any other hobby should be positioned so that it shines down onto the work. *Rise and fall pendants* are useful for this, especially if you work at the dining table. *Recessed strip lighting* is useful for providing countertop light in a kitchen.

Accent lighting is used to show off plants, pictures, collections, and interesting architectural features. There are many different types, which can be used to light objects from above, below or behind, or at an angle.

A *narrow beam halogen down light* may be used to light a single vase or piece of china. The lower part of the object remains in shade, so this gives a dramatic floating effect.

Pictures are often lit from above. An adjustable *eyeball* or *ceiling spotlight* focused on the picture, or a special *framing spotlight*, which will flood the painting with light but leave the walls around it in shadow, are worth considering, as well as the traditional brass *picture light*.

A *table lamp* with a wide based shade will throw a pool of light onto the surface below it and is an attractive way to light a small collection or some framed photographs.

Floor standing *drum torchères* can be positioned below large plants to create dramatic leaf patterns on the walls and ceiling. You can light objects on glass shelves very effectively by positioning a row of small *halogen spotlights* below the bottom shelf. *Wall-mounted sconces, wallwashers*, or tall *floor lamp-style* designs will illuminate the detail on an interesting cornice or ceiling.

Small *floor torchères* positioned behind a sofa or armchair will wash the walls with light and make the room seem larger.

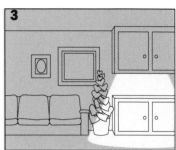

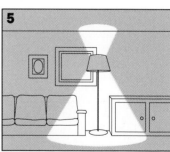

KEY TO LIGHTING PLANS

1. Recessed down lights
2. Wallwasher
3. Recessed strip light
4. Wall, floor, and lamp torchères
5. Floor lamp
6. Table lamp
7. Wall light
8. Ceiling pendant
9. Spotlights on track
10. Desk lamp

◀ *A row of down lights placed along the center of an entrance hall give a bright, welcoming light. They prevent the space from appearing too narrow and confining.*

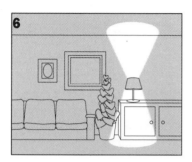

▲ *Task lighting can be stylish as well as functional. In this bathroom, Hollywood-style bulbs surround a mirror, with frosted glass to prevent glare. Once task lighting is in place, you can experiment with background lighting.*

▶ *A stylish sconce creates a mellow atmosphere by bathing the wall and ceiling in warm light and leaving the elegant daybed in partial shade.*

◀ *Different light for specific functions is the key to successful lighting – this modern hanging light illuminates the table, creating an island of light.*

A LIGHTING CHECKLIST

In order to analyze the lighting requirements for a particular room, first draw up a checklist.

• Does the room have several functions?

Many rooms have to be multi-functional; clever lighting can make one room seem like several, illuminating dining, working, reading, and sitting areas in different ways, and allowing one area to be lit separately from the rest.

• What mood do you want to create?

In the living room you'll want a different mood from that in the kitchen or bathroom – make sure you define your needs clearly when you set about your planning.

• Are there special lighting needs?

Children may need somewhere to do their home-work, in which case you will need to provide a good desk light. If you have an elderly member of the family, you'll want an armchair with a cord-switched reading lamp within easy reach.

• Will young children use the room?

Always use safety plugs, make sure hot bulbs are out of reach and table or floor lamps are stable, and avoid trailing light cords.

• Are there practical limitations?

The extent to which you can rearrange the lighting in a room depends on how flexible the existing electrical supply is. Are you prepared for the expense and disruption of putting in new wiring and outlets? Complete rewiring will almost certainly mean a great deal of redecoration.

• What is your budget?

If you decide exactly what you are prepared to spend before you start, you won't find the costs running away with you. Even if the ideal solution is beyond your means, with a little ingenuity you can probably find a less expensive alternative.

PRACTICAL POINTERS

If you live in an area where burglary is a risk, install security lighting. An outside light operated by a sensor will switch on when anyone approaches the house – useful both as a deterrent, and to help you find your keys, or park in the garage after dark. You can buy security bulbs and timers for use inside the house too. A simple security bulb will switch on when darkness falls and off again at dawn. More sophisticated versions switch on and off several times during the night. Timer switches can be set to switch lights on and off at varying times in different rooms.
Wiring work must be carried out by a qualified electrician.
Trailing extension cords can be dangerous. If necessary, install floor outlets so that table lamps can be plugged in without trailing cords across the floor. Never run cord under a carpet. It can overheat and cause a fire. Always check that the power is off before you change a light bulb.

▶ *Good lighting in the kitchen is essential. Two rows of elegant decorator bulbs create an effective but far from utilitarian scheme.*

◀ *A floor lamp is a versatile addition to general room lighting. Overall lighting can be kept low, while the lamp gives enough light to read by.*

▲ *A floor torchère bounces light off a wall to create a pattern of light and shade, and makes much of a simple house plant.*

▼ *A modern kitchen calls for modern lighting. Directing light exactly where it is needed, this halogen lighting system illuminates the working area without casting a harsh glare around the rest of the room.*

BUYING LIGHTING

Specialist lighting stores offer the best range of fittings and advice. Some have a design service, which is well worth considering if you want to fit a sophisticated low-voltage system.

Before you buy a lamp or other fixture, ask to see it lit so you can judge the effect. Remember that shade colors change when the light is on.

Make sure that the shade you intend to use is suitable for the bulb. Some paper and fabric shades can be scorched by powerful bulbs.

Is the lamp or fixture the right size? Measure the diameter of the table or cabinet before you buy table lamps and check that pendant lights won't be an obstruction for the taller members of your family.

Make sure you know how the fixture works and how to replace the bulb before you leave the store.

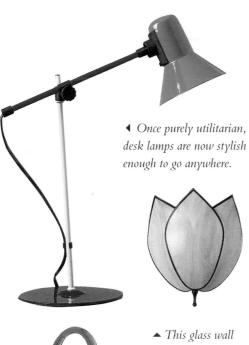

◀ *Once purely utilitarian, desk lamps are now stylish enough to go anywhere.*

▲ *This glass wall light will add a delicate accent to any scheme.*

◀ *Give your sitting room a Victorian air with a brass stemmed wall light.*

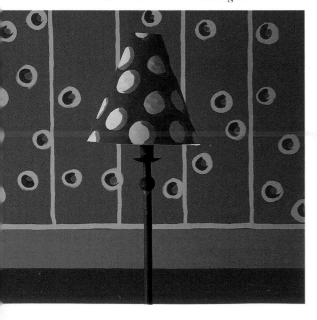

▲ *An ornament in its own right, this paper cone lamp is an attractive way of adding a soft, diffuse light.*

◀ *A lampshade chosen to complement the room scheme is the ideal accessory for adding a decorative flourish.*

▶ *A mock candle wall light provides any room with a soft glow — for a really authentic effect, try bulbs that flicker like real candles.*

CHOOSING CURTAINS

Take time to choose the best curtain treatment for your home – the right choice will not only enhance the windows but turn an ordinary room into a really special place.

When it comes to choosing curtains, there's no end to the different treatments and finishing touches available, in an exciting range of styles and fabrics. With so many options, the key to success is to approach the task methodically. Consider the style, size, and shape of the window, and what you want the curtains for. Are they simply decorative, or must they also keep out drafts? Should they be pulled back off the windows to let in light and frame a view, or is the scene outside better hidden? If privacy and insulation aren't important, could you dress the window by draping fabric over a rod – a simple and effective treatment if you don't need to draw the curtains?

Think about the room – its proportions and what it's used for, the upholstery, and accessories. Do you want the curtains to be a focal point, or to convey an understated elegance? Lined curtains drape well and provide better insulation than unlined, but easily laundered unlined curtains may be more practical in a playroom or kitchen.

Once you have sorted out your initial thoughts, work through the checklist overleaf to help you choose a curtain style that suits your needs.

▲ *Full-length curtains with a box-pleated valance are a good match for a large sash window. Using tiebacks to hitch the sheers up with the curtains softens the imposing effect to suit the bedroom.*

STYLE CHECKLIST

When choosing curtains it's a good idea to clarify your thoughts by separating some of the different elements involved. Below is a quick checklist of questions to ask yourself; look through them, then read on for possible solutions and a fuller description of any particular effects you want to create.

- What length?
- Hung from a rod or a track?
- Which heading?
- With or without a valance or pelmet, swags and tails?
- Hung straight, or held with tiebacks?
- Lined or unlined?
- Combined with sheers, shades, or blinds?

LENGTH

Sill-length curtains work well in cottage-style rooms with recessed windows, or with horizontal windows in modern homes. Curtains should barely touch the sill.

Below-sill length can look untidy when drawn back – use a tieback or curtain holdback to drape them attractively. If you have a radiator under the window the curtains should end just above it.

Floor-length curtains work best at sash windows, in bays and bows, and on French or picture windows. The curtains should almost touch the floor with no visible gap. Where the curtains won't get underfoot, you can let the fabric tumble, or puddle, onto the floor in arranged folds.

Café curtains give privacy at the lower half of the window while letting in light at the top.

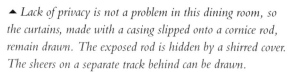

▲ *Lack of privacy is not a problem in this dining room, so the curtains, made with a casing slipped onto a cornice rod, remain drawn. The exposed rod is hidden by a shirred cover. The sheers on a separate track behind can be drawn.*

◄ In a child's bedroom, using a curtain rod and snazzy fabrics for the sill-length curtains and shade hits just the right note of fun.

► Hung on a bowed track with a formal, goblet pleated heading, these elegant curtains set the tone of the whole room. They are fixed at the center and held back permanently by high, tasseled tiebacks to emphasize the height of the window.

▼ These inspiringly simple curtains are suspended from two delicate brass rods by means of loops, or tabs, of the red border fabric.

RODS AND TRACKS

Rods are a decorative and versatile option for hanging curtains. Points to consider include:
- Rods with a brass or metal finish for a formal look.
- Wood or plastic rods for an informal style.
- Slim, discreet rods for short informal curtains.
- Large rods for long straight runs, and to carry the weight of heavy floor-length curtains.

Curtains can be hung from rods in a number of ways. The fullness of the curtain can be taken up with a heading tape, then hung from rings. The curtain can be made with a tab heading (loops of fabric that go over the rod) or it can have a casing (a horizontal pocket that slides over the rod) and cannot be drawn. For dramatic effects with a rod, try draping swags or hanging a valance.

Tracks have a streamlined effect that suits many modern furnishing styles. Although most are functional rather than stylish, some decorative types are available. The curtains are hooked onto runners designed to glide smoothly along the track. Points to look out for include:
- Special lightweight plastic and aluminum tracks can be bent to fit bow and bay windows.
- Steel tracks are available for the heaviest of curtains.
- Combination tracks make hanging two curtains, or a curtain plus valance, extremely easy.

The fullness of the curtain can be gathered up in a range of heading styles which play an important role in the final look of the window dressing. The curtain heading usually covers the track; if there is no pelmet or valance, the curtain is best left undrawn, and held off the window with tiebacks so that it always conceals the plain track.

HEADINGS

Headings determine the way that the fullness of the curtain or valance is gathered up. They range from simple gathered headings to elaborate smocked and pleated types. The most commonly used headings are gathers, and pencil, triple, cylindrical, and cartridge pleats.

Casings are the simplest ways to hang a curtain. A hem is stitched along the top of the curtain, then it is gathered onto the rod. The width of the hem can vary from a meager 1in to a casing wide enough to take deep continental or cornice rods. The casing can be stitched with or without a heading, which sits above the rod as a frilled edging.

Lightweight, short curtains made with a casing can be supported on tension wire – an ideal solution for sheers in a small window or across a dormer window.

VALANCES

A valance hides the curtain rod or track and heading and adds a decorative finish to a window. Depending on its height and depth, a valance can be used to alter the proportions of a window, making it look taller or shallower.

A **soft valance** is a deep frill that hangs in front of a curtain to give a soft, pretty finish to a window and, depending on the type of heading and trim used, is suitable for most rooms. Soft valances can be straight or shaped, and edged with braids or fringing.

In a **hard valance** the fabric is stiffened with a backing fabric, or stretched over a wooden frame. A hard valance can be straight, cut with a decorative edging, or bound or trimmed with cord, braid, or fringing.

SWAGS AND CASCADES

Swags and cascades are a dramatic treatment for windows. The swag is a drape of fabric which hangs in front of the curtains; the cascades are the elegant lengths of fabric that frame the window on either side. The more formal version is fixed to a valance board, but fabric can be draped informally over a rod as the only form of window dressing. Although the formal swags look best on tall windows, dressing full-length curtains, they can be effective scaled down to suit smaller windows.

▲ *Here, the lower edge of the valance has been cleverly cut to follow the floral garland and ribbon design on the curtain fabric. The depth of the valance, along with drawing the curtains beyond the window on either side, visually reduces the height and narrowness of the window.*

▶ *Elaborate swags and cascades are ideal for creating a dramatic window dressing. In this hallway, the window treatment takes advantage of a coordinated range of fabrics, by using a lighter version of the main curtain fabric for the swags and cascades. The plain linings and tiebacks pick up the yellow of the roses in both floral fabrics.*

◀ *Choose your curtains to enhance your decorating style. Here, the plain, pale curtains hanging straight down to the floor, and swags and tails draped casually over the pole rods, suit a light, minimally furnished room.*

▼ *Floor-length curtains with a box-headed valance make a handsome contribution to this stylish living room. Details, like matching the binding and piping on the valance and tiebacks to the piped trim on the armchairs, pull the room scheme together.*

TIEBACKS

Curtains that are hung straight suit a very small window, or where you want a simple style, perhaps for a cottage look or a nursery. A straight curtain can look handsome, but consider tiebacks for a more decorative or elegant finishing touch.

No-sew tieback options include using a heavy cord and elaborate tassel, or you can loop the curtains behind metal or wooden holdbacks.

LINING

Lining adds insulation, protects the curtain fabric from the sun, and prevents fading. It also makes the curtains drape well. To add interest, use a contrast lining with a pattern or a coordinating color. Specialty linings, including room-darkening or thermal fabrics are available.

Interlining curtains with a soft layer of padding between the curtain fabric and lining makes them hang beautifully and gives extra insulating properties.

SHEERS, SHADES, AND BLINDS

One solution for problem windows, or bay or shaped windows, is to combine the curtain with a shade, blind, or separate sheer curtain.

A blind or shade works well on windows that are covered by curtains at night, but need alternative screening from excessive sunlight or prying eyes during the day, and they can be styled to match curtains.

A sheer curtain is another answer on windows where you need to hide a view, or have daytime privacy, because it allows light to filter into the room.

CURTAIN ACCESSORIES

Gleaming metal and softly draped fabrics are a magical combination in a window dressing. In a traditional style, hanging the curtains from a brass rod or on metallic rings, or securing them away from the window with wooden or brass tiebacks, looks luxurious.

For simple yet exciting window treatments, contrast the richness and softness of curtain fabrics against the ruggedness of iron rods. Draping delicate sheers over a matte black iron bar is very dramatic, and well suited to a modern decorating scheme.

▲ *When fastened horizontally beside a window, this molded brass bracket is an elegant way of holding back formal curtains.*

▲ *One solution for hanging lightweight curtains is to improvise a rod from a strip of dowel and slip ornamental rings over the ends as decoration.*

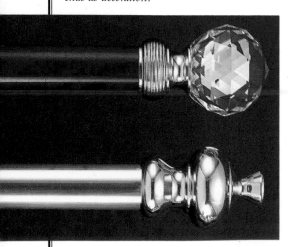

▲ *With its end coiled into an artistic spiral, a slim iron bar makes an excellent rod for hanging a tabbed curtain.*

◄ *The ornate knobs, or finials, used to decorate the ends of a curtain rod come in many shapes and materials.*

▲ *A brass rosette is strong enough to hold back even a heavy curtain. You simply unhitch the fabric to draw the curtain.*

▼ *Tiebacks restraining lightweight curtains can be looped over little brass hooks fixed to the wall or window frame. Look for pretty designs, like these leaf and floral hooks.*

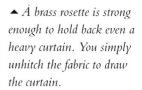

A GUIDE TO SHADES & BLINDS

Blinds or shades make versatile window coverings; there are many styles and materials to choose from. On their own or teamed with curtains they give shade and privacy.

▲ **Roller blind or shade** This is a smooth, stiffened panel of fabric that winds around a roller at the top of the window. The shade is rolled up and pulled down via a spring-loaded mechanism or a pulley cord hanging at its side. The base edge can be straight or shaped.

▲ **Roman blind** When lowered, a Roman blind lies flat against the window; when raised – by means of cords and loops attached to the back of the blind – it folds into neat horizontal pleats. A wooden batten along the lower edge of the blind holds it straight, while smaller battens may also be inserted across each pleat to define the folds. Roman blinds may be lined or unlined.

▶ **Fan-tailed blind** This is a variation on a Roman blind, in which the lower edge folds into a pleated semi-circle or "fan" shape. If desired, the fan can be released to lie straight, as on a Roman blind.

▲ **Austrian blind** When lowered, an Austrian blind hangs like a single gathered curtain, but with soft folds along the base edge; when raised – by a series of cords running up the back of the blind – it pulls up into ruched swags. Austrian blinds are always cut slightly longer than the desired finished drop, so that the lower edge remains swagged when the blind is fully lowered. The blinds may be lined or unlined. You can emphasize the ruched effect with a frill along the side and base edges.

◀ **Festoon blind** A festoon blind is similar to an Austrian blind, but is permanently ruched into flounces all the way down its length, whether raised or lowered; special festoon blind gathering tape is used to create the ruches. The blinds are often made from sheer fabrics and teamed with curtains.

▲ **London blind** In its simplest form, a London blind has no gathers or pleats across the width, and is pulled up into soft, horizontal folds by two tapes stitched to the back of the blind, close to the side edges. To give a fuller effect, the blind is made with an inverted pleat over each side tape. Another alternative is a wide blind with a third, central tape. The blinds may be lined or unlined.

▲ **Tied blind** A tied blind is a smooth panel of fabric hung in front of the window. It is rolled or loosely gathered by hand to the desired height, and secured with fabric ties. The base edge may be held straight by a wooden dowel, or left to hang in soft folds at each side of the supporting ties. Tied blinds are very simple to make, but are more awkward to raise and lower than other styles.

▶ **Venetian blind** A Venetian blind is made up of horizontal slats of wood, plastic, or aluminum. When the blind is raised, by means of a pulley cord, the slats stack neatly on top of one another. When the blind is lowered, you can angle the slats – usually by pulling on a second cord – to control the amount of light that filters in.

◀ **Pleated blind** Pleated blinds are traditionally made from sun- and water-resistant paper, but nowadays you can also buy them in polyester. The blinds have permanent concertina-style horizontal pleats, with cords to raise and lower them. A range of plain colors and flecked finishes is available.

▶ **Vertical louver blind** These blinds are made from vertical louvers, the angle of which can be altered by means of a cord, to let in or shut out light – much like Venetian blinds. A pulley cord draws them back to the side of the window. They are useful for large windows and patio doors, and come in a wide choice of colors and materials.

▲ **Roll-up shade** Non-fabric roll-up shades may be made from a number of materials, including woven grass, bamboo, split cane, reed, and vinyl. They are raised and lowered via a pulley system.

SHELVING

Shelves are the simplest, least expensive, and most versatile type of storage you can buy. Your choice should depend on practical considerations, such as strength and adaptability, as well as on good looks.

I t's tempting to imagine that the first item a cave-man invented was a shelf. At the very least, he would certainly have utilized any flat ledge in the cave to store his tools and cooking pots. Finding somewhere to keep all your possessions, and leave space for your future belongings, is still an ongoing challenge in any home. To solve any shortage of storage and space, a combination of functional and decorative shelving is an attractive solution.

There are basically two main types of shelving to choose from – fixed, wall-mounted systems, including self-assembly kits, all-in-one bracket-and-shelf units and built-in shelves, and freestanding, movable units. Shelving is made in a variety of materials to suit all tastes and budgets. The least expensive are the sturdy metal, wooden, and plastic systems designed for offices and garages. Medium-priced shelving is often made from particleboard with a wipe-clean melamine

coating or hardwood veneer. Solid timber and glass or clear acrylic shelving costs a little more.

Before deciding on the best type of shelving for your budget, you should assess what you want to store. Your choice of shelving needs to take into account practicalities such as load-bearing capacity as well as how well the shelves fit in with your decor. Most manufacturers provide guidelines on this, but always ask for information if you need it.

Take a look around your home for any under-exploited spaces – alcoves, under the stairs, or over doorways or windows, for instance – where you could fit a shelf or two. Accessibility is important too, both in terms of where the shelves are situated and how you arrange items on them. Frequently used items need to be within easy reach. Deep shelves are rarely an advantage, as the last thing you want is to be constantly moving one row of things so you can reach another.

▲ *The functional appearance of these shelves suits the modern layout of the room. At the same time, the galvanized tracks and stylish wooden boards provide useful storage and display surfaces.*

WALL-MOUNTED SHELVES

There are three distinct types of wall-fixed shelving: self-assembly kits, lightweight all-in-one bracket-and-shelf units, and shelving built into alcoves. Most home supply stores stock a wide range of shelf boards, tracks, and brackets. Useful accessories include clip-on book ends, grooved shelves for displaying plates, and corner shelves that enable you to run a continuous length of shelving around a room.

Wall-mounted shelving is either set or adjustable. If you are reasonably sure that the contents of your shelves won't change, there is little point in buying adjustable shelving. However, if you think you may want to extend the shelving or alter its function over time, an adjustable system is the most practical.

▸ *Corbel-style brackets make excellent mini-shelves for holding individual ornaments, potted plants, or a vase of flowers. Several grouped in an arrangement on the wall can look extremely effective.*

▾ *Adding an edge trim to the shelves and filling them with an assortment of objects turns an ordinary track system into a stylish array of shelving on a whole wall.*

▸ *A single glass shelf, supported on two decorative brass brackets, provides an unintrusive surface for showing off anything from pictures to flowers and decorative pieces.*

SELF-ASSEMBLY KITS

Apart from being inexpensive, the great advantage of self-assembly shelving kits is that you can tailor them to any items you want to display or store, from cassettes to candlesticks, books to bottles, and arrange the shelves where and how you want them. Shelving and fittings are normally sold separately, allowing you to buy as much or as little as you like.

When you are planning to install several shelves in a stack, always measure the height of the items you want to store, and space the gaps between the shelves accordingly. Whichever shelving material you use, your shelves must be well mounted and supported so that they do not come away from the wall or sag.

Brackets and boards Right-angled brackets screwed directly into the wall are commonly used to support shelves. A wide range of designs is available. With brackets and boards, you can devise all kinds of shelving arrangements – from covering a whole wall to putting up a single display shelf. The main disadvantage is that the shelving takes a long time to put up, as each board has to be individually levelled and each bracket screwed to the wall.

Track systems In this very functional form of shelving, tiers of adjustable, wall-mounted shelves are fixed to metal tracks with rows of slots punched along their length for fastening the clips or brackets that hold the shelves at any height. The major advantage is that once one shelf is level, all the others will be automatically level. Unfortunately, the tracks tend to show up clearly against the wall.

◄ *Regularly spaced L-shaped brackets and wooden boards form the basis of a strong, practical, and attractive storage system in this kitchen.*

◄ *Adjustable track shelving is highly flexible. You can slot in shelves at any height with variable spacing between them. Here in a child's room the shelves are arranged at the head of the bed, providing storage for toys, games, stuffed animals, and books, and a place for the bedside lamp.*

◄ *These shelves are supported along their back edges by an ingenious wall-fixed strip. Note how a shelf across the corner becomes a useful desk.*

◀ *A simple bracket shelf unit with an integral towel rail fits neatly into a small bathroom. It's easily attached to the wall with only two screws.*

▼ *These modern shelf units, which are fastened to the wall and floor, combine the stability of wall-mounted shelving with the mobility of freestanding shelves.*

PREASSEMBLED UNITS

With preassembled units, you can fasten the shelves to the wall in one try, and transport them as one piece if you move.

All-in-one brackets and shelves You can buy small, lightweight shelving units, combining brackets and a shelf or shelves, to screw to the wall. They may be designed to hold specific items such as jars of spices or videos. Some are decorative, others more functional. Some designs incorporate other features underneath the shelf, such as a single drawer, a towel rack, or curtain rod, and are excellent space-savers.

Stacked shelf units You can hang a set of shelves fitted into a frame on the wall. Some versions involving lightweight frames supporting wooden shelves are floorstanding but need to be fastened to the wall at the top for stability.

POINTS TO REMEMBER

Check what the walls are made of before putting up the shelves. On most walls, screw the shelf supports into the studs for weight-bearing strength, rather than use hollow-wall fasteners.

•

Use a wiring detector to check that there are no electric cords, gas or water pipes hidden in the plaster where you want to mount the shelves.

▲ *In its simplicity, a lightweight, wooden unit with three shelves is in keeping with a country style of decorating.*

▶ *A combination of wooden and glass shelving on either side of this fireplace illustrates the value of alcove space for storage and display.*

◀ *A compact unit with well-lit glass shelves is tailor-made to fit into the alcove above this countertop. The shelves are carefully spaced to accommodate the specific items on them.*

▼ *Dividing the shelves built in along one wall into cubicles like this turns standard living room storage into an original design and display feature in a minimalist setting.*

BUILT-IN SHELVING

Tailoring shelves to fill an architectural gap, such as an alcove beside a chimney breast, an understairs triangle, or over a door, is an extremely practical use of space. For the most exclusive custom-built shelving that adds classical storage facilities to a room, you should call in a carpenter. Then you can decorate the shelving with paint finishes and shelf-edge trims, and add display lighting to your own specifications.

As well as the track-and-bracket systems, the most common methods of installing alcove shelving yourself are listed below.

Wooden battening is the easiest type of shelf support to fit along two or three sides of an alcove. The batten is clearly visible, but if you can, paint it the same color as the wall so that it merges into the background. Measure and install each shelf independently because the walls of the alcove are unlikely to be true.

Shelf-end supports, made from thin strips of aluminum or steel fitted to the sides of a narrow alcove, are an unobtrusive option for short shelves that don't need to carry too much weight. There are various types, ranging from slotted metal strips with small studs that fit into them to carry the shelves, to plastic or metal studs that screw into wood lining the side walls. Alternatively, you can install a right-angled metal strip on each side of the alcove – and along the back for a heavy load – and either rest the ends of the shelves on top, or buy a grooved shelf that slides over the bracket and hides it completely.

FREESTANDING SHELVING

Freestanding shelving fits inside a wooden or metal frame that you can place against a wall or set up so that it projects into the room, forming a high or low-level room divider.

You usually buy the shelves and supports together, either ready-assembled or as a flat-pack, which is the less expensive option. In either case, they are transportable so you can take them with you whenever you move.

Freestanding shelving takes up more space than wall-mounted kinds and is often more expensive because it needs a strong frame. But it is flexible. You can easily add on extra sections when you run out of storage space and rearrange the units whenever you want.

Industrial shelving is excellent for a garage or a tool shed, but its uses don't end there. Tough and considerably less expensive than other types of shelving, it can be installed in a kitchen, teenager's bedroom, or even a living room. The frames are made from steel, thick battens of wood, or brightly colored plastic tubing bolted together, and usually have adjustable shelving, available in a choice of several widths.

▶ *The dividing line between freestanding shelving and modular storage systems is often very fine. Integrating shelves with matching cabinets and drawers lets you hide some items and display others.*

POINTS TO REMEMBER

When you buy kit shelving, try to see an assembled sample beforehand to make sure it is well designed and sturdy – especially if you want to use it as a room divider.

•

If you are buying more than one shelving unit, ask for the manufacturer's brochure to study the full range of accessories.

•

To prevent too much dust collecting when you use shelving as a room divider, include some closed cupboard units at floor level.

▲ *A freestanding stack of four sturdy wooden shelves on a strong metal frame makes a handsome and useful piece of furniture wherever it is located.*

▶ *For trendy shelving at a bargain price, a commercial shelving system fits perfectly into a teenager's room.*

CHOOSING TILES

Whether you opt for hard tiles, such as ceramic, marble, terra cotta, or stone, or the softer finish of vinyl or cork, you'll find that tiled surfaces offer many decorative and practical advantages over other forms of wall and floor covering. Tiles are divided roughly into two categories:

Hard finish includes ceramic, terra cotta, quarry, slate, stone, marble, and terrazzo, offering a vast choice of color, texture, and finish. On the whole more expensive and trickier to lay than soft finish tiles, these are nevertheless the most durable options – some, such as terra cotta, will last a lifetime and more, and even improve with age.

Soft finish includes vinyl and cork tiles, all softer and warmer underfoot than most hard tiles and generally less costly. These tiles are easy to clean and lay, and, in the case of vinyl, available in an extensive range of designs. Although they are hardwearing, they don't offer the same strength and longevity as most hard tiles.

Before you decide on a particular type and style of tile, you need to make sure it is suitable for its intended position and application. For example, not all floors are strong enough to bear the weight of quarry tiles, and not all ceramic tiles may be used on kitchen countertops or in showers. If in doubt, always ask the tile retailer for advice.

▸ *Black and white ceramic floor tiles, laid in a checkerboard design with a matching geometric border, are a traditional favorite which suits both period and contemporary room schemes. These hardwearing tiles are a good choice for heavy traffic areas such as hallways.*

BUYING TIPS

• Most tile suppliers will send you samples of your chosen tiles, so you can see how they look in the intended setting before you buy. Check how the tiles look in both natural and artificial light before making a final decision.

• If buying several boxes of tiles, check that they are all from the same batch – this is indicated by a code number on the box. Colors sometimes vary between batches. If tiling a large area, you may need to buy from two or more batches and mix them together.

• Always allow a few extra tiles in case of mistakes in measuring or laying. Ask the tile retailer if they have a return policy, in which case you will be able to get credit for unused boxes of tiles.

FLOOR PREPARATION

• Floor tiles need to be laid on a sound, dry, and level floor, or they are likely to lift or wear unevenly.

• You can fill cracks and hollows on concrete floors using a cement mix, but on a very uneven floor you need to apply a self-leveling compound.

• On a plank floor, secure loose boards and make sure that protruding nails are firmly punched below the surface. For a perfectly flat finish, nail sheets of plywood or hardboard to the floorboards before laying the floor tiles.

• Note that some types of floor tiles – generally heavy, hard flooring, such as quarry, stone, and terra cotta – should always be laid by an expert. Your retailer will advise you.

CERAMIC TILES

Hardwearing, water-resistant, and easy to clean, ceramic tiles are a practical as well as an attractive finish for walls, floors, and other areas in the home, such as countertops and fireplaces. Prices range from budget to expensive, depending on whether you opt for a mass-produced or handmade tile. The tiles are sold singly, by the square yard (meter), or in boxes of various quantities.

TYPES OF TILE

Ceramic wall tiles are available in a vast range of designs, shapes, sizes, and finishes. In addition to basic plain and patterned wall tiles (known as "field tiles"), many coordinated designs offer matching individual decorative tiles with smooth or relief designs; tile panels or plaques to create a feature (see Focal Point, below); border tiles; listello or slip tiles; and wainscoting and cornice tiles to give a well-finished look. You can also buy stronger, heat-resistant countertop tiles and fireplace tiles.

Ceramic floor tiles are thicker than ceramic wall tiles, and fired at a higher temperature to make them stronger. Like wall tiles, they are available in an extensive range of types, shapes, and styles, mass-produced and hand-made, glazed and unglazed (unglazed tiles must be sealed before use). Border and inset floor tiles are available to add interest to the main floor tiles.

▲ *Ceramic tiles are the perfect choice for bathroom walls and floors, where steam and splashes can soon damage wall coverings or paint. Use wainscoting and decorative tiles to break up large expanses of wall and add interest.*

FOCAL POINT
A ceramic plaque, such as the handpainted, relief design of fruits and vegetables shown here, creates a handsome feature on a tiled wall. This plaque is part of a coordinated design, which includes plain and patterned field tiles, matching decorative and listello tiles, and coordinating trims such as the deep blue wainscoting tiles.

ENCAUSTIC TILES
Encaustic tiles are hand produced using a technique similar to marquetry, except the stoneware or clay is still in a semi-liquid state while the design is formed. So, unlike an ordinary tile with a surface decoration, the pattern actually runs into the tile. Encaustic tiles exhibit a soft merging of color areas, which gives them the mellow look of an authentic antique floor.

5

PRACTICAL HOME DECORATING

BASIC TOOL KIT

Having a basic set of tools ensures that you can tackle most decorating tasks quickly and easily. Buy good-quality tools – they last longer and give better results than inexpensive ones. It is usually more economical to borrow or rent rarely used items as you need them.

Wire brush for scraping rough surfaces to remove rust, loose flakes, and other debris.

Saws: Hacksaw (1) is an all-purpose saw for metal, plastic, and wood. Panel saw (2) (optional) is for cutting large pieces of wood. Tenon saw (3) is for making accurate cuts in wood.

Try square for marking and checking the accuracy of right angles.

Adjustable wrench to tighten and loosen nuts and bolts. One that opens to 1³⁄₈in (3.5cm) is fine for most situations.

Measuring tape: Choose a retractable steel tape.

Level to check whether a surface is exactly horizontal or vertical.

Utility knife for cutting materials such as vinyl and cardboard. For safety, buy one that has a retractable blade.

Awl to make starter holes in wood to take screws, hooks, and eyes, and for drilling.

Screwdrivers: Slot head (4) and Phillips-head (5) types in a range of sizes.

Metal ruler (straight-edge) for marking straight lines.

Drill and drill bits: A two-speed drill (6) copes with most household jobs. You will also need various sizes of twist bits (7) for wood, and masonry bits for harder surfaces.

Combination pliers to grip, straighten, and bend metal, and to cut wire.

Abrasive paper for sanding rough or uneven surfaces and for roughening smooth surfaces before painting.

C-clamp to secure wood when sawing or to hold glued joints while the adhesive sets.

Cord and pipe detector to check walls for hidden electric wires or water pipes.

Steel wool for cleaning small or recessed areas or for roughening a surface for painting.

Nail set (optional). Use with a hammer to drive nail and tack heads below the surface.

Hammers: A medium-sized claw hammer (8) for most hammering jobs and to pull out nails. A tack hammer (9) for smaller jobs and for working in narrow spaces.

DECORATING TOOLS

Paint bucket for mixing and holding small amounts of paint.

Paint brushes: A set of brushes in sizes ranging from ½-4in (1-10cm) handles most painting tasks. Use an angled cutting-in brush (1) for window frames.

Paint roller and tray for painting large areas quickly and evenly. A narrow roller (2) is for narrow spaces and painting stripes.

Low-tack masking tape to cover particular areas when painting or staining.

Chalk line (optional) for marking a long guideline on a surface.

Scissors: 8in (20cm) paperhanger's scissors for making long, clean cuts in wall coverings. Use smaller scissors for precise cuts.

Pasting table: A foldaway table for holding wall covering while you apply paste. The standard size is 6 x 2ft (180 x 60cm) when open.

Plumb line enables you to mark a vertical guideline for tasks such as hanging wall covering.

Seam roller is rolled along the seam between sheets of non-textured wall covering to give a smooth finish.

Scraper for removing old wallpaper and paint.

Wallpaper brush to smooth out pasted wall coverings once in position.

Paste brush to apply wallpaper paste quickly and evenly. Buy a purpose-made one or use an old, wide paint brush.

Putty knife for spreading and smoothing spackling. If possible, get a wide and a narrow one.

PREPARING FOR PAINTING

Whether you are painting a plaster wall, a metal radiator, or wooden furniture, it's essential to prepare the surface first. The preparation needed depends on the type of surface you are painting, any previously applied finishes, and the paint you intend to use.

You need to apply primer or sealer to most bare surfaces before you paint them. This seals porous surfaces and helps the paint to adhere. It's essential to choose a primer that is suitable for the surface to be painted, and is compatible with the paint you intend to apply. The charts below and overleaf give you a guide to which primer you should use. Read the manufacturer's recommendations for the paint and primer before you buy.

In addition to the primers in the chart, you can buy quick-drying primers for most surfaces. Some primers are suitable for interior or exterior surfaces only, while others may be used for both; follow the manufacturer's recommendations. To save time and trouble, a two-in-one primer and undercoat is available. Avoid using lead-based metal primers where possible.

Surface	Preparation	Primer/sealer
Exterior walls (masonry)	**1** Remove dirt and loose paint with a stiff brush **2** Kill mold and algal growth with fungicidal wash; rinse off **3** Seal surfaces that remain powdery or chalky with stabilizing primer **4** Fill minor cracks and holes with exterior filler; for larger defects, use ready-mix cement	**Stabilizing primer** seals and stabilizes powdery masonry surfaces to give a sound base for masonry paint
Exterior woodwork	**1** Treat rotten wood using a wet-rot repair kit or replace the wood **2** Remove flaking paint with a stiff brush, and sand smooth **3** Kill mold and algal growth with fungicidal wash **4** Fill cracks and chips with exterior filler **5** Apply knotting solution where necessary **6** Dust off; apply primer to bare wood	**Stain killer** seals knots and resinous areas of bare wood to prevent resin seeping through **Aluminum wood primer** is for use on previously creosoted exterior wood. It contains minute flakes of aluminum which prevent the stain coming through new paint **Preservative wood primer** is used to seal and protect bare exterior wood
Bare plaster	**1** Leave new plaster to dry for 4–6 weeks; use only latex paint for the first 6 months **2** Fill cracks and holes with filler; sand uneven surfaces **3** Dust with a soft brush, or vacuum with a soft brush attachment **4** Apply primer/sealer	**General-purpose (multi-surface) primer/sealer** or **PVA solution** (dilute to the recommended consistency, following the manufacturer's instructions) **Stain sealer** prevents common stains, such as grease, ink, and cigarette tar, from showing through new paint

Surface	Preparation	Primer/sealer
Unfinished drywall	**1** Dust with a soft brush, or vacuum with a soft brush attachment **2** Apply primer/sealer	Prime as for **Bare plaster** **Metal primer** or **general-purpose (multi-surface) primer/sealer** should be applied to nail heads
Previously painted plaster/drywall	**1** Scrape or sand off flaking, cracking, or peeling paint, then touch in bare areas with a little paint to even out the surface; leave to dry **2** Repair cracks and holes with filler, and self-adhesive joint tape on drywall, if necessary **3** Wash down with a mild solution of soap or detergent. Rinse and allow to dry thoroughly **4** Lightly sand the surface, then dust it off	No primer necessary
Previously wallpapered plaster/ drywall	**1** Remove wall covering unless it is designed to be overpainted – fiberboard or lining paper, for example **2** Lightly wash down **3** Stick down lifting seams with repair adhesive	No primer necessary
Bare wood	**1** Fill cracks and chips with wood filler **2** Apply knotting solution where necessary **3** Lightly sand the surface, then dust off **4** Apply primer	**Stain killer** seals any knots and resinous areas **General-purpose wood primer** or **general-purpose (multi-surface) primer/sealer**
Previously painted/ varnished wood	**1** Scrape or sand off flaking, cracking, or peeling paint/varnish, then touch up bare areas with a little paint/varnish; leave to dry. If paintwork/varnish is in very poor condition or there is a thick build-up, remove it using a chemical stripper or hot air gun **2** Wash down the surface with a mild solution of soap or detergent; rinse and allow to dry **3** Lightly sand the surface, then dust it off	No primer needed
Bare metal	**1** Rub off light rust with steel wool or wet-and-dry abrasive paper dipped in mineral spirits; remove heavier rust using a wire brush **2** Wipe over the surface with a cloth dampened in mineral spirits **3** Apply primer, working it well into holes and fittings	**General-purpose metal primer** for steel, ironwork, and most ferrous metals **Special metal primer** for non-ferrous surfaces, such as galvanized metal, aluminum, brass, chrome, and copper **Quick-drying metal primer** for new galvanized metal such as window frames **Radiator primer** on bare radiators prior to painting with radiator enamel **Rust-inhibiting primer** for outdoor metalwork, such as exterior pipes, gutters, and railings
Painted metal	**1** Sand off flaking, cracking, or peeling paint using a wire brush; if the paintwork is in very bad condition, strip it off using a chemical stripper **2** Wipe the surface with a cloth dampened with mineral spirits **3** Sand the surface using steel wool or wet-and-dry abrasive paper dipped in mineral spirits **4** Apply primer to any patches of bare metal	Prime bare areas as for **Bare metal**
Concrete	**1** Leave new concrete to dry for two months **2** Prepare as for exterior walls (masonry) **3** Leave to dry thoroughly. Remove any white crystalline deposits using a stiff, dry brush **4** Apply primer/sealer	**Concrete floor sealer** is available to stabilize and seal concrete floors **General-purpose (multi-surface) primer/sealer** may be used on other concrete surfaces

TYPES OF INTERIOR PAINT

When you are choosing a paint, the color is likely to be your first consideration, but you should also bear in mind the properties of different paints and the finish they produce (see charts overleaf).

Paints are classified in two groups – water-based and alkyd-based (also known as oil-based). Water-based paints are quicker drying and, in general, easier to use than alkyd-based types, and they don't have such a strong smell, but they are not usually as longwearing. For a more durable finish you can seal them with a coat of varnish. Use water to thin the paint for some paint effects and to clean painting tools.

Alkyd-based paints are slower drying and more durable than water-based paints but they give off fumes that some people may find unpleasant. If using these paints in an enclosed space, keep the room well ventilated. Use mineral spirits to thin the paint for some paint effects and to clean painting tools.

CREATING COLORS
Mass-produced water- and alkyd-based paints are widely available in a broad range of colors.

Alternatively, if you want a specific color, a mixing service is available in most paint and home decorating stores.

You can also add tints to create colors yourself, but these are expensive and sold in small quantities only. The shade may be difficult to match if you run out.

A less expensive but equally effective way to paint is to use artist's acrylic or artist's oil paints for water- and alkyd-based paints respectively.

PREPARING SURFACES
Before applying paint, you need to prepare the surface using one or more of the following specialist products:

Sealants These seal surfaces to prevent paint soaking in so you need fewer coats. Seal bare plaster with interior primer. On bare wood use stain killer. This prevents resin from seeping out of knots of wood and staining the paintwork. There are other sealants that prevent paint, grease stains, or rust from bleeding through.

Primer Use this to prepare bare wood or metal to take undercoat and top coats. Prime bare plaster with thinned latex paint. Universal primers are available for all surfaces, although specific primers are recommended.

Undercoat Use this after primer when building up a paint system on new wood or metal, or on old paintwork when changing the paint color significantly. Undercoat is not necessary if you're using a single-coat paint. Combined primer and undercoat is also available for some surfaces.

PAINT FACTS

WATER-BASED PAINTS

Paint	Surface	Drying	Preparation	Comments
Color washes	Walls/ceilings	2-3days	Seal bare surfaces	Semi-transparent, slow-drying finish. Mainly used for paint effects such as colorwashing and dragging. Buy ready-mixed or as base to dilute with latex paint and water. Varnish areas that require regular wiping.
Eggshell (latex)	Walls/ceilings/ wood	2-4hrs	Seal and prime bare surfaces; may require undercoat	Washable, fairly hardwearing, low-sheen cover. Ideal for kitchens and bathrooms. Thin with water to use as glaze.
Floor (latex)	Concrete/wood	1-4hrs	Seal; prime bare surfaces with diluted floor paint	Washable, longwearing, dirt-resistant finish.
Gloss/satin semigloss	Wood	4-8hrs	Seal and prime bare surfaces and apply undercoat – unless self-undercoating	Washable, dirt-resistant, very longwearing, shiny finish. Unsuitable for heated surfaces. Shows up surface irregularities so thorough preparation is necessary.
Kitchen & bathroom	Walls/ceilings	1-5hrs	Seal bare surfaces	Washable, moisture-, mold-, dirt- and grease-resistant finish. Shows up surface irregularities so thorough preparation is necessary.
Flat latex	Walls/ceilings/ wood	2-4hrs	Seal and prime bare surfaces; undercoat bare wood	All-purpose, non-shiny finish. Non light-reflective, so helps to conceal surface flaws on plain walls. Shows scuff marks and likely to develop sheen with washing. Unsuitable for kitchens and bathrooms unless sealed with PVA or varnish. Varnish if used on wood. Non-drip solid latex is ideal for ceilings.
Silk/satin latex	Walls/ceilings/ wood	2-4hrs	Seal and prime bare surfaces; undercoat bare wood	Washable, fairly longwearing, mid-sheen finish. Good for textured wall coverings but will highlight irregularities on a plain wall. Varnish if used on wood. Non-drip solid latex is ideal for ceilings.
Textured	Walls/ceilings	4-8hrs	Seal bare surfaces	Gives relief effect that can be patterned using special tools. Good for disguising imperfect walls. Difficult to wash or remove.
Wood color stain	Wood	4-6hrs	Apply to bare wood	A semi-transparent stain designed to add color to trim and other wood. Available in natural tones as well as subtle colors. Lightly sand with fine sandpaper and apply a protective coat of varnish.

ALKYD-BASED PAINTS

Paint	Surface	Drying	Preparation	Comments
Eggshell	Walls/ceilings/ wood	12-16hrs	Seal and prime bare surfaces; may require undercoat	Washable, fairly hardwearing, low-sheen cover. Thin with mineral spirit to use as glaze.
Flat oil	Walls/ceilings/ wood	8-12hrs	Apply undercoat only	Washable, fairly longwearing, flat matte finish. Shows scuff marks. Can substitute with undercoat.
Floor	Wood/tiles/ stone/brick/ concrete	16hrs	Seal; prime bare surfaces with diluted floor paint	Washable, longwearing, dirt-resistant finish.
Gloss and semigloss	Wood/metal	12-16hrs	Seal and prime bare surfaces and apply undercoat – unless self-undercoating	Washable, dirt-resistant, very longwearing, shiny finish. Shows up surface irregularities so thorough preparation is necessary.
Satin	Wood/metal (special paint)	16hrs	Seal and prime bare undercoat – unless self-undercoating	Washable, very longwearing mid-sheen finish. Shows up surface irregularities so thorough preparation is necessary.

PAINTING WALLS AND CEILINGS

Painting walls and ceilings is one of the easier decorating tasks, but you need to follow some guidelines for professional results. You can paint walls and ceilings using a paintbrush or a roller. Either way, a three-step process is involved: the paint is applied, distributed evenly, and finally smoothed out.

If you decide to use a roller, you still need a paintbrush for painting into corners and for "cutting in" edges – where walls meet ceilings, baseboards, and door frames, for example. Always begin by painting the edges of the surface, then move on swiftly to paint the middle – if the edges dry before you have completed the rest of the surface, there will be unsightly lap marks.

Paint the ceiling before the walls, and in both cases work in overlapping bands, blending the edges carefully. Always paint away from the wet paint edge, so that the paint thins out and doesn't form a ridge. As a general rule, paint away from the main source of natural light, so you can see clearly the area you've just painted.

USING A PAINTBRUSH

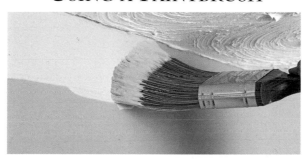

Start by flicking the bristles of the brush across your hand a few times, to tease out any dust and loose bristles.
Loading the brush Dip the brush into the paint, loading one-third of the bristle length. Tap the bristles against the side of the can or paint bucket to remove excess paint.

1 To cut in the edges of the surface, hold the brush against the edge, angling it as shown and pressing just enough to flex the bristles. Draw it along the surface, keeping an eye on the paint edge and painting with long, slow strokes.

2 Use the wide edge of the brush to paint along the angle of wall corners, working from the top of the wall to the bottom.

3 Start painting the main surface area immediately. Apply the paint with diagonal strokes. When the bristles show signs of emptying, distribute the paint evenly by brushing across it with gentler, horizontal strokes.

4 Smooth off the surface by drawing the brush vertically from the top to the bottom of the painted area. Use light strokes and lift the brush from the surface at the end of each stroke.

USING A PAINT ROLLER

Before you begin painting with a roller, use a paintbrush to cut in the edges of the surface, following the first two steps of "Using a paintbrush" on the previous page. Then pour paint into the well of the paint tray.

Dip the roller into the paint in the well, then roll it back and forth on the ramp to distribute the paint evenly throughout the pile. The roller should be full but not dripping when you lift it from the paint tray.

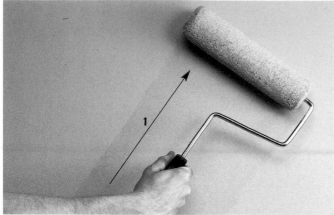

1 With the loaded roller, make a diagonal sweep (1) across the surface. On walls, roll upward on the first stroke to prevent dripping. Use slow roller strokes so that the paint doesn't spatter.

2 Draw the roller straight down from the top of the diagonal sweep (2). Move the roller to the beginning of the diagonal and roll up (3) to complete the unloading of the roller.

3 Use horizontal back-and-forth strokes to distribute the paint evenly over the surface.

4 Smooth off the painted area by lightly drawing the roller vertically from the top to the bottom of the painted area. Lift the roller and return it to the top of the area after each stroke. Reload the roller and repeat until the whole surface is painted.

SMOOTH FINISH
Although you can't use a roller to paint right into an edge – at the join between wall and ceiling for example – you can get very close by slipping the sleeve slightly off the roller. This will help blend in the brush marks where you have painted along the edge, giving a more uniform finish.

PAINTING CEILINGS

Fit an extension rod – available from home decorating stores – to your roller when painting ceilings and high wall areas. This saves you the trouble of having to set up a work platform.

It's a good idea to wear safety goggles to protect your eyes from splashes of paint when you are painting overhead.

PAINTING WOODWORK

Woodwork around your home is subject to considerable wear and tear, and often needs repainting before other surfaces. The key to a good finish – once you have washed it down and prepared the surface – is as much about painting in the right order as being skillful with a brush.

Take time to plan the job. Aim to paint any movable woodwork, such as window frames and doors, early in the day and preferably in fine weather, so that they will be dry enough to close by nightfall.

As with walls and ceilings, always work outwards from a wet paint edge, to prevent ridges forming.

WINDOWS

ORDER OF PAINTING

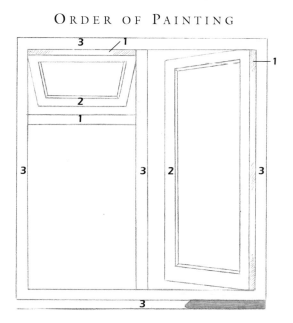

Casement windows Have the opening casements wide open while you paint, following the sequence in the diagram.

Sash windows
Paint following the sequence given here, sliding the top and bottom sashes up and down to expose different areas as required.

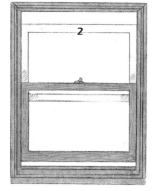 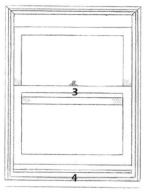

Before you begin, remove stays, catches, locks, and any other fittings, if convenient.

1 Using an angled cutting-in brush, begin by painting the wood next to the glass. Use the narrow edge of the brush, and overlap the paint on to the glass slightly, to create a weather seal.

2 Clean excess paint off the glass before it dries, using a putty knife wrapped in a clean cloth. Re-wrap the knife often – always wipe with clean fabric. Leave approximately $\frac{1}{16}$in (2mm) paint overlap on the glass.

3 Paint the rest of the frame, working out toward the walls, following the numbered order (see left).

DOORS

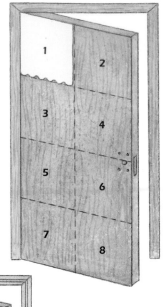

Flush doors
Paint from the top to the bottom, working quickly and following the sequence in the diagram.

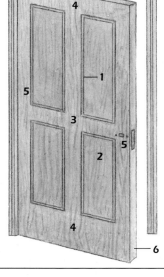

Paneled doors
Paint in the order given here, working quickly to avoid join marks between sections.

• Before you begin, remove any door furniture and wedge the door open.

• Paint the door in sections (see Order of Painting, left), working quickly to avoid join marks between sections.

• Apply the paint sparingly to avoid drips and runs.

• Paint out to the edges of the door, taking the brush right off the edge, beyond the door, rather than stopping at it – this might cause the paint to "catch" and run.

• Finish each painted section with brush strokes along the grain of the wood – this means you need to use both vertical and horizontal strokes on a paneled door.

• Paint the molded rebates on a paneled door using a small brush, as if they were separate pieces of wood. This will help prevent drips on the panels.

• Paint both sides of cupboard doors to give an even moisture seal and prevent warping.

TRIMS

Baseboards Protect the floor with a broad filling knife or paint shield. Use this technique also to protect walls when painting wall moldings.

Decorative moldings Using a stiff-bristled brush, such as a stencil brush, and small circular strokes, work paint into the hollows and recesses of ornate moldings.

GLOSSARY OF PAINT EFFECTS

An illustrated A-Z guide to a selection of distinctive and popular paint effects.

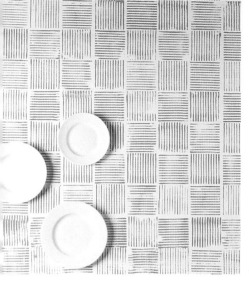

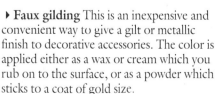

◀ **Block printing** Block printing is a means of decorating surfaces using handprinted motifs. The block can be made from a number of materials – for example, wood, potato, or sponge – and has a raised motif or pattern. Paint is applied to the raised motif which is then pressed against the surface to print the motif.

▶ **Colorwashing** Colorwashing has a soft, weathered look created by brushing one or two thin washes of diluted paint, normally latex, over a smooth base coat. The wash can tone or contrast with the base coat and is generally a slightly darker color. Apply the base coat with a roller, allow to dry, and brush the diluted wash on top so the softened brush strokes and a hint of the base coat are visible.

◀ **Crackleglazing** This technique mimics the look of aged paint with applications of incompatible layers of paint and glaze, or layers of varnish. If paint is used, you apply a coat of crackleglaze between a base and top coat of latex. With varnish, a quick-drying water-based varnish is applied over a slow-drying alkyd-based one. Crackleglaze and crackle varnish kits are available from art and craft stores.

▶ **Distressing** This technique combines a variety of methods to give a weathered and battered appearance to wooden furniture. To simulate the layers of paint and wear acquired over time, several layers of different colored paints are applied to the item, then sanded unevenly to expose patches of underlying colors and bare wood.

◀ **Dragging** This grainy effect, similar to woodgraining, is achieved by applying a semi-transparent glaze over a different color of base coat, then pulling or dragging a dry brush across the wet glaze to reveal thin lines of the base coat. Apply the base coat and glaze with a paintbrush and use a dragging brush or a coarse, longhaired paintbrush for dragging.

▶ **Faux gilding** This is an inexpensive and convenient way to give a gilt or metallic finish to decorative accessories. The color is applied either as a wax or cream which you rub on to the surface, or as a powder which sticks to a coat of gold size.

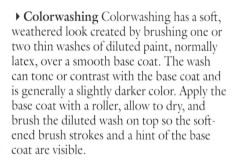

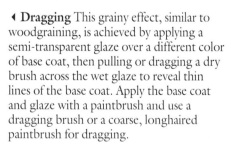

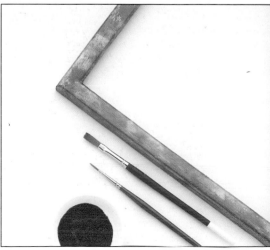

Faux marquetry This technique uses wood stains and stencils to imitate the patterns and colors of genuine wood veneer marquetry. Starting with a bare wood surface, you can apply the wood stains directly to the wood, through a stencil or use masking fluid to create negative stencil patterns.

Gilding Real gilding is the process of overlaying sheets of metal leaf onto a solid surface. The simplest gilding process, known as oil-gilding, involves sealing the surface with shellac varnish, applying a coloring paste to complement the metal leaf, then applying a coat of oil size before laying on the metal leaf. Metal leaf is available in pure gold, fake gold, silver, aluminum, and copper.

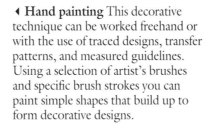

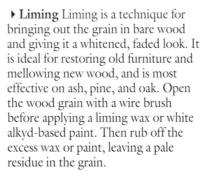

Hand painting This decorative technique can be worked freehand or with the use of traced designs, transfer patterns, and measured guidelines. Using a selection of artist's brushes and specific brush strokes you can paint simple shapes that build up to form decorative designs.

Liming Liming is a technique for bringing out the grain in bare wood and giving it a whitened, faded look. It is ideal for restoring old furniture and mellowing new wood, and is most effective on ash, pine, and oak. Open the wood grain with a wire brush before applying a liming wax or white alkyd-based paint. Then rub off the excess wax or paint, leaving a pale residue in the grain.

Lining Lining is a traditional decoration for wooden furniture and accessories. A continuous fine line, in gold or another color that contrasts with the base coat, is handpainted just inside the edge of the item with a fine artist's brush.

Marbling This paint effect mimics the look of real marble, with layers of glaze sponged over a base coat, then darker feathered lines resembling veins added on top, using a fine brush or the tip of a feather. Oil-based paints are the traditional choice for this effect because they are slow-drying but you can use water-based paints instead. You can apply various color combinations depending on the type of marble you are copying.

◄ Oil-glazing Also known as scumble glazing, this gives a soft, broken-color finish. A transparent oil or scumble glaze is tinted with artist's oil colors and brushed over an oil-based base coat. While still wet, the glaze is worked either with a cloth for a rough, natural texture, or a brush for a controlled, neat finish.

▶ Paneling This is trompe l'oeil paint effect in which light and dark tones of the same color paint – representing areas of shadow and light – are used to create the illusion of wooden or plaster paneling on walls and doors. Most paneling designs comprise a series of square or rectangular shapes outlined on two adjoining sides with bands of darker paint and on the remaining sides with bands of lighter paint.

◄ Ragging Ragging is a broken-color effect, using rags to make blotchy patterns in thinned paint. There are three methods of ragging: *ragging off*, where a scrunched up rag is pressed against the surface to lift off patches of wet paint; *rag rolling*, where a rag is rolled along the surface to remove the paint; and *ragging on*, where the thinned paint is applied with a scrunched up rag.

▶ Roller effects In this technique, textured paint rollers with precut shapes, such as stripes or diamonds, are used to apply latex paint. A variety of patterns and shapes can be created by applying the roller in a continuous line or in specific areas and arrangements, such as the checkerboard pattern shown here.

◄ Sponging In this technique, a sponge is used to apply one or more colors over a solid base color. For a soft, all-over mottled effect, sponge at least two close tones of the same color over a similar base color. Use a natural sponge for even blending. Sponging can be used in conjunction with other effects – for example, "Stenciling" or "Stripes" on page 262.

▶ Stamping A quick paint effect, stamping involves the use of precut rubber or wooden stamps to print decorative motifs on a flat surface. The stamp is coated in paint, using a roller or an ink pad, then pressed firmly against the surface to print the motif. To create regular stamped patterns (see right) you need to measure and mark the position of each stamp precisely.

◀ Stenciling With stenciling, color is brushed, sponged, or sprayed over a cut-out shape, which is then removed to leave the decorative image on the surface. You can buy stencils ready cut or make your own from acetate sheeting or stencil cardboard.

▶ Stippling Stippling is a type of oil-glazing. A stippling brush or other flat-faced brush is used to lift off a thin layer of oil glaze, revealing fine speckles of a toning or contrasting base color beneath. Oil-based paints are used in preference to water-based ones because they are slower drying.

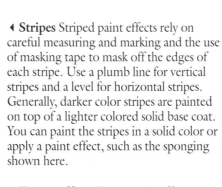

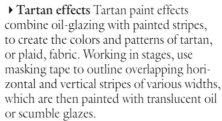

◀ Stripes Striped paint effects rely on careful measuring and marking and the use of masking tape to mask off the edges of each stripe. Use a plumb line for vertical stripes and a level for horizontal stripes. Generally, darker color stripes are painted on top of a lighter colored solid base coat. You can paint the stripes in a solid color or apply a paint effect, such as the sponging shown here.

▶ Tartan effects Tartan paint effects combine oil-glazing with painted stripes, to create the colors and patterns of tartan, or plaid, fabric. Working in stages, use masking tape to outline overlapping horizontal and vertical stripes of various widths, which are then painted with translucent oil or scumble glazes.

◀ Textured painting Textured paint can be used to create a range of three-dimensional patterns on walls. The thick paint is applied evenly with a roller or paint brush, then while still wet, worked with a textured roller, brush, or other tool to give a rough rustic finish or decorative pattern. Using thick stencils made from corrugated cardboard, you can use textured paint to create relief stencil patterns.

▶ Verdigris Verdigris is a faux paint effect that mimics the powdery, blue-green corrosion of metals containing copper. Using latex paint or artist's acrylics, a burnt umber base coat is applied first, then shades of green paint are stippled or sponged on top. Highlights can be added to match examples of real verdigris.

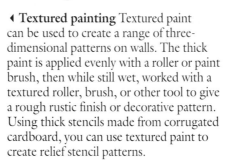

◀ Woodgraining Woodgraining is a traditional paint effect used to imitate the grain of real wood. There are a range of methods depending on the type of wood you want to simulate. You can use natural wood shades or more fanciful colors. The simplest technique uses a light base color with a darker glaze applied on top. The wet glaze is dragged, then combed and rolled using a custom-made woodgraining tool.

CHOOSING WALL COVERING

There is a vast range of wall coverings available. When making your choice, it is wise to consider a number of practical factors (as listed overleaf) as well as finding a design you like.

Printed wall coverings may be hand or machine printed. Machine-printed papers (1) make up the largest group of wall coverings. Prices vary greatly, depending on the quality of the paper and the number of colors used. Many are finished with a clear plastic coating, making them washable – a good choice for areas subject to wear and tear, although they are not as tough as vinyls (see below). Hand printed papers (2) are expensive but offer superb designs and colors. However, they are generally not washable.

Vinyl wall coverings (3) have the design printed on a thin layer of vinyl which is fused to a paper backing. Vinyls are very durable. They can be washed and even scrubbed. Many are ready-pasted. Vinyls are generally easier to remove than coated printed papers because the vinyl layer can be peeled off first. Textured vinyls (4), such as expanded or blown vinyl and sculptured vinyl, undergo various heat treatments during manufacture to produce a relief pattern. They provide slightly more insulation than standard vinyls, so are a good choice for condensation-prone rooms.

Relief wall coverings (5) have deeply embossed or relief patterns. They come in plain white or cream, and most are designed to be painted over. They are durable, and help disguise bumps and other surface defects.

Woodchip or panelboard wall covering (6) has a subtle overall raised design created by small wood particles sandwiched between two sheets of paper. It is inexpensive and useful for covering poor plaster.

Specialty wall coverings include metallics (7), fabrics, and foam polyethylene. Some are easy to hang while others, such as unbacked fabrics, are best left to a professional.

Lining paper (8) can be applied to the surface before papering or painting, to help improve the finish. Hang it horizontally if you are going to wallpaper the surface, and vertically if you are going to paint it.

WALL-COVERING BORDERS

Decorative borders are available in a wide choice of designs and depths, often as part of a coordinated design. As well as adding color and pattern interest, they can enhance the proportions of a room by breaking up a bare expanse of wall – in the same way as moldings, such as wainscoting and picture rails.

Some types of wall-covering border are pasted in the same way as conventional wallpaper; others are ready-pasted for soaking and sticking; or you can buy self-adhesive borders with a peel-off backing. Avoid using borders with high relief wall coverings.

THE RIGHT CHOICE

For the best results, you need to take the following factors into account before choosing your wall covering:

• **Wall condition** If the wall surface is uneven, avoid thin wall coverings and wall coverings with a glossy finish or regularly striped pattern – these will emphasize lumps and bumps. Textured papers are best for disguising uneven walls.

• **Room shape** If the room has an irregular shape, with alcoves, recessed windows, and obstacles such as radiators to paper around, opt for a wall covering with a small-scale, overall design and a small pattern repeat rather than one with large, obvious motifs.

• **Durability** If the wall covering will need to withstand a lot of wear and tear, choose one with a washable or scrubbable finish. Vinyls are the toughest papers. If the wall covering is to be exposed to a lot of bright sunlight, choose a light-fast paper which won't fade.

• **Ease of use** Ready-pasted wall coverings are easy and less messy to apply than standard papers, but they are more expensive. Beginners will find it easier to work with small patterns or plains, rather than large-scale designs, which are trickier to match. If this is your first attempt at papering, you should avoid expensive, hand-printed papers, that may be ruined if you get paste on the front, and very thin, inexpensive papers which stretch and tear easily.

• **Delivery time** Some wall coverings have to be ordered weeks in advance, so plan ahead or your choice will be limited to designs stocked in the store.

• **Removal** If you re-decorate quite often, choose a paper that is relatively easy to remove – non-coated printed papers are generally the easiest.

WALL-COVERING SYMBOLS

Most wall-covering manufacturers use these standardized symbols on their roll labels and pattern books, to give an at-a-glance guide to the characteristics of the wall covering.

spongeable

washable

extra-washable

scrubbable

moderate color fastness

good color fastness

excellent color fastness

paste the wall

ready-pasted

paste the covering

strippable

free match

offset match

peelable

straight match

reverse alternate lengths

wet removable

WALL-COVERING BASICS

Make sure the wall surface is clean and sound before you apply a wall covering. Remove any old wall coverings, make good poor plaster, and fill cracks. Clean painted walls with a degreaser such as baking soda dissolved in hot water, or detergent, then rinse thoroughly.

Roughen gloss-painted walls with abrasive paper. Size (seal) bare plaster and spackle-filled areas with diluted wallpaper paste or sizing.

Remove fixtures and fittings where possible, turning off the electricity while removing and papering around electrical fixtures. Once you have removed the fixtures, apply masking tape over the exposed outlets to keep out any water and paste.

YOU WILL NEED

- WALL COVERING
- SCISSORS
- PASTE
- PASTE BRUSH
- PASTING TABLE
- WATER TRAY (FOR READY-PASTED WALL COVERING)
- STEEL TAPE MEASURE
- PLUMB LINE

- PENCIL
- LEVEL
- WALLPAPER BRUSH
- BROAD FILLING KNIFE (OPTIONAL)
- UTILITY KNIFE (OPTIONAL)
- SEAM ROLLER
- OVERLAP OR REPAIR ADHESIVE

MEASURING AND CUTTING

Hold the wall covering against the wall. Allow a full pattern repeat at the ceiling line. The wall covering should overlap the ceiling and baseboard by about 2in (5cm). Cut the first strip with scissors. Unless using patterned wall covering, cut subsequent strips to the same length.

Matching patterns Hang the first strip in place as described overleaf. Hold the wall covering against the wall, adjacent to the first drop, matching the pattern. Measure and cut the second drop. Continue in this way.

PREPARING WALL COVERING

Wall coverings may be ready-pasted or unpasted. If using an unpasted wall covering, you need to buy a suitable paste. Ready-pasted wall covering should be soaked in water, a strip at a time, to activate the paste.

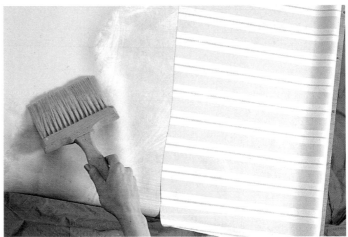

Ready-pasted wall covering Half fill a water tray with water, and stand it next to the wall where the first strip is to be hung. Roll the cut strip loosely from the bottom, adhesive side out. Leave the roll to soak for the manufacturer's recommended time. Hold the top edge of the strip with both hands and lift it from the water; check the pasted side to make sure the strip is evenly wet. Leave the bottom edge of the strip in the tray so water will run back into it off the strip.

Unpasted wall covering Lay the strip wrong side up on the pasting table, weighting it down if necessary. Using a pasting brush, apply the paste over half the strip, working from the center out to the side edges and taking care not to get any paste on the table. Fold the pasted section back on itself – or in concertina folds if working with a very long strip – with the pasted sides together. Paste the rest of the strip and fold this end, too. Leave to soak for the recommended time.

HANGING WALL COVERING

1 Measure and mark in from one corner of the room a distance equal to the wall covering width minus ½in (1.3cm). Draw a vertical line from ceiling to floor at the marked point, using a level. Cut and prepare the first strip as shown on the previous page.

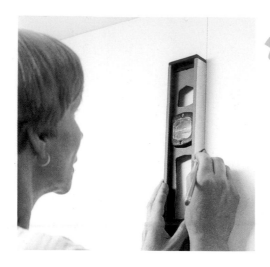

TIP

STARTING POINT
If the wall covering is plain or there is no strong motif in the pattern, start at an inconspicuous point in the room, such as a corner, where it won't matter if the first and last strip don't match exactly.
If the wall covering has a bold pattern center the first strip on the most prominent wall in the room – for example, the chimney breast, or the wall opposite the door – then work from the center strip out in both directions.

2 Unfold the top section of the pasted strip. Position the strip lightly on the wall, so one long edge is flush with the vertical line and the opposite edge wraps around the corner of the wall. Use your palms to slide it into place. Overlap onto the ceiling by about 2in (5cm), so there is a full pattern repeat at the top.

3 At the top of the wall where the paper creases into the corner of the room, make a vertical snip in the upper edge of the wall covering so that it lies smoothly. Starting at the upper edge and using a wallpaper brush, smooth it from the center out in both directions. Check for air bubbles, pulling the strip away and smoothing it out as necessary.

4 Unfold the lower section of the strip, using your palms to position it against the vertical line. Smooth out the wall covering with a wallpaper brush, checking for bubbles and repositioning as necessary.

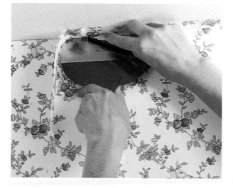

5 Press the paper into the ceiling angle with a broad filling knife. Trim the excess with a sharp utility knife; keep the knife blade in place while changing the filling knife position. Or gently press the paper into the angle of the ceiling with the back of the scissor blades; peel back enough to expose the crease, and cut along it with the scissors. Smooth back in place. Wipe off excess paste.

6 Hang the next strip in place, matching the pattern if there is one and butting the edges together. Use a seam roller to roll the seam (except on wall coverings with a raised design).

WORKING AROUND CORNERS

These steps show you how to apply wall covering around corners. You can paper around internal and external corners in the same way.

With vinyl or vinyl-coated wall covering, you may find that it doesn't stick to itself when you overlap it at the corner. If this is the case, you will need to use overlap or repair adhesive to stick it down (see step 5, below). You can buy this from home-decorating stores.

1 Cut a full strip in the usual way. Measure from the edge of the previous strip to the corner of the wall, at the top, middle, and bottom. At inside corners add ½in (1.3cm) to the longest of these measurements. At external corners add 1⅜in (3.5cm).

Electrical fixtures Turn off the power supply. Put masking tape over the exposed outlets. Hang the paper in the usual way. Pierce the paper over the center of the outlet and make small diagonal cuts to the corners. Trim to the edges of the outlet with a utility knife.

2 Cut the strip lengthwise to the new width; paste it as before. Position on the wall, butting the uncut long edge against the previous strip. Take the strip around the corner, snipping it at the top and bottom. If wrinkles occur at an internal corner, clip the overlapping edge. Smooth with a wallpaper brush, and trim the excess at the upper and lower edges.

3 Measure the width of the remaining piece of cut wall covering. Measure and mark this distance from the corner of the wall across the bare wall. Draw a vertical line at this point from the ceiling to the floor, using a pencil and a level.

4 Paste and position the remaining cut width of wall covering on the wall, with the cut edge at the corner and the finished edge against the vertical line. Smooth flat with a wallpaper brush; trim the excess at the upper and lower edges.

Vinyl wall covering To stick down the overlap on vinyl or vinyl-coated wall covering, peel back the overlapping edge; apply overlap or repair adhesive to the lapped seam, and press the wall covering back in place. Wipe off any excess adhesive with a damp sponge; once dry, it is permanent.

WORKING AROUND WINDOWS AND DOORS

These steps show you how to apply wall covering around doors and windows with a frame.

1 Position the wall covering strip on the wall, butting it against the edge of the previous strip in the usual way, with the opposite edge extending over the window or door frame. Use a wallpaper brush to smooth the flat areas and press the strip tightly into the angle between the wall and frame.

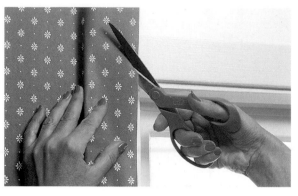

2 Use scissors to cut diagonally from the edge of the strip overlapping the window or door to the upper outer corner of the frame. For a window, repeat at the lower corner.

3 Trim the excess wall covering to 1in (2.5cm) from the outside edge of the frame. Smooth out again, pressing out any air bubbles.

4 Hold the wall covering against the outer edge of the frame with a broad filling knife, and trim the excess with a utility knife. Or crease the paper and trim with scissors, as in Hanging Wall Covering, step 5, page 266. Trim the excess at the ceiling and baseboard. Wipe off excess paste.

5 Cut and apply short strips of wall covering to the section above the door or window, matching the pattern. Repeat below the window.

6 Position the next full-length strip on the opposite side of the window or door, butting it against the previous strip, with the pattern matching. Cut diagonally to the outer corners of the frame and trim the excess, as in steps 2 and 3.

7 For a window, match the pattern on the lower half of the strip, below the window. Trim the excess wall covering to 1in (2.5cm) from the outer edge of the frame; smooth the strip with a wallpaper brush. Trim the excess along the lower edge, using a filling knife and a utility knife, or scissors (see Hanging Wall Covering, step 5, page 266). Wipe off excess paste.

PAPERING A STAIRWELL

Before you start wallpapering, you must protect the floor and construct a safe work platform. Although it is a nuisance, it's better to remove the stair carpet altogether instead of trying to cover it up. The bare boards provide a firm base for the work platform and enable you to screw wooden battens to the stairs to stop the feet of the ladder from slipping.

If you can't take up the carpet, cover the treads individually with strong brown paper or pieces of dropcloth, taped or pinned in place. Do not use plastic sheeting as this is dangerously slippery on top of a carpet.

Although the layout of your staircase may differ slightly from the standard types, you should be able to adapt a platform arrangement to fit your needs. If necessary, hire equipment to build the platform.

You should also have someone to help you, especially where long drops are involved.

1 Prepare the walls in the normal way, stripping off the existing wall coverings. If necessary, size bare plaster with diluted wallpaper paste. Remove the stair carpet or cover it with brown paper or a dropcloth. Erect a work platform on the staircase and ensure that the structure is sound. Set up the pasting table in a convenient position close to the stairs. Lock any doors opening onto the work area.

2 Always hang the longest length of paper first, even if it goes against the normal procedure of working away from the light. If the longest drop is at a corner or adjacent to the head wall of the stairwell, measure 19¾in (50cm) out from this point and hang the first drop at this position. This allows you to get the feel of hanging the paper before you tackle a more awkward area.

3 To ensure the wallpaper hangs straight, suspend a plumb line to mark the position of the first drop. Mark the vertical line of the plumb line on to the wall.

4 Measure the length of the first drop from ceiling to stair baseboard. Remember to measure the longer edge of the paper so you allow for the slope of the stairs. Add 6in (15cm) to this measurement to allow for trimming. Measure and cut out the first paper drop to this length.

◀ *The standard technique for wallpapering a stairwell is to hang the longest drop first – even if, as on this staircase, it goes against the rule of working away from the light.*

▸ *Choosing a simple wallpaper design, such as this one, makes life a lot easier when you have to match up the long drops of paper needed to cover a high stairwell.*

5 Paste the paper generously so that it does not dry out as you work. Loosely fold it concertina-wise, and drape it over your assistant's arm. While your assistant stands on the stairs at the position of the first drop, climb onto the work platform. You must not have more than one person on the platform at a time.

6 A long piece of pasted paper is heavy and can easily stretch or tear so you need to support the length. Take the top edge of the paper, while your assistant supports the weight of the lower section, and slide the top edge into place. Align the side edge of the paper with the vertical guideline, and at the top edge overlap the ceiling by about 2in (5cm). Working downward, press the paper in place, brushing out air bubbles in the usual way.

7 Mark the edge of the baseboard by creasing the paper with the back edge of a scissor blade. Carefully peel the paper away from the wall and cut along the crease line with a pair of long-bladed wallpaper scissors. Brush the paper back into position. Trim the top edge of the paper in the same way.

8 Check that the wallpaper pattern matches with its adjoining length before measuring and cutting out each new length. Continue hanging the paper around the stairwell on either side of the longest drop.

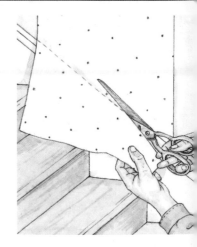

REMOVING WALL COVERING

If you want to hang a new wall covering on a wall that's already papered, you must remove the existing wall covering first. There are two methods you can use:

Soaking and stripping This involves soaking the walls with warm water and a little dishwashing liquid or wallpaper stripper to loosen the paper, then scraping it off with a stripping knife. For coated papers, such as vinyl, you need to score the surface first to help the water to penetrate.

Steam stripping A steam stripper removes heavy and/or coated papers quickly and effectively. The electrical stripper consists of a heated water tank, which supplies steam to a flat plate. You hold the plate against the wall covering and the steam softens the paper, making it easy to scrape it off. You can buy a steam stripper from home-decorating stores, or hire one. Various models are available; always follow the instructions for your particular model.

The stripping method you choose will depend upon the type of covering you have on your walls. The table below shows you which of the techniques to select, and the steps overleaf show you what you need to do.

▶ *Heavy-duty wall coverings, such as this painted relief paper, are easier to remove if you soften them first using a steam stripper.*

IDENTIFYING WALL COVERINGS

Type	How to identify it	Stripping technique
Uncoated printed	Absorbs water	Soak and strip
Coated washable	Doesn't absorb water; coating doesn't peel off	Score surface, then soak and strip, repeating as necessary. Alternatively, use a steam stripper
Vinyl	Doesn't absorb water; coating peels off	Dry-strip vinyl layer, then soak and strip backing paper
Painted	Coating chips off	As for coated washable paper
Fabric	Surface texture	Dry-strip fabric layer from paper backing or plaster. Alternatively, use a steam stripper. Soak and strip backing paper

SOAKING AND STRIPPING

1 Protect the floor with dropcloths. Score the surface of washable or painted wall coverings with a utility knife or scoring tool. Don't press too hard or you will score the wall.

2 Add a little dishwashing liquid or wallpaper stripper to warm water. Use a plant mister to spray the wall covering, leave to soak for about 10 minutes, then spray and leave again.

3 Use a wide stripping knife, keeping the blade at a shallow angle to avoid gouging the plaster. When it is finished, wash the wall with water to remove any leftover strands of paper.

USING A STEAM STRIPPER

Wear work gloves and a long-sleeved shirt, and work from the bottom of the wall up, so the rising steam will soften paper higher up the wall.

1 Protect the floor with dropcloths. Fill the stripper's reservoir, plug it in and switch on. With steaming plate vent side up, wait until steam starts to emerge. Then press the plate against the wall for 15 seconds.

2 Lift the plate off the wall and scrape off the damp paper using a broad stripping knife. Apply more steam for stubborn paper, but avoid steaming an area for more than 30 seconds at a time. While scraping with one hand, use the other to steam the adjacent area. Wash down the wall to remove any traces of paper and paste.

STRIPPING VINYLS

For easy stripping, the top layer of a vinyl wall covering is designed to peel away from the backing paper. Find a lifting seam or edge near the top of the wall, and tease the vinyl away from its backing. Peel back gently, then grasp the vinyl in both hands and pull outward and downward to remove the whole strip. Remove the backing paper by soaking and stripping.

TONGUE-AND-GROOVE PANELING

Installing tongue-and-groove wooden paneling is a fairly simple job, especially if you use one of the cut-to-size kits available from major home-decorating centers.

▲ *Staining the tongue-and-groove paneling to look like antique pine brings a mellow country air to this dining area.*

Vertical planks fitted to wainscoting height – about 3ft (90cm) above the floor – form a protective and attractive covering for the lower wall area. This is particularly useful in halls and on stairways where the lower wall receives plenty of knocks and scrapes. Paneling is also an excellent way of hiding crumbling or patched plaster, and concealing unsightly pipes and cords. It is not, however, a cure for damp walls; you must fix these first.

One edge of each tongue-and-groove board has a groove machined along it, while the other has a matching tongue which slots into the groove of the next board. Interlocking tongue and-groove boards allow room for the wood to expand and contract with changes in temperature and humidity.

Tongue-and-groove boards, moldings for neatening corners and for fitting around doors and windows, baseboards, wainscoting, and battens are available from lumber yards and home-decorating stores. When estimating quantities, sketch a plan of the wall or room and take it with you. Most boards come in 3–4in (75–100mm) widths; allow extra for the overlaps.

Alternatively, you can buy wainscoting paneling kits with boards already cut to length, plus rail, baseboard, and cap moldings.

WAINSCOT PANELING

In a kit, the boards come cut to length. Otherwise tongue-and-groove boards are sold in 6ft (1.8m) lengths that you can cut in half before you start.

FITTING THE BATTENS

Wainscot paneling is fixed to three horizontal wooden battens attached to the wall, to correspond with the top, middle, and bottom of the boards. Buy enough battens for the length of the wall being paneled, and cut to length.

Getting the top batten perfectly horizontal is very important. Few walls are truly vertical or really smooth – they may lean into or away from the room and have minor bumps and hollows that coincide with the fastening points. You have to correct for such imperfections by packing odds and ends of hardboard or plywood between the battens and the wall to prepare a perfectly flat face. An extra pair of hands can be helpful when fitting battens.

Floors too can be uneven or tilted. You may need to alter the length of individual boards by trimming them or lifting one off the floor when fastening it in place – the bases of the boards are masked later by baseboard. Use paneling over baseboard that is thinner than the battens. Remove baseboard that is thicker.

▸ *Paneling the wall to wainscoting height and painting the boards a strong shade of green gives a bathroom a clean finish. The shelf along the top is useful for keeping*

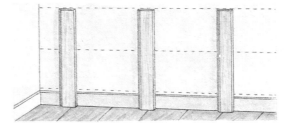

1 ▸ To fix the top batten flush with the top of the boards, mark the height of a wainscoting board at regular intervals along the wall. Using a pencil and a straight edge as a guide, draw a horizontal line joining these points.

2 Mark the bottom batten ½in (12mm) above the baseboard (or floor). To position the central batten, draw a horizontal line midway between the upper and lower lines.

3 Using a drill and wood bit, drill holes through the battens at 18in (45cm) intervals. Finish each hole with a countersink bit.

4 Hold the batten along drawn line and mark the wall through a screw hole at one end. With a masonry bit, drill at the mark. Insert a wallplug. Fit screw to hold.

5 ▾ Lift the batten up against the top line and with a level check that it is horizontal, re-marking if necessary. Use wainscoting boards to check the height along the batten and make a note if any need shortening.

6 Holding the batten horizontally, mark through the other screw holes onto the wall. Drill, plug and install screws as for the first, but do not tighten. Fasten the central and bottom battens in the same way.

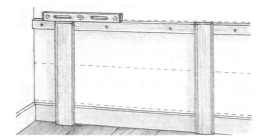

7 ▴ To check that the three battens form a flat vertical surface for the boards, hold a level vertically across them. If the battens are not even, push odds and ends of hardboard or plywood between the wall and the relevant batten until it is. Repeat at intervals along the wall. When battens are true, tighten all the screws. Continue around the room.

FASTENING THE BOARDS

As much as possible, plan your paneling so that a major feature such as a doorway is flanked by whole boards, and paneling across a chimney breast is symmetrical, with trimmed, narrow boards hidden away in inconspicuous corners. Work in one direction around the room when fitting the boards so that the molding on the panels looks consistent. Where necessary, trim the boards flush with the top batten.

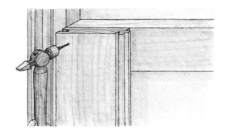

1 ▸ Starting in a prominent position, beside a door frame for example, place the first board with the groove on the inside. Use a level to check that it is vertical. Hammer a panel nail straight through the board into each batten, ½in (12mm) in from the groove.

2 ◂ Using a tack hammer, knock a panel nail into each batten at an angle of 45 degrees where the tongue joins the board so that the tongue is free to slot into the next board. Drive the nail in with a nail punch.

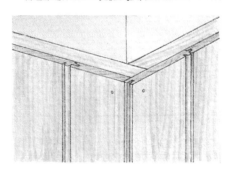

3 ▴ Slot the groove of the next board over the tongue of the first. Nail through the tongue of the second board as in step 2.

ELECTRIC FIXTURES

Always turn the electricity off at the power source before moving sockets and switches in the paneled area. Call in an electrician if in doubt.

•

If the fixture is surface mounted, unscrew the box, pull it forward, and refix it onto the front of the boards, having cut out a suitable hole in the boards with a coping saw to pull the wires through.

•

If the fixture isn't surface mounted, remove the box from the wall, pack out the back to the thickness of the batten and board, refit the box to the wall, cut a hole in boards for box, then fit the cover.

4 ▴ On the first wall, fit boards up to the end of the batten, trimming the last board to size if necessary, and nail in position. On the adjacent wall, fit the first board to overlap the last board, nailing straight into the batten. Neaten the corner with angle molding later.

5 ▾ Since the last board of a run into an internal corner is unlikely to fit exactly, cut it to size along the tongue edge. Chisel off the back of the groove and simply lay the board on the battens. Face nail the panel to the battens on both sides of the board. If you are going to continue paneling along the adjacent wall, butt the grooved end of the first board against the final board on the other wall and nail it into position.

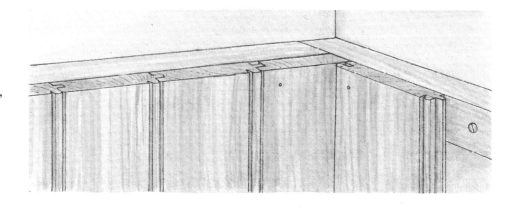

FINISHING

Having installed the boards, complete the paneling with a new baseboard, a wainscoting rail, and strips of wooden molding along the top, around the corners, and beside doors.

Using a nail punch, drive each exposed panel nail just below the surface of the board and fill the holes with wood filler. Before the boards can be damaged or marked, apply stain, paint, or varnish finish to the wood.

▶ **Door frames** Cover any gap between the board and the architrave with a strip of quadrant molding, glued and nailed in place.

◀ **Windowsills** Most windows will be higher than wainscoting level, but if you do have to panel around one, finish the paneling just short of the reveal and cover the batten and board edges with a piece of strip molding or lath.

◀ **Wainscoting rail** Nail and glue the rail flush with the top of the boards. Nail and glue a strip molding along the top to cover exposed batten.

Corners Nail and glue on strips of angle molding to define internal and external corners.

Baseboard Nail and glue new baseboard along the bottom of the boards.

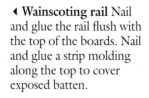

WOODSTRIP FLOORING

Wood has a timeless beauty that complements traditional and contemporary decorative schemes. Woodstrip flooring provides an attractive and practical wood or wood-effect surface you can lay yourself.

It is hard to beat the appeal of natural wood as a flooring material. But, unfortunately, beautiful bare floorboards are not hidden beneath every old floor covering – you may instead reveal a surface of unsightly, mismatched floorboards or one made of concrete. If this is the case, you can lay a good-looking and long-wearing wooden floor yourself using packs of woodstrip flooring and a flooring kit.

A woodstrip floor has a similar appearance to standard floorboards, although the boards are narrower and fit flush together with tongue-and-groove joints. It is made either from solid wood or from particle board with a wood veneer or wood-effect laminate surface, and is available in a range of different wood or wood effects,

each with its own distinctive coloring and grain.

Woodstrip flooring is a practical surface. It is warm underfoot, durable, resists stains and indentations, is easy to keep clean, and needs only minimal maintenance. Certain types can be sanded and resealed if the original finish becomes worn. Unlike some patterned floor coverings, it goes well with virtually any decor or color scheme, and large expanses can be broken up with colorful rugs.

Properly sealed, woodstrip flooring can be used in most areas of the house, except where it is likely to suffer damp, for example in a bathroom. In entrance halls and at other outside doorways, a substantial door mat is a must to prevent wet and dirt being brought in.

▲ *Flush fitting woodstrip flooring is a practical and good-looking choice for a kitchen. It is smooth and easy to clean, making it very hygienic, and its longwearing finish is robust enough to stand up to household traffic.*

LAYING WOODSTRIP FLOORING

The instructions given here are for floating wood-strip flooring, which is sold in packs and is one of the easiest types of wood flooring to lay. The woodstrip boards are glued or clipped to one another but are not secured to the underlying floor – hence the term floating. A floating woodstrip floor can be laid on top of almost any existing floor surface – wood, concrete, tiles, vinyl, and even carpet – as long as it's level, sound, and dry. If a plank floor is very uneven, use sheets of plywood to level it; with an uneven concrete floor, use self-leveling compound. Allow a new concrete floor at least one month to dry before laying woodstrip.

PLANNING

The first planning decision you need to make is whether or not to remove the existing baseboards. If you do remove them, you can replace them above the woodstrip once the floor is laid, but this does involve a lot of work. An easier method is to leave the baseboards in place and fit strips of wood molding around the edge of the floor.

Work out the number of boards you need by measuring the dimensions of the room and drawing an accurate scale plan on a piece of graph paper to calculate the total floor area. Add an extra 5 percent for cutting and wastage. Woodstrip is sold in a variety of lengths and widths – 78¾ x 7⅛in (200 x 20cm) is the most common size, which covers 3½sq yd (3.2sq m). Most manufacturers provide guides on the average coverage for a pack of boards.

Mark the board positions on the scale plan, laying them across the floorboards of a plank floor or parallel to the main source of natural light or the longest walls. If you find that the last row of boards across the floor is less than 2in (5cm) wide, cut the first strip down as well so that you have a row of equal width at each side.

To accommodate the natural expansion and contraction of wood, leave an expansion gap of about ⅜in (10mm) all around the edge between the woodstrip and the walls. This gap is covered with the replacement baseboard or a wood molding.

MATERIALS

It's a good idea to use a cork, felt, or rubber under-lay beneath the woodstrip. This has good absorbing qualities, allows for a slight unevenness of the underlying floor, and provides a warmer, more comfortable surface. Concrete floors may need a polythene moisture barrier beneath the underlay.

To join the boards, use either the clips supplied with the woodstrip, or moisture resistant white glue. Installation kits, which may be sold separately from the boards, include a pull bar, to draw the out-side strips into place, a buffer block to protect the boards when hammering, and spacer wedges for expansion gaps. Alternatively, use a small prybar in place of a pull bar, make a buffer block from a scrap of softwood and use ⅜in (10mm) thick pieces of wood as spacers.

YOU WILL NEED

- **WOODSTRIP FLOORING**
- **POLYTHENE MOISTURE BARRIER (optional)**
- **UNDERLAY (optional)**
- **SPACER WEDGES**
- **TRY SQUARE**
- **PANEL SAW**
- **STEEL TAPE MEASURE**
- **JOINING CLIPS (optional)**
- **WATER RESISTANT WHITE GLUE**
- **BUFFER BLOCK**
- **PULL BAR OR SMALL PRYBAR**
- **ELECTRIC DRILL AND FLAT BIT**
- **WOOD MOLDING (optional)**
- **THRESHOLD STRIP**

▲ *Woodstrip flooring will outlast many types of soft and hard floor covering and has a natural appeal that never fades. Warm and comfortable underfoot, it ensures a cozy feel on its own or combined with colorful floor rugs.*

1 ▾ Prepare the floor as necessary, making sure it is sound, level, and dry. Lay the recommended moisture barrier on solid floors and any underlay as required.

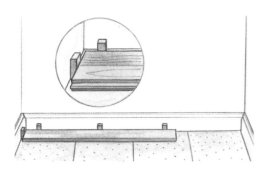

2 ▲ Place the first board with its grooves facing the walls. Insert spacer wedges between the end and side of the board and the walls, and push the board against the spacers.

3 ▲ Lay further boards end to end to complete the row, cutting the end board so it falls ⅜in (10mm) short of the wall. To do this, place the end board wrong side up next to the last fitted board, so it butts against a spacer. Use a try square to mark the cutting line as shown, and cut to length with a saw.

4 If your scale plan shows that the last row of boards is less than 2in (5cm) wide, you need to trim the first row lengthwise so the first and last rows are equal width. Use another piece of board to mark the cutting line on the boards in the first row and use a panel saw to trim.

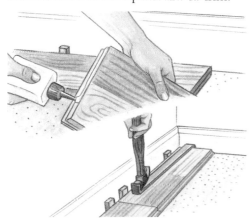

5 ▲ If adjacent rows are secured with clips, lift the boards and fit clips following the manufacturer's instructions. Apply adhesive to the end-to-end, tongue-and-groove joints and tap them gently into position, using the pull bar and hammer to draw them together.

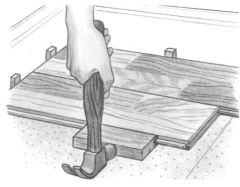

6 ▲ Use the offcut from the end of the first row to start the second row. Complete the row, trimming the end board as before. Depending on the installation system, lift the boards and fasten clips as recommended, or apply adhesive at intervals along the tongue-and-groove joint. Fix the boards using a buffer block and hammer to knock them home.

7 Continue laying the boards across the room, using the offcut from the previous row to start the next row and staggering the end joints in adjacent rows by at least 12in (30cm). See overleaf for and fitting around obstacles like pipes.

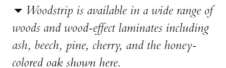

▼ *Woodstrip is available in a wide range of woods and wood-effect laminates including ash, beech, pine, cherry, and the honey-colored oak shown here.*

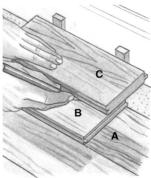

8 ▲ Lay the boards to be cut (B) on top of the last fitted boards (A). Place an offcut of board (C) so it overlaps with B and its tongue butts against the wall spacer. Use the grooved edge of C to mark a cutting line on B. Trim along the cutting line and fit in place using the pull bar to draw them together. Remove all the spacer wedges.

FINISHING

Once the woodstrip is laid, you need to conceal the expansion gap either by replacing the baseboard or by fastening a quarter-round or other shoe wood molding over the gap. At doorways, you also need to fit a wood threshold strip that allows for the expansion gap. Wood moldings and threshold strips are available from woodstrip suppliers in colors to match the flooring or from specialist lumber yards. Wood and plastic radiator pipe covers are also available from woodstrip suppliers.

While laying the floor there are a few obstacles you're likely to encounter. You may need to cut out a section of woodstrip to fit around a radiator pipe; trim a door or door frame to allow for the raised floor level; or make an inspection hatch for access to underfloor plumbing or electrical wiring.

Most woodstrip floors come ready-sealed, but in areas of very heavy wear they benefit from a single coat of floor varnish or sealer to prevent moisture from getting into the joins. Unsealed woodstrip needs three or four coats of sealer.

▼ **Concealing the expansion gaps** Either cut strips of wood molding and nail them over the expansion gap, or replace the baseboard using a block of wood to hold it down while you nail it in position. To ensure the flooring is free to expand and contract, secure the baseboard to the wall, or the molding to the wall or baseboard – not to the woodstrip.

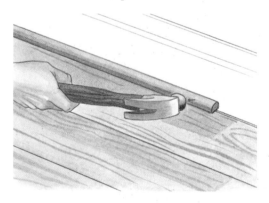

▲ *Maintaining a woodstrip floor is as simple as daily vacuuming or sweeping and if necessary a wipe with a damp mop. Apply a floor polish only if it is recommended.*

▼ **Trimming door frames** Place an offcut of woodstrip against the door frame, with a piece of underlay underneath. Resting a panel saw on the woodstrip, trim the base of the door frame. Check the woodstrip fits under the frame and trim slightly if necessary to fit.

Trimming doors Laying woodstrip raises the floor level so you may need to trim the lower edges of any doors opening into the room. Scribe the cutting line using a scrap of board, then trim the door at the line.

Fitting threshold strips Select the threshold strip depending on whether the woodstrip is at a higher level or flush to the adjacent floor. Manufacturers make different profile strips to allow for different floor levels. Cut the strip to length and nail or glue it to the floor underneath – not to the woodstrip.

▼ **Cutting around pipes** Measure and mark the position of the pipe on the relevant board. Drill a hole at the mark slightly larger than the pipe. Make angled saw cuts up to the hole as shown. Remove the plug of wood, fit the board around the pipe, then glue the plug back into place behind the pipe.

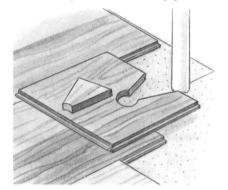

SANDING A WOOD FLOOR

The cost of a beautiful new floor surface could be as little as lifting your carpet and spending two or three days sanding and sealing the wooden floorboards hidden beneath.

Pine or oak floorboards, sanded and sealed, make a handsome floor surface to suit any style of home decoration. The natural simplicity of the wood works as well with the rustic feel of a country cottage setting as with the streamlined look of an airy modern apartment.

If the floorboards are in good condition, you need only clean and lightly sand them. However, if lifting your existing floor covering reveals boards that are unfit for display, they will need a really thorough sanding. This removes any dents, stains, and blemishes, and flattens out any warped boards to expose smooth, clean wood.

Coating the clean boards with a protective sealer afterward gives a really durable and attractive finish.

To sand a floor by hand would take a long time, even in a small room, so it's much more convenient to use specialist power sanders. Sand the bulk of the floor with a drum sander, which looks much like a lawnmower, and use an edging sander to sand the edges and awkward corners. You can rent both these items from a tool-rental store. It is a good idea to reserve them in advance, especially if you want to work on the weekend, because demand often exceeds supply.

▲ *Sanding and sealing these floorboards brings to life their warm, rich colors. The soft sheen of polished wood contrasts well with the surrounding matte paintwork.*

281

PREPARING THE FLOORBOARDS

TIP

Time is money when you are working with rented tools, so clear the room of furniture and prepare the floor before you pick up the sanding machines. And always be sure to return them on time.

Before sanding your floorboards you should examine them to see what condition they're in. Check for sagging boards which often signify damaged joists. Pry up the boards to examine the joists beneath – if they are rotten you may need to get a professional to treat or replace them. Treat signs of woodworm with a woodworm killer.

If your floorboards are in a really bad state – thin and splintering, a mismatch of shapes and sizes, or with large gaps in-between them, they may not be worth exposing. Under those circumstances, woodstrip laminate or another floor covering is a better option.

1 Clear the room of all furniture and floor coverings and take down the curtains. Vacuum the floorboards. If necessary remove a heavy build up of wax by rubbing the boards with steel wool soaked in mineral spirits.

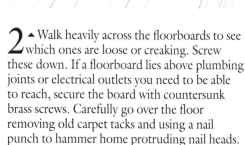

2 Walk heavily across the floorboards to see which ones are loose or creaking. Screw these down. If a floorboard lies above plumbing joints or electrical outlets you need to be able to reach, secure the board with countersunk brass screws. Carefully go over the floor removing old carpet tacks and using a nail punch to hammer home protruding nail heads.

3 Cut slivers of wood to fit into any large gaps between the floorboards. Spread wood glue on both sides of each sliver. Wedge the wood into the gap and hammer the wood in place using a wooden block to protect the floorboards. Allow the glue to dry and plane the wood flush if it protrudes above the floorboards. If necessary stain the wood to match the color of the boards.

4 Using a filling knife, insert wood filler into the gaps. Color the filler with wood stain to match the color of the boards. Sand it smooth when it's hard.

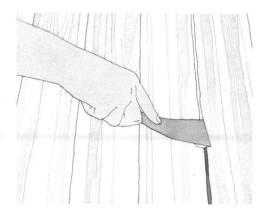

◀ *The rewards of a few days spent renovating wooden floorboards are enormous — you can soon achieve one of the least expensive yet most beautiful types of floor surface.*

SANDING THE FLOOR

When you pick up the sanders from the rental store, ask for a demonstration so that you know how to operate them and how to replace worn sanding sheets. Buy plenty of sanding sheets of all grades as it is better to have too many sheets than too few.

Wear a face mask, safety goggles, and ear plugs to protect your eyes, nose, throat, and ears. It is also a sensible idea to wear overalls and old clothes.

YOU WILL NEED

- DRUM SANDER
- EDGE SANDER
- VARIOUS COARSE SANDING SHEETS
- MASKING TAPE
- OVERALLS
- EAR PLUGS, FACE MASK, AND GOGGLES
- HOOK SCRAPER
- SANDING BLOCK
- VACUUM CLEANER
- MINERAL SPIRITS

▶ *The honey colors and deep patterned grain of these pine boards reflect those of the ornate wooden legs on the banquette in this sunny living room.*

1 Bring all the equipment you need into the room you are sanding. Close the door and seal around the door frame with masking tape. Open the windows for ventilation. Put on your safety goggles, face mask, and ear plugs.

2 ▶ Fit a coarse sanding sheet to the drum sander, locking it firmly in place. Plug the sander in, drape the cord over one shoulder and keep it behind you. Take the sander to one corner of the room. Tilt the sander backward and switch it on. Gently lower it to the floor.

3 ▶ Allowing the sander to move forward under its own pull, work diagonally back and forth across the room. Make sure each run slightly overlaps the previous one. To stop the sander biting into the floor, tip it back at the end of each run and when you stop the machine. Unplug the machine and change the sanding sheet when it wears or clogs with dust. Empty the dustbag into a thick garbage bag at regular intervals.

4 ▶ Repeat step 3 working across the opposite diagonal. Using a medium-grade sanding sheet, sand parallel to the floorboards, slightly overlapping each run. Then switch to a fine-grade sanding sheet and sand parallel to the floorboards.

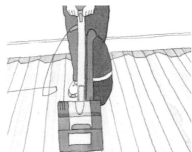

5 ▲ Fit a coarse-grade sanding sheet into the edge sander. Work all around the perimeter of the room moving the sander along the grain. Repeat the process using a medium- and then a fine-grade sanding sheet. In corners and around pipes use a hook scraper and then a sanding block.

6 Vacuum the floor thoroughly, along with the baseboards, door, and window frames. Don't sweep the floor as this stirs up the dust. Leave for 24 hours to let the dust settle before vacuuming again. Wipe the boards with mineral spirits to remove the last specks of dust before sealing.

SEALING THE FLOOR

After exposing the floorboards you need to protect them with a durable sealer. The best choice is a water-based floor varnish made from acrylic and polyurethane resins. This gives a tough, scratch-resistant surface, has a low level of odor, and rapid drying time. Each coat is dry to the touch in thirty minutes, and you can apply another coat after a few hours. Otherwise, use an alkyd-based polyurethane varnish. In either case, apply at least three coats of varnish for a longwearing finish.

Varnishes are available either clear or in a range of natural wood colors. Whatever varnish you choose it makes the floor darker than when newly sanded, and each coat darkens the wood a little more. If you are using a colored varnish and think you've achieved the right color after the first coat, use a clear varnish to finish.

Using a wood stain is another way to add color to your floor. These are available in a range of shades which you can mix together if required. Apply the stain right after sanding and then varnish the stained wood to seal it.

▶ *Floorboards are a perfect canvas for the bright colors of patterned rugs.*

YOU WILL NEED

- WOOD STAIN (optional)
- ALKYD-BASED WOOD VARNISH (clear or colored)
- MINERAL SPIRITS
- SOFT CLOTH
- FINE WET-AND-DRY ABRASIVE PAPER
- VACUUM CLEANER
- 4in (10cm) PAINT BRUSH

▶ *Sealing the floor with coats of varnish protects it from future wear and tear – essential in a hallway where the boards have to endure continuous comings and goings.*

1 ▶ (Optional) Working along the grain, one board at a time, use a soft cloth to apply the stain. When it is dry, remove any excess with a clean cloth. If you're using a water-based stain which raises the grain, lightly sand the floorboards with dampened wet-and-dry paper. Remove the dust by vacuuming and then wiping the floor with a cloth soaked in mineral spirits.

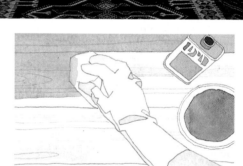

2 Thin 10 parts varnish with 1 part mineral spirits. Using a soft cloth, rub the diluted varnish into the floorboards. Allow the varnish to dry, sand the surface, and remove any dust with a vacuum cleaner.

3 ▾ Brush one coat of undiluted varnish onto the floorboards, first across and then along the wood grain. Keep the varnish damp to prevent brush marks from showing when it dries. When the floor is dry, sand and remove the dust as before. Repeat with one or two more coats of varnish.

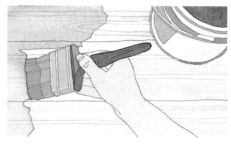

CLEAR WOOD FINISHES

Use one of the special finishes to protect and enhance the natural beauty of wood.

There's a clear finish for wood to suit every situation in the house, from an old chair in need of a quick facelift to sanded floorboards that must withstand hard wear. Look through the list to find the finish that suits your needs, then check the details in the chart on the next page. Remember, some finishes protect the wood, others don't; some are easily sanded off, others are difficult to remove. Whatever finish you choose, practice on an inconspicuous piece of wood first, and always follow the manufacturer's instructions.

Varnishes and lacquers seal the wood to form a tough protective surface coating – you can stand a hot mug or damp glass on a varnished table without causing damage. Special formulations are available for floors.

Varnishes are either clear or tinted. Clear varnishes allow the natural wood color to show through, while tinted ones are colored with dyes or translucent pigments and allow a color and finish to be applied in one go. Tinted varnishes come in a range of natural wood colors. Water-based varnishes are odor free and easier to use than alkyd-based. To remove varnishes you sand them off.

Lacquers give a tough, glossy finish. They come in two parts that are mixed together before application.

Wood stains change the color of the wood without altering the character of the grain. They are available in wood tones – used to improve the natural shade of wood or to imitate a more expensive wood – and bright, rainbow colors. Stains seep into wood without sealing the surface so, if you want a protective coating, stained wood must also be varnished. Once they have been applied, stains are difficult to remove.

Traditional finishes include wax, oil, French polish, and shellac. They are not as tough or durable as varnishes; a hot cup of tea will mark a French polished or waxed surface. If you like the soft sheen of wax or oil but want to protect the wood, apply them to a surface that's lightly varnished.

GENERAL PREPARATION

Surface imperfections in the wood will show under a clear finish, so you need to prepare the wood first. The ideal surface is a fine or medium grain which simply has to be sanded down. On old wood, preparation depends on any existing finish, and the type of finish you plan to apply.

Previously varnished wood – strip off and sand down any cracked or peeling old varnish. To re-apply varnish to previously varnished surfaces that are in good condition, lightly sand them down. A previously varnished finish must be removed before it can be stained.

Waxed and oiled finishes must be completely removed before applying any new finish – to do this use grade 00 steel wool dipped in mineral spirits and rub along the grain. Wipe off with a dry rag before the mineral spirits evaporate.

French polish must be sanded off before applying a clear finish. Think twice before removing French polish in fairly good condition from fine furniture. It may be wiser to have it renovated by an expert.

SPECIAL PREPARATION

To lighten wood, or if you want to stain it to a shade paler than its natural color, use a special wood bleach. This comes as two solutions applied separately. Always bleach as your first step because the bleach may raise the surface of the wood, which must then be sanded smooth.

To fill cracks or cover dents or nail heads, use a wood filler in a shade that matches the finished surface. Apply sparingly as you lose the effect of the grain on filled areas. Plastic wood filler can shrink, so apply in small amounts and leave to dry. For a perfect color match if you are staining the wood, apply the stain first, then buy a filler to match the newly stained surface.

To fill the grain of coarse open-grained woods such as oak, use a grain filler. If necessary color the filler with wood stain, so staining and filling can be done in one operation. Apply filler with a coarse cloth, wiping against the grain.

A varnish is ideal for bathroom use, as it both seals and enhances the wood. To choose a tinted varnish, place a special test strip on the surface to be varnished.

At-a-glance guide to clear wood finishes

VARNISHES	Application	Durability and use	Effect
CLEAR (ALKYD- & WATER-BASED)	Brush on lightly along the grain: it may be easier to apply a first thinned coat with a cloth. Aerosol varnishes are useful for tricky surfaces such as wicker. Some varnishes are dry to the touch in 30 minutes.	Tough finish, particularly good for areas subject to heavy wear and for surfaces that would otherwise be painted, such as doors and baseboards. Extra tough matte or satin types are available for floors.	Gloss, matte, or satin finish. Alkyd-based gloss is shinier than water-based. Some varnishes give a slight orange tint. Water-based acrylic varnishes yellow less with age than alkyd-based.
COLORED (ALKYD- & WATER-BASED)	As above, with the advantage that color and finish are applied in one step. Good on pine, which doesn't absorb stain evenly, and for surfaces where the existing varnish has not been stripped off.	As above.	Gloss, matte, or satin in a variety of colors which deepen with each layer. If the color intensity you want is not available in the right finish, build up color and then apply the appropriate clear top coat.
TWO-PART LACQUER	Apply to a smooth surface and work in a well-ventilated room.	Very durable finish, so it is good for countertops, table tops, and floors.	Dries quickly to a very clear finish, which can be polished for a high gloss or rubbed down with steel wool and wax-polished for a softer effect.

WOOD STAINS	Application	Durability and use	Effect
ALKYD-BASED	Apply lightly and evenly to bare wood with a cloth to avoid a patchy effect, as the stain soaks in and cannot be removed. On very new pine and on end grain, use several coats of very diluted stain.	Stains but does not seal bare wood – use on furniture, baseboards, doors, floors, and paneling. Some stains contain translucent pigments to stop them fading.	A matte finish in various colors, including wood effects. Stains from the same product line can be mixed to create the color of your choice.
WATER-BASED	Apply as alkyd-based. Water-based stains are quicker drying and easier to apply than alkyd-based. They tend to raise the grain of the wood so light sanding down may be needed after stain has dried.	As above. Water-based dyes are not as colorfast as alkyd-based, but their slightly faded look can be attractive.	As above.

TRADITIONAL FINISHES	Application	Durability and use	Effect
OIL	Easily applied with a cloth; re-apply often in areas of heavy use. Raw linseed oil takes up to three days to dry; boiled linseed oil and Danish oil take about 18 hours. Teak oil is specially formulated for teak.	Repels water but does not completely seal the surface. Use for traditional wooden drainboards and drying racks, kitchen countertops and tables, porch chairs and benches.	Dark, rich, slightly lustrous finish. Danish oil is particularly lustrous but has less sheen than teak or linseed.
WAX	The oldest method of treating wood and one of the easiest to apply, but needs lots of effort for a really good shine. Apply several coats of a proprietary brand of traditional wax polish. Re-apply frequently as necessary.	Popular for stripped pine, but does not seal the surface – susceptible to heat, water and alcohol, and not very practical for floors unless traffic is light.	Soft, satin sheen.
FRENCH POLISH & SHELLAC	Traditional application requires some skill; it is much easier to brush the polish on and then wax it. On pale or bleached wood use white French polish. Shellac is applied with a brush whereas French polish is rubbed in.	Not very durable – particularly susceptible to heat and alcohol. Traditional finish for furniture.	Deep, lustrous, high gloss if traditionally applied – finish with wax for a softer look.

CARPET TILES

Once you have mastered the basic technique of laying carpet tiles, why not experiment with decorative borders and patterns or by cutting different colored squares into assorted shapes?

Carpet tiles have a great many advantages. They combine the warmth and style of a carpet with the longwearing, washable qualities of a tiled floor. This makes them a practical and reasonably inexpensive option for any of the well-trafficked and accident-prone areas of your home, particularly hallways, bathrooms, kitchens, and children's bedrooms.

The tiles are squares of carpet made from polypropylene fibers bonded onto an asphalt backing, and are available in a wide range of patterns and colors. They are light to work with and easy to cut, so you need no special tools or experience to fit them. The only tiles which require sticking down are the tiles around the edge of the room and the very first one you lay. Use double-sided tape to stop them from moving and to anchor the rest of the flooring; lay the remainder loose, without using tacks or adhesive.

Regular vacuuming picks up everyday dust and dirt. If there is a particularly stubborn spill or stain on an individual tile, lift it up to rinse it under the faucet. Remember to dry it well before putting it back. If a single carpet tile gets worn out or damaged, simply replace it, without the hassle of disturbing the surrounding pieces.

Each floor tile has an arrow on the back to show the direction of the pile. For a smooth look, lay all the tiles with the arrows pointing in the same direction. For a checkerboard effect, lay alternate tiles with the arrows pointing at right angles to each other.

▶ *By cutting carpet tiles of different colors into regular shapes, you can create interesting designs on the floor. Here, a geometric pattern of squares within squares in light and dark blue looks remarkably stylish in a kitchen.*

LAYING CARPET TILES

When laying carpet tiles it is important to start with a smooth, flat floor surface. If a solid floor is rough, you can use a floor-leveling compound to level it. With an uneven wooden floor you should cover it with sheets of plywood or hardboard, nailed or stapled to the floorboards.

Before laying carpet tiles, leave them unwrapped for 24 hours to adjust to the temperature and humidity of the room – this ensures a better fit.

CALCULATING AMOUNTS

Most individual tiles are either 16in (400mm) square or 20in (500mm) square. The pack indicates how many square yards (meters) the tiles will cover. To work out the number of tiles you need:

Measure the length of the room at its widest point and divide it by the tile size to find out how many tiles you need in the longest row, counting any part tiles as whole tiles.

Measure the maximum width of the room and divide it by the tile size, again counting any part tiles as whole ones.

Multiply the two figures together to find out the total number of tiles required.

Buy 10 per cent extra to allow for mistakes in cutting or fitting and replacement.

CUTTING CARPET TILES

As the carpet tiles are unlikely to fit the room exactly, you should always lay them from the center of the floor out toward the walls so that any part tiles end up around the edges. To make sure that the edge tiles are wider than half a tile's width, see step 3.

To cut tiles to size, you need a cutting board, a very sharp utility knife, and a steel ruler. Always cut through the carpet pile from the back of the tile. Make one firm, careful stroke, then bend and crack the tile along the cutting line. If the knife blade gets covered with tile backing and becomes tacky, clean it with a cloth and mineral spirits to keep it sharp.

YOU WILL NEED

- CARPET TILES
- STEEL MEASURING TAPE
- BALL OF STRING
- CHALK
- DOUBLE-SIDED ADHESIVE TAPE
- UTILITY KNIFE
- PENCIL AND STEEL RULER
- CUTTING BOARD – a scrap of fiberboard or particleboard is ideal
- PROFILE GAUGE AND PAPER

▼ Longwearing yet attractive, these lavender carpet tiles provide the perfect backdrop to a wide variety of accessories.

---

1 Find the mid-point of each wall (**A** and **B**) and stretch two lengths of string tightly across the room between these points on opposite walls – where they cross is the center of the room. Hold the ends of the string in position with panel nails driven into the baseboard.

2 ▼ To check for fit, start at the center and work out, laying a complete row of tiles along each guide string. Butt the tiles tightly together. Here, three gaps at the edge are too narrow – less than half a tile.

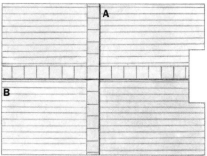

3 ▾ If, as here, some gaps at the edge are too narrow, move the guide strings. With two narrow edge gaps (row **A**), move the guide half a tile either way. With one narrow edge gap (row **B**), move the guide until the gap is wide enough. Re-lay the trial run of tiles to check.

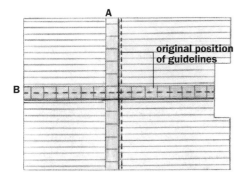

4 When you are happy with the edge gaps, lift off the trial run tiles. Rub chalk liberally on the guide strings. Lift each string, and hold it taut then let it snap back against the floor to mark it with two distinct chalk lines. Remove the strings before laying the first row of tiles from the center point of the floor (marked by the chalk lines) out toward the walls.

5 ▸ Secure the first tile at the center point with double-sided adhesive tape, noting the direction of the pile indicator arrow before sticking it down. Continue laying loose tiles along the chalk guidelines to within a tile's width of the walls, butting each tile quite hard against the previous one. Keep checking that the pile arrows are pointing in the correct direction.

6 ▾ Place a whole tile, pile upward and facing in the right direction, exactly over the last tile in the row. Lay another tile on top, butting its outer edge up to the wall. Use a knife to nick the edges of the middle tile where the top tile overlaps it. Turn the tile over and join the nicks with pencil on the underside.

7 Place the marked tile face down on a cutting board and, using a firmly held steel ruler as a guide, cut along the pencil line. Slot the cut tile in place over a strip of double-sided adhesive tape with the cut edge against the baseboard.

8 Fit the remaining whole tiles between the two intersecting rows of key tiles, always starting at the center and working outward. Cut and fill in with edge tiles after all the whole tiles are in place, anchoring each one on a strip of double-sided carpet tape.

FITTING AROUND OBSTACLES

▸ **Fitting around corners** Lay the tile to be cut over the last whole tile (**C**) on one side of the corner and use steps 6–8 above to mark it for cutting. Without turning the marked tile, lay it on the last whole tile of the other wall and repeat steps 6–8. The tile now has a mark on all four edges. Turn it over and pencil in the cutting lines. Cut out rectangle (**D**), leaving an L-shaped piece of tile (stippled line in diagram) to fit around the corner.

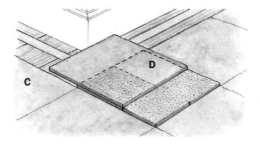

Fitting into corners Fit the corner pieces last. Mark against both walls and cut the tile as for "Fitting around corners," but this time discard the L-piece and fit rectangle (**D**) into the corner.

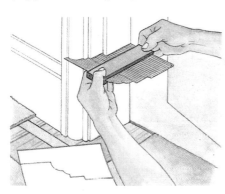

▸ **Cutting around a curved object** Cut a paper template around the base of the object as shown, trace the outline of the shape on to the underside of the tile or tiles with a pencil, and cut to fit.

◂ **Cutting around an architrave** To cut around an intricate shape such as an architrave, press a profile gauge against the molding so that its sliding strips of plastic take on the required shape. Transfer this outline on to a piece of paper and cut it out. Flip the pattern over, mark it on the back of the tile, and cut around the detail.

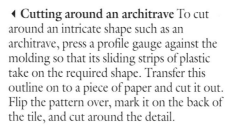

▾ **Fitting around a pipe** Mark the position of the pipe on the underside of the tile, and cut a slit and a hole to fit it. If you have a spare piece of pipe the same size, you can twist this into the slit you've made in the tile and cut around it for a perfect fit.

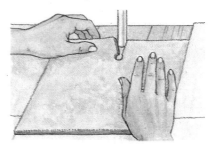

CREATING DESIGNS

Once you have got the knack of laying carpet tiles in one color, you can start inventing designs which use tiles of different colors to form overall patterns or borders.

The simplest way to create a pattern is to lay two different colored tiles alternately across the floor for a chessboard effect. Alternatively, you could add a border in a contrasting color to highlight the outer edges of a room. For a more intricate result, you can cut different colored tiles into smaller shapes and rearrange them, jigsaw fashion, into a design over the whole floor or just around the perimeter.

When you're adding insets of color, lay the background carpet tiles over the whole floor first, then lift and cut the appropriate tiles to allow for the insets.

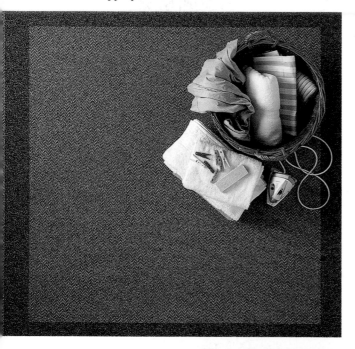

◀ *A subtle wine-colored border, placed around a block in the center of the room, accents heather color tiles for a restful combination.*

▲ *Experiment with a large, bold pattern of contrasting colors to make a striking checkerboard design for a garden room.*

▶ *This vibrant jazzy pattern of primary colors in modern diamond design — with its striped border — is perfect for a child's playroom.*

LAYING SHEET-VINYL FLOORING

Sheet-vinyl flooring is tough, good-looking, and simple to lay.
Gather a few basic tools, make an accurate floor plan, and take your
time trimming the vinyl so it fits snugly.

Sheet vinyl is longwearing and easy to clean, making it a popular choice for kitchens, bathrooms, hallways, and children's bedrooms. There is an exciting range of colors, textures, and patterns to choose from – including designs based on traditional ceramic floor tiles and some realistic marble and wood effects.

There are two types of sheet vinyl – standard hard-backed vinyl and the softer, cushioned variety which is padded and warm underfoot. The sheets usually come in 79, 118, and 157in (2, 3, and 4m) widths, enabling you to cover a fairly large room in a single sheet, although the larger widths can be awkward to work with.

Some vinyls are designed to lie flat and remain in place without adhesive. This makes the job of laying it straightforward, so it may be a feature to look out for when choosing a new flooring. Whatever type of vinyl you choose, it's a good idea to fit a metal threshold strip over the cut edges across a doorway to prevent the vinyl from curling up.

▲ *Sheet vinyl is an ideal floor covering in a kitchen/dining room – an area that's bound to receive a lot of wear and some occasional spillage – because it is easy to mop clean.*

291

LAYING SHEET VINYL

To make sure you buy enough vinyl to cover the floor in one try, without having to patch an alcove or doorway, measure the maximum length and width of the room and add at least 8in (20cm) for a trimming allowance. If the room is seriously out of square, add 16in (40cm) for the trimming allowance. Draw a 1:20 scale floor plan and mark on all the room dimensions.

If the design has a large pattern repeat, center the pattern across the floor, so the pattern breaks are equal at either side of the room. Manufacturers usually specify the size of the pattern repeat on the label.

Where the size and shape of the room makes it impossible to use a single piece of vinyl, use your floor plan to work out the best position for a join. A join is likely to be scuffed and damaged so try to position it away from doorways in an area that receives light wear. Add extra to the trimming allowance to allow for pattern matching and overlapping.

1 Place the vinyl in a room that allows space to work, or on a clean surface outside – provided the weather is fine. Unroll the vinyl wrong side up. Following your scale plan, using a pen and sharp scissors or a utility knife, mark and then cut the vinyl roughly to size allowing at least 4in (10cm) trimming allowance on all sides.

2 Roll up the vinyl loosely and transfer it to the room in which you are laying it. Leave it to acclimatize in this room for one or two days. If the weather is quite cold, turn on the heating to make the vinyl more flexible and easier to work with.

3 Unroll the vinyl in position in the room, with the right side up. Align the pattern with the longest wall or a dominant feature. View it from the main doorway to check the vinyl is straight and adjust it if necessary. Ease the vinyl into place so that the excess rides up by about 4in (10cm) all around.

4 ▸ Brush the surface with a soft broom to remove any air pockets. Use scissors to make vertical release cuts at all the corners and trim the excess vinyl to a 1in (2.5cm) overlap. Then leave the vinyl in position for a week, to allow it to settle – you can use the room as normal during this time.

▲ *This woodblock-effect vinyl is an inexpensive alternative to the real thing.*

YOU WILL NEED

- SHEET-VINYL FLOORING
- TAPE MEASURE
- PEN
- UTILITY KNIFE
- SHARP KITCHEN SCISSORS
- SOFT BROOM
- METAL RULER OR BLOCK OF WOOD
- VINYL ADHESIVE AND SPREADER if required
- BLOCK OF WOOD 4in (10cm) square
- THRESHOLD STRIPS for doorways
- PROFILE GAUGE
- DOUBLE-SIDED ADHESIVE TAPE
- VINYL SEAMING ADHESIVE (from vinyl supplier)

Sheet vinyl must be laid on a clean, dry, level floor. Any bumps and hollows will eventually show through, and damp can rot the backing. If you lay vinyl over floor tiles, stick down any loose tiles and level the joints with filler.

CUTTING

To cut and trim the vinyl, use a sharp utility knife or a pair of sharp kitchen scissors. If possible, make the first rough cut of the vinyl in a larger room or even outdoors as long as the weather is fair.

There are two ways to cut vinyl so it fits flush with the wall – *scribing* and *direct trimming*. Experts usually trim all sides by direct trimming but this is difficult to get right the first time; it's easier to fit at least the longest side by scribing. Practice cutting the vinyl on a spare piece. Trim off less than you think first time and re-trim if necessary.

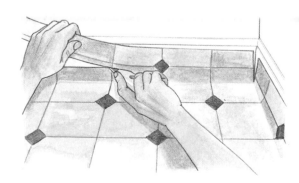

5 ▸ Lift back the vinyl at each corner and mark it where it meets the corner. At *internal corners* make a diagonal cut across the corner just above the mark. Trim the cut to a V-shape until the vinyl fits into the corner. For *external corners* make a vertical cut up to the mark, then trim the cut to a V-shape so the vinyl runs smoothly around the corner.

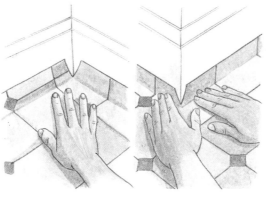

6 ▸ Slide the vinyl slightly away from the longest or most prominent wall, maintaining the pattern alignment. Place a block of wood against the wall so it overlaps the vinyl edge. Hold a pen against the outside edge of the block. Draw the block and pen along the wall so the pen marks the wall profile. Cut along the line and slide the vinyl back against the baseboard. Scribe and cut the remaining edges in the same way, or cut directly as in step 7.

7 ▾ (Optional) Press the vinyl hard into the angle between the baseboard and the floor using a block of wood or metal ruler. Using the wood or ruler as a straight edge, run the blade of the utility knife firmly along the crease line to trim off the excess vinyl. Alternatively, if you prefer to use scissors, fold back the vinyl, mark where it meets the baseboard, and cut along this line.

8 (Optional) If necessary, apply adhesive to the underside of the vinyl, following the manufacturer's instructions. To glue all over, fold back half the sheet, apply the adhesive, and press it back in place. Repeat to stick down the other half of the sheet. To stick the edges only, turn them back, apply the adhesive, and press them back in place using a block of wood wrapped in fabric to smooth them down.

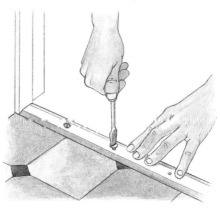

9 ▴ Use a soft broom to sweep the floor from the center outward, removing any air bubbles. Screw threshold strips in place across the doorways to stop the vinyl from catching or curling up.

◂ *Cushioned vinyl that is softly padded and warm to the touch makes a comfortable floor covering for a sitting room.*

SPECIAL TECHNIQUES

When laying vinyl you may need to fit the sheet around a fixed obstacle in the room. To accommodate a large item, such as a washbasin, the best technique is to make a brown paper template of it and then transfer it on to the rough-cut vinyl. However, if there are several obstacles in a small room – less than 79in (2m) square – it's easier to cut and tape several sheets of paper together so they extend over the entire floor area, and fit around each obstacle. You can then use this as your cutting pattern.

To fit vinyl around a small obstacle, such as a pipe, simply measure and mark its position and dimensions and transfer these onto the vinyl.

Sometimes the shape or size of a room means you have to use more than one piece of vinyl. If this is the case, it's important to secure the vinyl along the seam lines with double-sided adhesive tape or vinyl adhesive, so it stays in position and does not curl up.

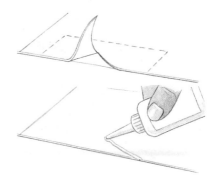

▶ *Vinyl is available in a wide range of designs, including some that give a handsome tiled effect.*

▲ **Fitting around an obstacle** Cut a paper template to fit around the base of the obstacle; it may be easier to use several sheets of paper, cut the template in sections and then tape the sheets together to make up a complete outline. Trace the template in position onto the vinyl, then use a utility knife to cut away the waste. Make a straight cut to the edge of the sheet where the join won't be noticeable – right at the back of a washbasin stand, for example.

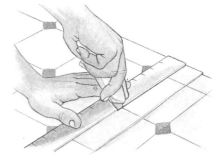

▲ **Trimming around a door frame** Press a profile gauge against the door frame so the sliding strips take the shape of the molding. Transfer the profile, at the appropriate position, onto the vinyl. Cut away the waste.

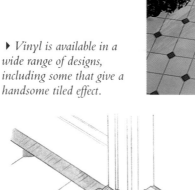

TIP

PUNCHING A PIPE HOLE
If you have a spare piece of pipe the same diameter as a fixed pipe, use this to punch a hole. Mark the pipe position as usual. Sharpen the inside rim of the pipe with a metal file. Resting the vinyl on a piece of wood, position the sharpened end of the pipe between the marks on the vinyl. Hit the other end of the pipe with a hammer so the pipe cuts through the vinyl.

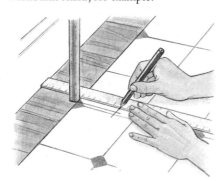

▲ **Fitting around a pipe** Butt the vinyl up to the front of the pipe. Use a straight edge to mark off the position of both sides of the pipe on to the vinyl. Measure from the wall to the front of the pipe and transfer this measurement onto the vinyl between the two marks. Using the marks as a guide, use a utility knife to cut a hole, the same diameter as the pipe, in vinyl. Make a straight cut to the edge of the sheet.

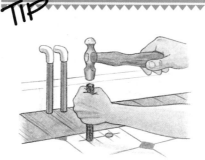

▲ **Joining sheets of vinyl** Add extra to the trimming allowance for pattern matching and overlapping. Matching the pattern, fit adjoining sheets of vinyl in position so their edges overlap by at least 1in (2.5cm). Using a utility knife and metal ruler, cut right through the overlapping layers. Remove the waste strips. Apply vinyl adhesive or double-sided adhesive tape to the underside of the join and stick it to the floor.

▲ **Repairing an accidental cut** Cut a length of double-sided adhesive tape and stick it to the wrong side of the vinyl along the cut. Peel off the backing paper and stick the vinyl to the floor. Then run a thin line of seaming adhesive along the length of the cut to bond the edges together.

TILING WALLS

Tiles have a decorative quality unmatched by any other wall finish. Not only do they look good, they are immensely practical, longwearing, and waterproof.

There are plenty of excellent reasons for extending a tiled area beyond a small back-splash behind a basin or sink. In bathrooms, condensation alone plays havoc with wallpaper, and if you have a shower or children who enjoy splashing around, you definitely need a waterproof finish on the walls. In kitchens, tiles provide an easy-to-clean surface behind countertops and stoves. Tiles can be an expensive option, but they are durable and will provide long-lasting style.

The key to achieving a professional finish is to plan the job from beginning to end before you even buy your tiles. Knowing the tricks of the trade for dealing with awkward areas makes the world of difference between a first-class and an indifferent result; as does planning ahead for the careful positioning of any cut tiles. Working your way through the job on paper highlights these areas, allows you to experiment at no cost, and more than repays the time spent in the long run.

▲ *Ceramic tiles are an attractive and practical way to decorate a wall in a kitchen or bathroom. They're easy to clean, waterproof, and very longwearing, and there are designs to suit all tastes and decors.*

SETTING OUT

Setting out is the first stage of putting your tiling plan into action. Doing this properly ensures that cut tiles fall neatly on either side of the area to be tiled and that your tiles are positioned squarely. This is of critical importance to achieving a good result.

Normally you fit tiles working upward from the edge of a bath, the rim of a shower stall, a kitchen countertop, the top of a baseboard, or the floor, all of which are likely to be too uneven to use as a base. So your first job is to draw a horizontal baseline which ensures that every row of tiles is level. Then fix a straight batten along this line to support the first row of tiles.

You also need to set the width of the final vertical rows on either side of the tiled area. Mark each wall so that as far as possible you avoid cut tiles at external corners and at the sides of windows. Where cuts are required at both ends of a wall, find its midpoint and measure out from here so that each final column is even and, preferably, not less than half a tile in width.

HOW MANY TILES?

Find the area in square yards (meters) of each surface to be covered by multiplying its height by its width. Add the areas together and multiply by the number of tiles of your chosen design it takes to cover a square yard (meter) – this information is generally supplied on the packaging. Allow an extra 5 per cent for waste.

If you have an exposed edge or edges to your tiling area, make sure you have enough suitable edging tiles, with rounded or glazed edges, unless you are using angled, universal tiles or fitting an edge trim.

1 ▾ Using a straight edge and level, draw a line all around the bottom of the area to be tiled, approximately a tile's width above where the lowest tiles are to finish.

2 Take one tile and, holding it level with the base of the area to be tiled, mark the point where it rises highest above the guideline. Add ⅛in (3mm) to allow for the width of a grout line and draw the baseline around the bottom of the area to be tiled at this height, parallel to the guideline.

3 ▾ At 1ft (30cm) intervals, partly drive masonry nails into lengths of batten so that the points just show through. Position the top edge of one length of batten along the baseline and drive the nails into the wall until they hold, but no further than necessary – you will need to remove the batten later. Continue fitting battens along the baseline.

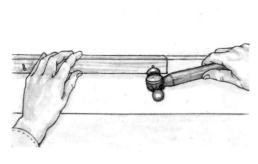

TIP
~~~~~~~~~~~~~~~~~~~~~~~~~~~~~~~~~~~~
MAKE YOUR MARK
Make a useful marking stick – a tool allowing you to gauge at a glance how many tiles fit between two points. Take a piece of 2 x 1in (50 x 25mm) batten, about 4ft (1.2m) long, and mark it off in whole tile widths, allowing for grout gaps if necessary.
~~~~~~~~~~~~~~~~~~~~~~~~~~~~~~~~~~~~

4 ▾ With your marking stick, work out where the last columns of whole tiles end on either side. Use a plumb line to draw vertical lines at these points.

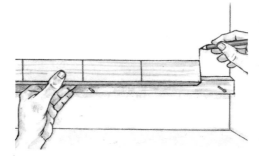

5 ▾ Fix further lengths of batten, at right angles to the first, along the outside of the vertical lines, as in step 3. Check that the battens are vertical with a level.

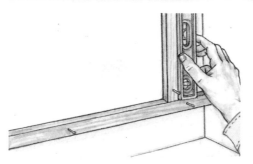

INSTALLING THE TILES

The tiles are installed in horizontal rows from the bottom of the area to be tiled upward. Work over a small area of the wall at a time so the tile adhesive does not dry out before you have a chance to embed the tiles.

1 ▾ Spread about 1 square yard (meter) of tiling adhesive on the wall, using a notched spreader to leave it in ridges. Fix the first tile in the corner of the two battens. Continue fitting the first row of tiles along the wall to the other vertical batten. With square-edged tiles, embed plastic spacers in the adhesive between the tiles; for tiles with angled edges or spacer lugs, push them up against one another.

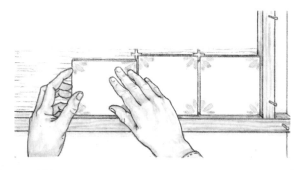

2 ▾ Fit successive rows of tiles between the battens, up to the desired height. Leave to set for an hour, then slide a knife blade along the batten edges to clear the joints. Remove the battens by pulling out the nails with needle-nosed pliers. Measure and cut tiles to fit the gaps and then fix them with tile adhesive.

▲ *A simple checkerboard pattern of yellow and deep green tiles is an effective choice for the walls of a utility room.*

3 Leave the tiles to set, usually for 12 hours. Cover the surrounding area before you start. Apply and finish the grout and seal any gaps along the adjoining bath surround, shower stall, or countertop with sealant.

◀ *Topiary trees are the unusual subject for the tiles of this kitchen backsplash. Using a border tile means that two complete tiles fit in each vertical row, while a third tile needs a little cutting to fill in the gap under the dishrack.*

CUTTING TILES

Generally, on a row of tiles along a wall, you will need to cut the tiles at each end to fit the area. When tiling a bath surround or the area behind a kitchen countertop, there should be no need for anything other than straight cuts, which are quite simple to make.

A tile-cutting jig is the best way to make straight cuts parallel to the sides of the tiles. The jig has a built-in marking gauge which you set to the width of the gap to be filled before cutting; it automatically allows for the width of one grout line.

However, because a tile-cutting jig can only hold the tile to be cut squarely, you cannot use it to score diagonal cuts on the tile. To fill slanting gaps, you have to mark the tile by hand with a felt-tipped pen, then score it with a handheld tile cutter against a straight edge.

1 ▸ Check that the space for a cut tile is uniform by measuring it top and bottom using the jig. If it is, you can use the jig to cut the tile. If not, transfer the measurements directly to the tile and make allowance for the grout line.

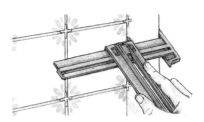

2 ▸ *In a jig:* position the tile in the jig. Holding the tile and jig steady with one hand, line up the tile-cutting tool in the guide and draw it firmly along the slot toward you. *By hand:* join the marks on the tile with a ruler and felt-tipped pen. Use a hand cutter along a metal straight edge to score the tile surface.

3 ▸ Grip the tile between the jaws of the cutting tool, with the jaws directly over the scored line. Hold the free side of the tile with your other hand, and squeeze gently with the tool to snap the tile. Check the fit and smooth the cut edge with a tile file.

TILING CORNERS

Almost every tiling job involves turning a corner at some point. Prepare for tackling corners during your planning and setting out.

▸ **Fitting into internal corners** At internal corners, overlap one set of cut edges onto another. Plan in advance which way to arrange the overlap, and allow for a grout line.

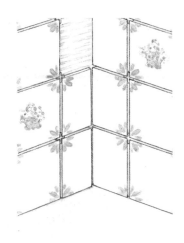

▸ **Fitting around external corners (1)** You can finish external corners with a double-edged trim strip. Embed the strip in the adhesive, then simultaneously place both columns of tiles so you can align them. You can use a single-edged trim strip for finishing off an exposed edge of a tiled area, especially when using plain-edged tiles.

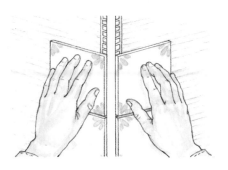

Fitting around external corners (2) Instead of using trim strip, overlap the adjacent tiles, making sure that the overlapping edge is glazed or rounded.

INSTALLING CURTAIN RODS AND TRACKS

When choosing a curtain rod or track, you need to take into account the size and shape of the window and the style and weight of the curtain.

Most rods and tracks are sold in kit form, although some of the heavier metal tracks and corded systems need to be installed by a professional. Always follow the instructions that come with the curtain fixture.

▸ *You can install flexible track in a bay window with the ends running to the edge of the bay or extending around the sides. Keep the curves gentle so they do not obstruct the runners. Some types of track may need to be softened first by immersing them in a bowl of warm water.*

POSITIONING RODS AND TRACKS

Wall-mounted The most common site for a curtain fixture is on the wall above the window or window recess, usually 3–5in (7–12cm) above the window frame. To allow the curtains to be drawn back from the window, and let in more light, extend the fixture 6–18in (15–45cm) on each side of the window. To make the window appear taller, position the fixture slightly above the window frame.

Frame-mounted If there is a narrow wall surround and you are hanging a light- or medium-weight curtain, you can secure the fixture to the wooden window frame.

Ceiling-mounted If the window reaches almost to the top of the wall, you can attach the brackets to the ceiling. Check that the fixture you buy is suitable.

Recess-mounted Net, café, and dormer window curtains can be mounted on a rod inside a window recess. Mount the fixture directly onto the wooden frame or on the sides or top of the recess.

CURTAIN RODS

• These decorative fixtures are made of wood, metal, or plastic. Ornamental end-stops, called finials, stop the rings sliding off the rods.

• Rods are most effective across a short, straight row of windows or across a recess.

• You can buy some metal types bent to shape for fitting in a bay – others require special angled joints.

• Use slim rods for short or light-weight curtains.

• Use thick rods – at least 1in (25mm) in diameter – for long or heavy, lined curtains.

• Cut wood or plastic types to size. Telescopic and sprung versions can be adjusted to fit. Corded rods may need to be re-corded if you shorten them.

CURTAIN TRACKS

• Made of plastic or metal, these are mainly fixtures that are designed to blend against the wall or be concealed behind a curtain, pelmet, or valance.

• Ideal for large or bay windows as you can bend certain types to fit the corners of the bay.

• Select the correct strength of track for the weight of curtain fabric.

• Some forms of track can be used with cording sets for ease of opening.

• Hand-drawn curtain tracks can be cut to size. Cord-operated tracks come in a range of sizes and may need re-cording if they are altered.

PUTTING UP RODS AND TRACKS

Short curtain rods need a bracket at either end. Rods longer than 5ft (1.5m) which are carrying heavy curtains need an extra central bracket or one every 4ft (1.2m) for very long rods. Curtain tracks need brackets every 6in (15cm), especially if they are supporting heavy curtains.

1 Measure the width of the window. If desired, add a 6–18in (15–45cm) allowance on each side of the window so the curtains can be held back. Buy the nearest longer length of rod or track. Cut a plastic or wooden fixture to length with a hacksaw.

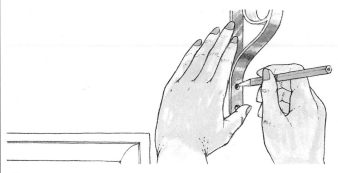

2 ▲ Hold one of the brackets or the bracket fixing plate at the desired height above the window: for a rod 3in (7.5cm) from the edge of the window; for a track 1in (2.5cm) from the ends of the track. With a pencil, mark the screw hole positions.

3 Mark screw hole positions for a bracket at the opposite end of the window, using a level to check it is level with the first bracket. For a rod longer than 5ft (1.5m), mark the position of an extra central bracket. For a track, mark further bracket positions at 6in (15cm) intervals across the wall.

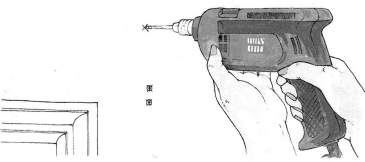

4 ▲ Using a power drill and masonry bit, drill holes at the marks. Insert a wallplug into each hole, then screw on any bracket-mounting plates and the brackets.

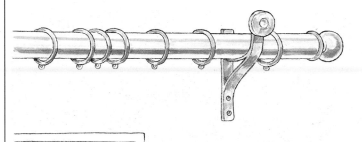

5 ▲ Put a finial or end stop on one end of the rod or track. Feed on the rings or runners – one for each curtain hook – and put on the other finial or end stop. Position the rod or track on the brackets, centering it over the window. If necessary, secure the rod or track to the brackets using the fittings provided.

YOU WILL NEED

- TAPE MEASURE
- CURTAIN ROD OR TRACK WITH BRACKETS AND FASTENERS
- LEVEL
- DRILL AND MASONRY BIT
- SCREWDRIVER

CONCRETE LINTELS

When installing above a window you might find there is a concrete lintel which is difficult to drill into, even using a hammer drill and masonry bit. In this case it's easier to screw a wooden batten to the wall, with the screw holes on either side of the lintel, then fasten the curtain brackets to the batten. The lintel can extend up to 5in (125mm) each side of the window opening.

1 Cut a 2 x 1in (50 x 25mm) batten the same length as the curtain fixture, ensuring it is at least 12in (300mm) wider than the window. Using a drill and wood twist bit, drill screw holes through the batten, 1in (2.5cm) from the ends. Hold the batten in position, using a level to check it is straight, and mark the screw hole positions on it.

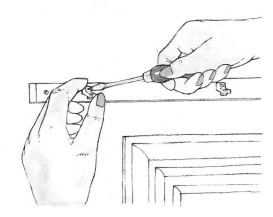

2 ▲ Drill screw holes in the wall, using a drill and masonry bit and insert wallplugs in the holes. Apply contact adhesive to the back of the batten and screw it in position. Screw the track or rod brackets to the batten, using a drill and wood bit to drill the screw holes.

TIP

FASTENING TO THE CEILING

You can also use a wooden batten when fastening to the ceiling. Use long screws that go through the batten and ceiling plaster, into the ceiling joists. To locate the joists, knock on the ceiling – they are 13–16in (35–40cm) apart and the spaces between them sound hollow.

INDEX

PICTURE CREDITS